WESTERN DISTRICT LIBRARY
ORION, ILLINOIS 61273

MW00994715

WITHDRAWN

Date Due

AG 26 '99			
AG 17 '00			
DEC 1 8 04			
AUG 02 08			
JUL 02 07			
JY 2 1 08			
MY 0 4 '10			
MY 3 1 '16			
JE 2 1 '16			

BRODART, INC.   Cat. No. 23 233   Printed in U.S.A

9/99 BN 9 $24.95(9.72)

HOMEBUILDING BASICS

CARPENTRY

HOMEBUILDING BASICS

CARPENTRY

LARRY HAUN

The Taunton Press

COVER PHOTO: Scott Phillips

Taunton
BOOKS & VIDEOS
for fellow enthusiasts

Text © 1999 by Larry Haun
Photos © 1999 by The Taunton Press, Inc., except where noted
Illustrations © 1999 by The Taunton Press, Inc.
All rights reserved.

Printed in the United States of America
10 9 8 7 6 5 4 3 2 1

The Taunton Press, Inc., 63 South Main Street, PO Box 5506,
Newtown, CT 06470-5506
e-mail: tp@taunton.com

Distributed by Publishers Group West

Library of Congress Cataloging-in-Publication Data

Haun, Larry
        Homebuilding basics : carpentry / Larry Haun.
            p.   cm.
        Includes index.
        ISBN 1-56158-167-4
        1. Carpentry 2. House construction. I. Title
TH5606.H38   1999   98-42608
    694—dc21   CIP

To carpenters everywhere—men and women, young and old—who are learning basic skills, becoming masters of their craft

ACKNOWLEDGMENTS

A book, like a house, is the product of many hands. It is created because people are willing to work together, with everyone employing the tools of their trade.

Thanks especially to my wife, Mila; my sisters, Loretta and Margaret; my brothers, Joe and Jim; my nieces, Debora, Christa, and Theresa; and all the other willing hands.

Thanks to Andrew Wormer, Jim Childs, Steve Culpepper, Julie Trelstad, Karen Liljedahl, Carol Kasper, Tom McKenna, Kevin Ireton, and Roe Osborn at The Taunton Press.

Thanks for the poetry from a dear friend and good carpenter, Phillip Rosenberg.

And thanks to Tom Vessella, who helped with math, and to Tony Mason, who helped with photography.

I also want to thank those who sent tools and gave me valuable information: Ray Abrams at R&A Tool; Donna Alexander and Liz Butler at Stanley Tools; Sil Argentin at Bosch-Skil; Jenni Cabral at Pacific Construction; Gerald Dalluge at Dalluge Tools; Mike Drungilas at National Nail; Liz Finnigan at Takagi Tools; Greg Gossage at Gossage Tool; Norman Griset at Griset Industries; Ted Hammers at Ted Hammers, Inc.; Dan Harrell at Zircon; Bob Hutchings at Big Foot Saw; Bruce Judson at Judson Enterprises; James Martin at Danair; Tom McEnaney at Calculated Industries; Burt Miraglia at Olive Knot Products; Courtney Newbill of Eisner Associates at DeWalt Tool; Rudy Pairis and Art and Gino at Pairis Enterprises; Anita Poindexter at Oxi-Solve; Mark Singer at Gorilla Glue; Jim Skelton at Diamond Back USA; Steve Sorton at Ator Tool Works; Darryl Thurner at Occidental Leather; Pam Tucker at Utility Composites; Ken Vaughn at New England Specialty Products; Jim Wienhold at Insty-Bit; Tom Woods at Empire Level; and Gary Young at the Los Angeles Apprenticeship Committee.

Thanks to the folks at Black and Decker, CEI, Faspac, Hida Tool & Hardware, Hitachi Koki, Japan Woodworker, Linear Link, Makita, McFeely's, Milwaukee, Pacific Cosntruction, Portable Products, Porter Cable, Prazi Beam Cutter, Proctor Products, Qual-Craft, RLD Tools, Senco, Simpson Strong-Tie, and Trus-Joist.

CONTENTS

INTRODUCTION

I've tried my hand at many jobs. I worked for several years as a farmer. I was a spiker once, laying railroad track. I taught Spanish and carpentry at night for years, and I even worked as a counselor for the deaf and for wounded Vietnam veterans. But I always came back to carpentry. It must have been the smell and feel of wood.

Not all of carpentry is easy. Moving and cutting lumber all day long can be hard work. Yet I hardly remember a time when I wasn't doing carpentry work. I was born in a farming-ranching region of western Nebraska, and carpentry— like sleeping and eating—was something everyone did.

I helped build my first house before I was out of high school. I worked with a kindly old man, a craftsman who taught me "white-overall" carpentry, the way houses were built from Civil War times until about World War II. Hand tools were used to cut the wood and build the homes because few power tools existed. I was deeply impressed by the beauty of the tools this old carpenter had and the skill with which he used them, and I'm thankful for the knowledge he passed along to me.

When I was still a teenager, the post-WWII housing boom was beginning, and I found myself in Albuquerque trying to

earn money to go to college by building houses with my older brother Jim. Because returning veterans were able to move into houses with nothing down and payments of $75 a month, the demand for housing was enormous. To meet that demand, we had to change the way we built. So, unlike Henry Ford, who took the automobile to the production line, we took the production line to the building site. We laid aside the white overalls and packed our pickups with tools built for speed. I set aside my handsaw and picked up a power saw that could cut wood to size in seconds, and I tossed my 16-oz. curved-claw hammer in favor of a 22-oz. straight-claw hammer that could drive a 16d nail with one lick.

In 1950, at age 19, I moved to Los Angeles to study at UCLA. I went to school three days a week and worked three days as a journeyman carpenter in the union. I got intellectual food for my mind and physical food for my body. On Sundays I rested.

By the mid-1950s, the building boom in Los Angeles was at its peak. Instead of building one house at a time, we were building 500 or even 5,000 at a time. Every person working in every trade was adapting. New tools, new procedures, and new materials were in evidence everywhere. It is a tribute to American ingenuity that we were able to build thousands of new homes without sacrificing quality for quantity. During these fast-paced days, I learned a lot about carpentry.

Nowadays I realize how fortunate I was to learn how to use hand tools from a traditional master builder when I was young. Today's carpentry is different in that we have all kinds of power tools, nail guns, and hand-held computers that help us build. But carpentry still requires that some basic knowledge of hand

tools and layout skills be acquired so we can move on to become masters of our craft. And this is my purpose in writing *Homebuilding Basics: Carpentry*. I want to share with others what I have learned from my teachers. Just as in my first book, *The Very Efficient Carpenter,* this second book continues the process of making information available to people about carpentry tools and the techniques for using them.

Homebuilding Basics: Carpentry is a step-by-step guide book to building. There is something in this book for anyone interested in carpentry or home improvement. In it, you will learn how to work safely and how to choose and use the basic hand and power tools for car-

pentry. You will learn the vocabulary of carpentry so that you can read plans and order building materials. You'll learn the basic steps of how to put together an entire house. And you'll see when precision counts and when it doesn't.

I no longer make my living as a full-time carpenter. Instead, among other things, I now spend a lot of my time writing and teaching the trade. But that doesn't mean I have stopped building. I help family and friends who need a willing hand. And my younger brother Joe and I work with Habitat for Humanity, building houses where we live in Oregon. Doing this physical work makes me feel good. It must be the smell and feel of wood.

1

HAND TOOLS

"Take your time"

"Use the right tools for the job"

"Keep them sharp and clean"

In the end, I think,

there are really only a few simple rules.

—Phillip Rosenberg,
A Few Simple Rules

When I started building houses, hand tools were the norm. Cutting wood, drilling holes, and driving nails all were done with hand tools. Even though today these tasks are often done with power tools, hand tools are still a part of every carpenter's tool collection.

When you're starting out as a carpenter, knowing which tools you'll need can be difficult. I've been in the trades for years, and choosing a tool is still not easy for me. Each time I walk into a tool center or receive a tool catalog in the mail, I am amazed by the dizzying array of carpentry tools offered for sale. Even buying something as basic as a hammer can be frustrating when there are 50 different models.

In this chapter I will introduce you to the basic hand tools every carpenter needs: fastening tools, cutting tools, shaping tools, gripping tools, bars, squares, tape measures, marking tools, and tools for checking level and plumb. I'll also show you a few ways to tote your tools from job to job.

FASTENING TOOLS

Hammers, screwdrivers, and staplers are useful to any carpenter. These are the beginning core of a hand-tool collection and can easily be kept close by—either on a toolbelt or in a toolbucket.

Hammers

The first hammer I owned as a 7-year-old had curved claws with a wooden handle. It was a 16-oz. model made of iron, and it wasn't much of a hammer. One claw was broken off, so it wasn't good for pulling nails, but I learned to drive nails with it. I can still remember the fun I had on warm days, using my hammer to build playhouses, forts, and boxes.

I have been in the trades for more than 50 years, and over that time I have collected and lost a good number of hammers of varying sizes. Depending on the kind of work you will be doing,

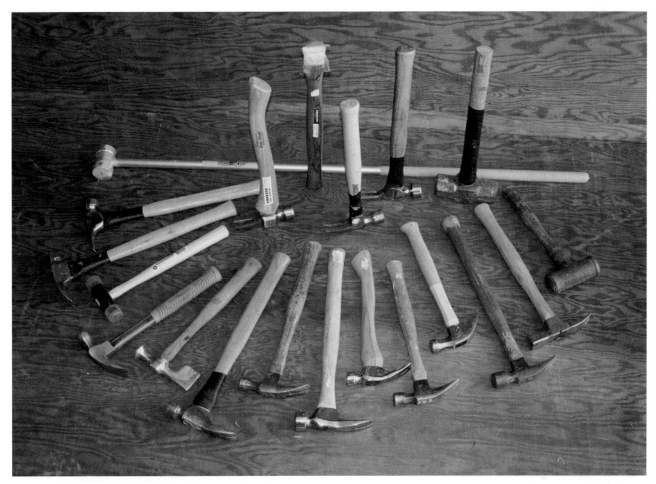

I have a collection of framing hammers, finish hammers, drywall hammers, mallets, and sledgehammers for a variety of jobs. I use the hammer in the back of the photo (with the long green handle) to tack housewrap and insulation panels to a building.

you'll more than likely build a collection of your own. But before you do that, take time to learn the parts of a hammer, the types of hammers, how to choose a hammer, and how to drive and pull nails with one.

Parts of a hammer The two basic parts of a hammer are the handle and the head. Most handles are made of wood, fiberglass, or steel. A wood handle absorbs some of the shock when hammering, but a fiberglass or steel handle

is so hard that it's virtually unbreakable. In most cases, I prefer wood handles, except when I do demolition work. For this job, I prefer to use a framing hammer with a fiberglass handle.

The head of a hammer includes the eye (where the handle enters the head), the cheek (the side of the head), the face (the striking end), and the claws. The face is either serrated or smooth (see the photo on p. 9). A serrated face won't become slick and slip off the nail head

Safety is a serious issue. On the job site, safe work practices should be followed at all times. Every day construction workers get hurt. Some are temporarily disabled by these accidents. Others are permanently disabled. Even worse, workers often die from job-related injuries.

Working safely is more than just protecting yourself physically with devices such as safety glasses. It's more than using tools correctly and making sure that blades are sharp. Humans simply cannot be plugged in like power saws and run all day long. Besides a body, you have a heart and a mind that also need protection. The first and most important safety rule I can mention is that you must have your mind on your work, especially when using power tools.

Most of my on-the-job injuries have occurred when I went to work with a battered heart. It can happen to any of us. A death in the family, a divorce, a car accident, or a sick child can make anyone lose concentration on what he is doing, resulting in a mistake. Unfortunately, a mistake on the building site can get someone hurt.

In the '50s, I built roofs with a partner. He was going through rough times at home with his family. Every morning his body was on the job at 7 A.M., but his mind didn't get there until around 10 A.M. During this three-hour period, he was basically unsafe at any speed. Twice he dropped a 2x rafter on my foot and injured me. One day he cut a huge gash in his forearm with a circular saw. This was before 9-1-1 existed, so I had to stop the bleeding, get him off the roof, take him to the hospital, and find another partner.

So, how can you keep your mind in focus even when times are hard? One thing that has worked well for me is to set aside a time every day for a period of meditation. I use this quiet time to bring my body and mind together. It helps me understand how I feel. Meditation takes some effort and practice, but after 50 years of pounding nails and running saws, I am here with all my body parts intact.

It is also important to admit when you are not mentally right. If you are having trouble focusing on your work, don't try to tough it out by yourself. It's okay to confide in the crew leader or a coworker and tell him you are having problems. It's okay to ask for help to get through the day.

Aside from staying mentally focused, what else can you do to be sure you are working safely? Throughout this book I have included specific safety guidelines for certain jobs and for using certain tools.

during hammering. The drawback of a serrated face is that it leaves a distinct checkerboard pattern on the wood after a missed blow. A smooth face, on the other hand, won't leave a checkerboard pattern when you miss. Unfortunately, a smooth face makes it easier for the face to slip off the nail head. To help a smooth face "catch" a nail head, you can rough it up a bit by using sandpaper or by rubbing it on concrete a few times. In general, a serrated face is used for rough framing, and a smooth face is used for finish work.

Most hammers, except for mallets, sledgehammers, and drywall hammers, have straight or curved claws that are used to pull nails. I prefer straight claws because they can also be used to move lumber around or to pry boards apart.

Types of hammers I knew a couple of brothers years ago who were framers around Palm Springs. They each had a 40-oz. hammer with a face about the size of a silver dollar. When framing 2x4 walls, they could roll out two 16d nails between thumb and forefinger, start both with one tap, and drive both home with one lick. My framing hammer is smaller, with a 21-oz. head, an 18-in. oval-shape handle, straight claws, and a serrated face. I like the oval shape of the handle because it fits well in my hand and gives me more control when nailing together rough framing lumber. Other framing hammers have 20-oz. to 28-oz. heads and shorter handles.

A finish hammer is used to nail on items like door trim, siding, and windowsills. I have two finish hammers—16 oz. and 20 oz. Both have straight claws and smooth faces, but the 16-oz. hammer has a 16-in. handle that works well for driving small nails. My 20-oz. hammer has an 18-in. handle, and I use it to drive larger nails through siding or exterior trim. My favorite finish hammer is made by Dalluge (see Sources on p. 198). It has a milled face like 120-grit sandpaper, is well balanced, and drives a finish nail without slipping off.

You don't need a power screwdriver to attach drywall to ceilings and walls. You can still get the job done with drywall nails and a drywall hammer. My drywall hammer weighs 16 oz., has a 15-in. wood handle, a rounded (convex) face, and a blade like a hatchet. The rounded face leaves a slight dimple (which is later filled with joint compound to hide the nail) in the drywall, and the hatchet blade is handy for prying or lifting sheets of drywall.

A mallet is a soft-faced hammer made of plastic, rawhide, rubber, or wood. It is often used to tap a wood chisel because it won't damage the chisel handle. Mallets come in different weights, ranging from 1½ oz. to 2 lb., with different handle lengths. The one I use weighs 10 oz. and has a 14-in. handle.

When driving stakes into very hard ground or doing heavy demolition work, you may need a 12-lb. sledgehammer with a 36-in. handle. This tool is also

The hammer on the right has a smooth face for finish work, while the middle hammer has a face with a sandpaper texture. The serrated face of the hammer on the left grips the nail head more aggressively for tasks such as framing.

used to nudge framed walls into position. Sledgehammers come in various weights, ranging from 4 lb. to 12 lb., with different handle lengths. I carry a 6-lb. sledgehammer with a 20-in. handle in my pickup.

NAILING WITH A HAMMER

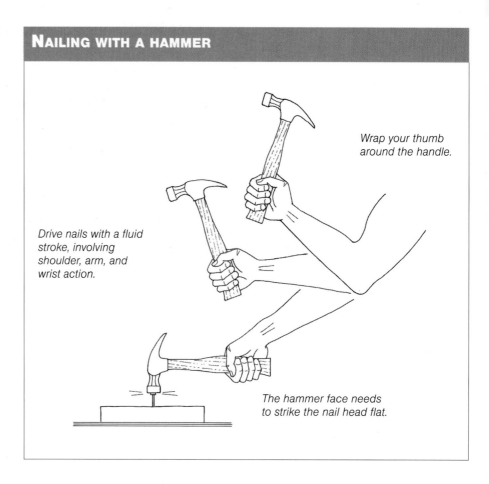

Wrap your thumb around the handle.

Drive nails with a fluid stroke, involving shoulder, arm, and wrist action.

The hammer face needs to strike the nail head flat.

Choosing a hammer A carpenter uses his hammer every day, so it's important to pick the right one for the job. A hammer will become an extension of your arm, so buy one that feels good to you.

Regardless of which type of hammer you need, whether it's for framing, finishing, drywalling, or demolition, always buy quality. A cheap hammer made of iron rather than hardened steel will most likely chip or break, like the one I had as a child.

Another consideration is the weight and length of the hammer. The best advice I can give regarding these two considerations is to buy a hammer that feels comfortable in your hands. Take a swing or two and see how it feels. If it's too heavy, try a lighter one. If it's top-heavy, try a shorter or longer handle. It's all a matter of fitting the hammer to your physical strength and comfort.

Driving nails Driving nails with a hammer has more to do with rhythm and coordination than it does with power and force. A long swing using shoulder, elbow, and forearm movement, with a decisive snap of the wrist at the end, is important for driving large nails (see the drawing above). Small nails can be driven mainly with simple wrist action. The key to nailing is to hit the nail head flat with the face of the hammer.

Practice hammering nails by driving them into a tree stump. Keep hammering until you develop a rhythm.

Otherwise, the nail will bend or pop out or the hammer will slide off and leave a mark on the wood.

Becoming a good nailer, like becoming a good typist, takes practice. I have heard old-time carpenters tell apprentices to sharpen their nailing skills and to stop leaving "Charlie Olsens" (the C- and O-shaped indentations left in the wood by the hammer face after missed hammer blows). To practice nailing, I suggest you get a box of 8d or 16d framing nails, find a hunk of wood or scrap 2x, and start hammering nails (see the photo above). Your grip on the handle is critical. There's no need for a tiring,

white-knuckle hold. Rather, grab the handle near the end with an easy, firm grip and make sure your thumb is wrapped around the handle. Hold the nail on the wood with one hand, start it with a tap, remove your hand from the nail, and drive the nail home. Keep driving until you develop a good rhythm. When driving nails through hard wood, try using softer, direct blows to keep the nail from bending.

There are times when you need to set (or start) a nail in a hard-to-reach or high-up place. Practice setting this nail with one hand. Wrap your hand around the hammer head, hold the nail with

Like most carpenters, I can tell tales of steel and nails sent flying from a hammer blow. Unfortunately, many of these tales don't have happy endings. Because the hammer is a striking tool, it can be dangerous, so protect yourself by following a couple of simple safety rules.

First, don't strike hard steel against hard steel, hammer face against hammer face, for whatever reason. Doing so can break off small pieces of steel (I call it job shrapnel), sending them flying—sometimes into unsuspecting bodies. I have carried a small piece of hammer steel lodged near the knuckle of my right index finger for 40 years.

Second, always wear safety glasses when you're hammering—no exceptions. Flying steel and nails can be crippling if they hit you in the eye. I know. It happened to me.

In the early '50s, I was framing walls on a very hot afternoon. Rather than stopping work to wipe the sweat off my glasses, I laid them aside.

I set a nail in a top plate and hit it with my hammer. Unfortunately, the blow barely caught the edge of the nail head, and the nail flew up and struck me in the right eye. It hurt some, but the pain was not intolerable. It felt like someone had poked me in the eye with their finger.

It took a few minutes before I realized that my vision was getting blurry.

The job site was near a hospital, so I drove my car to the emergency room. It took the doctor about 30 seconds to call for an eye specialist. The news was not great. The nail had hit me point-first and had punctured my eyeball, causing the fluid in my eye to leak out.

I was rolled into an operating room and was given a local anesthetic, so I got to watch as they stitched up my eyeball. I could sort of see a curved needle coming down to my eye as the doctor plugged the hole. I was sure wishing I had taken time to wipe the sweat off my glasses. After surgery, I was wheeled to a hospital bed with my head wrapped like a mummy.

After 10 days of wondering, waiting to find out if I would see again out of my right eye, the doctor took off the bandages. Good news. I still had to keep my eyes wrapped for another three weeks, but my vision was going to be more or less okay.

The effects of the accident still linger. Since then, I have had to wear dark glasses in bright sunlight because the eye is very sensitive to light, and stop lights look like amoebas. But I do consider myself lucky. I can see. Learn from my mistake and don't take chances with your eyes.

your thumb and forefinger flat against the head, and set the nail (see the left photo on the facing page). Some hammers are designed with a magnetic slot to hold a nail for setting in tight spots (Ted Hammers; see Sources on p. 198).

Once you have mastered the art of driving framing nails, practice with finish nails. The two methods differ. When driving finish nails, you need to be more accurate, because a missed hammer

blow could destroy an expensive piece of molding or other piece of finish work. To get more control, hold the hammer closer to the head. Practice the same way with finish nails as you did with the framing nails. Hold the nail, set it, and drive it.

Pulling nails Pulling nails with a hammer is easy. If you have one with a fiberglass or steel handle, simply hook the nail head with the claws and pull on

To set a nail with one hand, wrap your hand around the hammer head, hold the nail with your thumb and forefinger flat against the head, and stick it into the wood.

When pulling a nail using a hammer with a fiberglass or steel handle, slip a block of wood under the head to gain leverage. The block will also protect the wood.

the handle. To protect the wood from being marred and to gain better leverage, put a block of wood under the hammer (see the right photo above).

If you have a hammer with a wood handle, you have to be extra careful when pulling a nail to avoid breaking the handle. Slip the long part of the nail (called the shank) between the claws. Hook the shank by the inside ridge of the claws and push the hammer over to

one side (see the top photo on p. 14). Release, hook the nail again, and push the hammer to the opposite side. This should remove the nail or loosen it sufficiently for you to pull it out.

Screwdrivers

It's not always practical to grab a power drill to drive screws, especially if you only have one or two to set. So a couple of screwdrivers are still commonly found in a carpenter's toolbucket. There are two

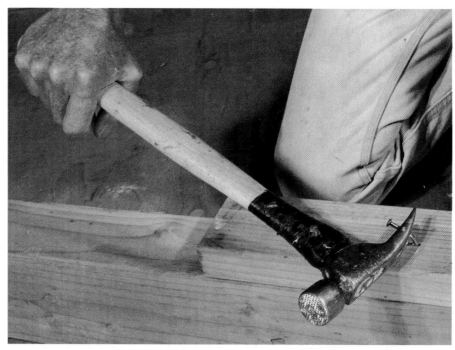

When pulling nails using a hammer with a wood handle, hook the nail and push the hammer to one side. Then release and repeat on the other side until the nail is loose.

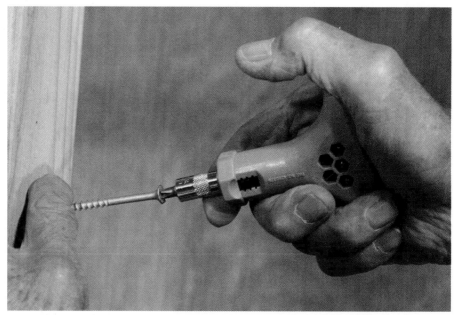

A T-shaped screwdriver with interchangeable bits is compact and holds several bits in the handle, so it's easy to carry. Its design also allows you to apply a lot of force to driving a screw.

common types of screwdrivers: standard and Phillips. The standard screwdriver has a flat tip shaped to fit a slotted screw. The Phillips has a tip shaped like a cross to fit a screw with a cross-shaped hole. Other types of screwdrivers include square and star-shaped tips.

All screwdrivers come in different lengths with different size tips and blade thicknesses. It's a good idea to buy a set of screwdrivers with a variety of tip types and sizes. Another option is to buy a screwdriver with interchangeable heads. This type will take up less room in your toolbelt or toolbox. I own a compact, T-shaped screwdriver (Judson Enterprises; see Sources on p. 198) that I carry in my toolbucket (see the bottom photo on the facing page). It's small but powerful, has a reversible ratchet, and the handle holds the extra bits. In general, I prefer to use Phillips-head screws and screw-drivers because the screwdriver is less likely to slip out of the slot in the screw.

Staplers

A stapler is a handy tool to keep around. Two types are commonly found on the job site: the hammer tacker and the staple gun. Most carpenters prefer the hammer tacker because it's fast and easy to use. The hammer tacker is about 1 ft. long and can be loaded with strips of staples. It got its name because you swing it like a hammer (see the photo above). When the tool hits a solid sur-face, it drives a staple. A hammer tacker usually accepts staples from ¼ in. to ½ in. long. It's most commonly used to tack down building paper, housewrap, plastic vapor barriers, the kraft-paper flanges on fiberglass insulation, and car-pet underlayment. On remodeling jobs, I use a hammer tacker to staple plastic over doors so that dust won't drift into other rooms.

The hammer tacker makes short work of stapling down felt paper.

A staple gun allows you to place staples more accurately. Most models drive staples from ¼ in. to 9/16 in. long. I use a staple gun for installing acoustical tile or for tacking down phone wires. The problem with a staple gun is that squeezing the trigger handle repeatedly can be tiring on the hand and wrist. If you have lots of staples to drive, you may want to buy a small electric stapler.

CUTTING TOOLS

Cutting material to size, whether wood, drywall, or even metal, is a big part of what a carpenter does. Today, most big cutting jobs are done with power tools. But there are times when a few simple hand tools are more appropriate. That's why it's important to keep a few saws, tin snips, and knives on the job site.

Japanese handsaws cut on the pull stroke rather than on the push stroke. For best cutting, keep the saw at a 10° angle.

Saws

The saws I keep on the job site are wood-cutting handsaws, a drywall saw, a coping saw, and a hacksaw. I seldom use a handsaw these days, but when I have only a cut or two to make, a handsaw is faster than plugging in my power saw. My two handsaws are both cross-cut saws. One is for cutting rough wood, like 2x4 studs, and has 8 teeth per inch. My finish saw has 12 teeth per inch and cuts a piece of molding without a lot of tearout.

I prefer Japanese handsaws (Japan Woodworker; see Sources on p. 198) over our standard American handsaws. Japanese handsaws are razor sharp and easy to use. Unlike standard handsaws, these saws cut on the pull stroke rather than on the push stoke. This makes them safer, because they won't buckle and bounce out of the kerf (or saw cut).

Some models even have teeth for cross-cutting on one side of the blade and teeth for ripping on the other. When cutting with a Japanese handsaw, cut at a lower angle than you would using a standard handsaw—about 10° (see the photo above).

I keep a drywall saw in my toolbucket because it's handy for cutting relatively soft materials like drywall and foam insulation board. A drywall saw tapers to a point, making it ideal for piercing and cutting in the middle of the material rather than from the edge, and its coarse teeth make quick (though ragged) cuts (see the photo on the facing page).

The coping saw is invaluable for trim work. It has a very thin blade with fine teeth and can be rotated to any angle to make intricate or curved cuts.

Occasionally, a carpenter will need to cut through metal. For nails or pipes, you'll need a hacksaw. It has a hardened blade designed to cut through all kinds of metal, and it's great for cutting through plastic PVC pipe.

Saw maintenance While drywall saws are cheap and easily replaced, my handsaws aren't, so I take good care of them. I keep them sharp (while it's possible to do this yourself, I find it easier to send them out to be sharpened) and store them in a cardboard sheath to preserve their sharpness. To keep the blades free from rust or corrosion, clean them with a rag or steel wool and paint thinner, then coat them with three-in-one oil or a silicone spray lubricant. Be mindful when using paint thinner, because it's toxic. Wear protective gloves, use a minimum amount, and don't dump the excess on the ground.

Knives

Knives have their places in a carpenter's toolkit. Most every carpenter has a utility knife, and many also carry a pocket knife. A utility knife can be used to open packages, to cut building paper, fiberglass insulation, composition shingles, linoleum, and drywall, as well as to

Start the cut by pushing the point of the drywall saw through the drywall. Then follow the cut line.

SAFETY FOR CUTTING TOOLS

• Keep the cutting edges of all tools clean and sharp. Dull tools are hard to use and to control.

• Cut away from your body.

• Don't put a sharp, unprotected tool in your nail apron. It might slice your nail apron or you.

• When using a cutting tool, don't force it. Just like people, every tool has its own pace.

• When working with sharp tools, pay close attention; don't allow yourself to be distracted.

A small block plane (in use) and a jack plane (right, on floor) can be used to shape and smooth wood. The Surform (left, on floor) is for shaping drywall.

SHAPING TOOLS

One of the first hand tools I learned to use as a young man was the handplane. I vividly recall watching a carpenter shape the edge of a door using a long, shiny jointer plane. Long curls of wood rose from the plane, covering his work area and filling my nostrils with the sweet smell of pine. Much of the shaping work I do these days is done with power tools, but I still find use for handplanes, chisels, files, and rasps.

Handplanes

I bring a jack plane and a small block plane to all my jobs. I use a 14-in. jack plane to shave a door to fit in its opening or to smooth the rough edges of a board. I use the block plane to round a corner of a board or to remove a bit of wood from a piece of molding. The small block plane is very handy because it fits easily into a toolbelt or toolbucket and can be used with one hand.

When a piece of drywall doesn't quite fit, I use a small, 5½-in. Surform to trim it down (see the top photo on the facing page). It resembles a handplane, but instead of a cutting iron, the Surform has a plate on the bottom that looks like a food grater. It's also handy for rough shaping other materials as well.

Using a handplane A handplane is easy to use if you follow a few simple guidelines. For optimum performance, keep the blade sharp and clean. A sharp blade will remove wood smoothly, leaving long shavings. A dull blade will chop at the wood, leaving a rough surface. Like any tool, it works better when it is kept clean. You can clean a blade with paint thinner or steel wool. When you are finished cleaning it, coat the blade lightly with three-in-one oil.

sharpen pencils. The most common utility knife has a retractable blade, so it's easy to carry it in a nail apron or on your toolbelt without fear of accidentally cutting yourself. Extra blades are stored in a compartment in the handle.

A pocket knife with a good carbon-steel blade is another tool that has many uses in carpentry work. I use mine to sharpen pencils, to cut strings, to open packages, and to trim excess caulk from around windows. Keep the blade sharp with a sharpening stone. If the knife becomes difficult to open and close, apply a little three-in-one oil on it.

It's also important to adjust the blade so you remove only a small amount at a time, keeping the shavings paper thin. Trying to remove too much wood will just clog the plane.

Hold the plane flat against the surface of the wood and cut with the grain. If you cut against the grain, you'll feel it. The plane will cut into the wood fiber and will jump, resulting in torn fibers and a rough cut. When you are finished with a handplane, retract the blade so that it won't get nicked. I wrap mine in a soft cloth for storage.

Chisels

Another shaping tool that comes in handy is a chisel. A chisel is often used to cut notches in wood (such as for a lockset) or to shave a bit off a joint to ensure a perfect fit.

Chisels come in various sizes. Most carpenters can get by with a set of chisels ranging in size from ¼ in. to 1 in.

Using a chisel As with a handplane, sharpness is essential when working with a chisel. A dull blade is dangerous and makes it difficult to achieve a smooth, clean cut. To keep the chisel sharp, don't use it as a screwdriver or as a pry bar.

A chisel has a straight side and a beveled side. When cutting, keep the beveled side facedown into the cut. Point the blade of the chisel away from your body to help prevent injury in case of a slip.

To protect the chisel handle, many carpenters use a mallet rather than a hammer to hit the chisel (see the top photo on p. 20). For best results, cut with the grain—otherwise, you'll tear out chunks of wood.

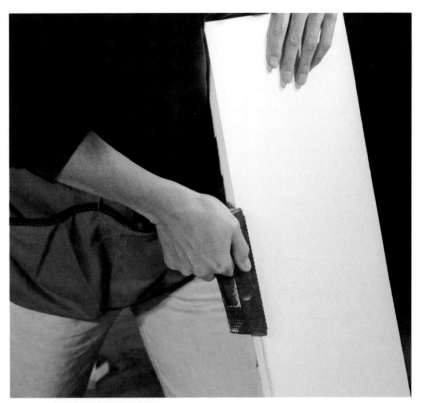

The Surform works well to trim a piece of drywall that doesn't quite fit.

Chisels are used to cut notches in wood or to shave wood off a joint to make a perfect fit. A standard set can have sizes ranging from ¼ in. (right) to 1½ in. (left).

A sharp chisel can make cutting a notch an easy task.

When not in use, protect the chisel's cutting edge with a couple of loops of electrical tape or wrap it in a clean cloth.

Files and rasps

Files and rasps are also handy items to keep around the job site. Files come in many different sizes (from smaller than a pencil to longer than a hammer), shapes, lengths, and cutting ability (roughness). Originally designed to shape metal, files can be used to smooth and form other materials as well, including plastics (such as Formica) and wood. Their teeth are shaped to cut on the push stroke. A good beginning set should include a three-cornered file, a flat one, and a round one.

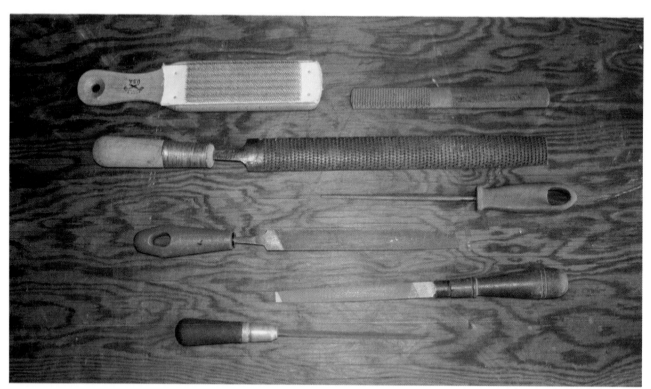

Files and rasps are handy shaping tools. The four tools at the bottom are files. The top right tool and the long one near the top are rasps. The wood-handled tool at the top left is a file card, which is used to clean both files and rasps.

Rasps have larger teeth than files do and are designed to remove a lot of wood. They, too, come in various sizes and shapes. A good rasp for a carpenter to own is the four-in-hand rasp. It has one flat side and one oval side, with four different cutting surfaces.

The cutting teeth of a file or rasp will eventually get plugged with metal or wood. When this happens, clean the teeth with a file card, which is a tool with short, stiff bristles that can remove any gunk with a few strokes.

GRIPPING TOOLS

Mechanical hands are what carpenters call the many pliers, wrenches, and clamps we use on job sites. When we can't tighten a nut by hand, we use a wrench. What we can't hold with our fingers, we hold with a pair of pliers. When we can't bring together a glued-up tabletop with our hands, we use a clamp.

Wrenches

Most carpenters carry a wrench or two in their toolbucket. I carry three types: a crescent wrench, an Allen wrench, and a pipe wrench.

I use the crescent wrench the most. The business end has a jaw that can be adjusted to different sizes by rotating a knob near the handle. When using a crescent wrench, make sure it fits snug on the bolt head or nut. A loose-fitting

Many items in construction are held together with bolts, so a carpenter needs to carry a few wrenches in his toolbucket. Shown clockwise from left are: two pipe wrenches, four crescent wrenches, and Allen wrenches.

wrench may slip when pressure is applied. To prevent the wrench from rapping your knuckles if it slips, pull it toward you rather than pushing it away.

A 6-in. crescent wrench is great for tightening circular-saw blades and doing maintenance work on power tools. A 12-in. wrench should work for most larger jobs.

A crescent wrench can be lubricated with a bit of graphite on the rotating knob. Graphite works better than oil, because oil picks up dirt that can make an adjustable wrench hard to open and close.

An Allen wrench is a hexagonal (six-sided), L-shaped steel rod used to tighten bolts and screws that have the same pattern in their heads (called hex heads). For convenience, buy a wrench set that comes nestled in its own case. This way they are all in one place and are protected by the case.

Pipe wrenches are large tools with adjustable, serrated jaws and are often used by plumbers. There are different sizes available, but I find that a 14-in. pipe wrench is very versatile. I use it during remodeling jobs in which I have to remove plumbing pipes under a sink. Rather than lubricating the moving parts of a pipe wrench, clean them with paint thinner if they become gummed up and hard to move.

Pliers

Although a carpenter won't use them every day, pliers are handy tools to have on the job site. There are many types and sizes out there, and I'd recommend keeping a few of these in your tool-

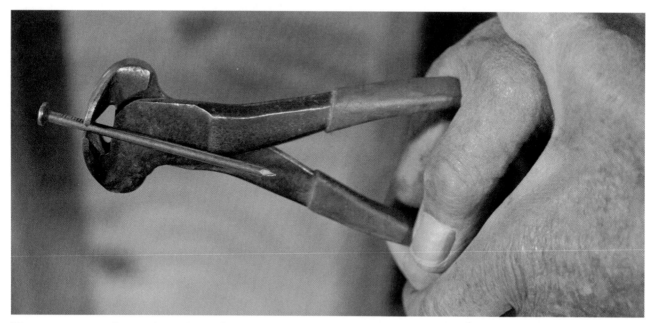

Nippers are great for cutting wire and rope and also work for pulling and cutting nails.

Side-cutting pliers are handy for cutting electrical wires.

bucket: a standard pair, nippers, side-cutting pliers, channel-lock pliers, and locking pliers.

Standard pliers, called slip-joint pliers, are used to hold things a bit tighter than you could with just your fingers. They can also be used to help turn a screwdriver or to hold a small nail for setting.

Nippers have sharp cutters on the end and are used to cut rope, wire, and nails (see the photo on the facing page). They also work well for pulling nails. I keep nippers in my bucket and frequently use them rather than a hammer or a bar (which can break off the head) to pull difficult nails. To pull a nail with nippers, grab the shaft of the nail with the nippers, rock back and forth on the handles to loosen the nail, and then pull it out.

Channel-lock pliers can be adjusted like a wrench to grip pipes and other large objects.

Side-cutting pliers, also called lineman's pliers, are useful for holding small items in the jaws, and they are great for cutting and pulling electrical wires (see the left photo above). Just be sure the power is off before working with any electrical wires.

Channel-lock pliers are adjustable and can be used to grip much like a wrench (see the photo above). To adjust a pair, open the jaws and move the groove on

Wide-jaw locking pliers can be used to secure wood to a bench or sawhorse.

A C-clamp can hold wood to a sawhorse while cutting with a circular saw.

one handle into a channel on the other handle. I use mine to hold a variety of things, including flat bars, square nuts, and round pipes.

I first saw locking pliers, more commonly known as Vise Grips, in 1946. Back then it was such a new invention that few people had a pair, but today they are as common as hammers. I never go to a job site without my pair.

Having a pair of locking pliers is like having a small portable vise in your hand. By turning a knurled knob at the end of the pliers' handle, the jaws can be opened and closed. When you squeeze the handles, the jaws lock by means of a spring-loaded clamp in the handle, holding the item securely. Flipping a lever on the handle opens the jaws. Special,

wide-jaw locking pliers can be used to clamp wood to a bench or sawhorse for cutting (see the left photo above).

Clamps

Clamps are valuable tools that serve as extra hands to hold whatever you are working on. If you had one of every type of clamp available, you would need a large truck to haul them. Carpenters use several types of clamps that are easily transported: the C-clamp, pipe clamp, bar clamp, and spring clamp.

The venerable C-clamp is the workhorse of the trade, offering straight-on holding power. This tool is a powerful holding device that clamps material steady while sanding, waiting for glue to dry, or sawing (see the right photo above). There are many sizes of C-clamps, ranging

Bar clamps (bottom) and pipe clamps (top) can hold wood securely during glue-up.

Spring clamps are quick and easy to use. Here they hold a straight-edge on a sheet of plywood.

glued-up boards or be expanded to grip long sections of cabinets. Pipe clamps are available that fit on either ½-in. or ¾-in. steel pipe. The advantage of this clamp is that it can be extended to any length of pipe, 20 ft. or more. The stationary part of the clamp is called the foot. The movable part is called the head (see the top photo on p. 25).

A bar clamp works the same way as a pipe clamp, but instead of a round pipe, the head slides on a flat bar (see the bottom photo on p. 25). Bar clamps are available in sizes ranging from 6 in. to more than 6 ft.

A spring clamp works like a large clothespin. It is easy to apply but doesn't have great holding power. Spring clamps vary in size from small ones that you can open with two fingers to large ones that take both hands to open. They work well for light holding jobs. I find my 6-in. spring clamps perfect for securing a straightedge to a door or sheet of plywood so I can make a straight cut with a circular saw (see the photo at left). They also work well for clamping two small glued pieces of wood or for holding one end of a chalkline. Better models have vinyl-coated tips so they don't mar finish wood.

BARS

Bars are solid-steel leverage tools. Depending on the size, a bar can be used for pulling nails, for prying open windows, or for demolition work. A carpenter uses several types of bars, such as the cat's paw, the flat bar, and the wrecking bar.

After the hammer, the nail puller most often used is the cat's paw. The cat's paw has a nail slot between two sharp claws, which are designed to dig into the wood around a flush-driven nail.

from 1 in. up to more than 1 ft. (the size of a C-clamp is determined by the size of its opening). My 6-in. clamps are the ones I use most on the job site.

A pipe clamp is a great job-site clamp because it can be adjusted to hold a wide variety of materials of various sizes. For instance, it can be used to clamp

To pull a nail with the cat's paw, place the claws on the wood in front of the nail head. If you need to, drive the claws straight in for a couple of licks to get them below the head. Once the claws are under the head, pull back on the handle to lift out the nail (see the photo at right). The striking face of a cat's paw is soft steel, so it's okay to hit it with a hammer. But wear safety glasses.

The flat bar is simply a flat piece of steel with a right-angle bend at one end. It comes in various lengths, but most fit easily in a toolbucket. The one I use is 1¾ in. wide and 1 ft. long.

Each end of a flat bar is sharpened and has a nail-pulling slot. I often use a flat bar to pry boards apart (see the photo below), to lift cabinet sections during

To remove a nail using a cat's paw, drive the claws of the cat's paw under the nail head, then pull back on the handle to lift out the nail. Wear safety glasses when striking this tool.

A flat bar can be used to pry apart two boards, but wear safety glasses when striking the bar with a hammer.

installation, and to scrape away old caulk. It is also handy for prying open windows that have been painted shut.

Don't leave a flat bar lying around with the right-angle bend facing up. Someone can step on it and get a hard rap on the shins.

The wrecking bar, which looks like a large cat's paw, is the tool I reach for when I'm doing demolition work. Wrecking bars are made of hardened steel, and most types have nail slots in both the flattened end and the curved end. Wrecking bars come in various sizes and styles. In general, the longer the bar, the more leverage you gain. The one I use is 3 ft. long. I keep it in my pickup with my sledgehammer and use it to remove flooring, siding, or roof

sheathing, to pull large nails, to jack up heavy objects, and to pull apart concrete formwork.

SQUARES

Most things a carpenter builds are either square or rectangular. So having a square or two around is just as important as having a hammer. The question is, which square among the many do you need? I have five types of squares that I find helpful: a small rafter square, a framing square, a combination square, a T-bevel square, and a drywaller's square.

Small rafter square

The small rafter square is a triangular square—90° on one side, 45° on the other—used to mark both square and angled cuts. It is available in two sizes: The small one measures 7 in. along a

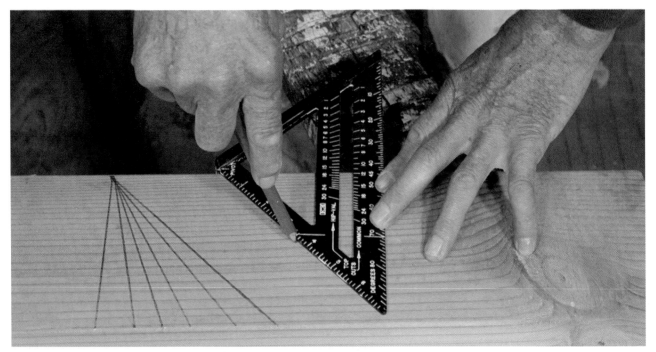

You can rapidly mark boards for angled cuts using a small rafter square. Simply align the degree of cut you want with the edge of a board, and scribe a line along the inch scale.

side, and the larger one measures 12 in. While I own both sizes, I prefer the smaller one because it is easy to carry in a toolbelt or toolbucket. You'll also have a choice between metal or plastic. I prefer the metal small rafter square because it is almost indestructible; mine is still legible and accurate even after years of use.

A small rafter square is very easy to use. On one side of the square is a scale in inches. Adjacent to this scale is a pivot point, and opposite the pivot point on the base of the square is a degree scale. To find any angle, say 20°, place the pivot point against the straight edge of a board and pivot the square until the 20° mark aligns with the edge. Then simply scribe a line along the inch-scale side, and the line will be 20° to the edge (see the photo on the facing page).

Framing square

I learned to use the framing square when I was a carpenter in the Navy in the early '50s. First introduced almost 150 years ago, the venerable framing square is still hard at work. Made of steel or aluminum, it has a 16-in. tongue and a 24-in. blade set at right angles to one another. Not an easy tool to carry in your toolbelt, it is nevertheless handy for quickly checking if walls are perpendicular to each other when setting cabinets and for marking square across 2x12 joists.

I use small stair gauges with my framing square when laying out stairs (see the photo below). The gauges are simply screw clips that are fastened to the edge

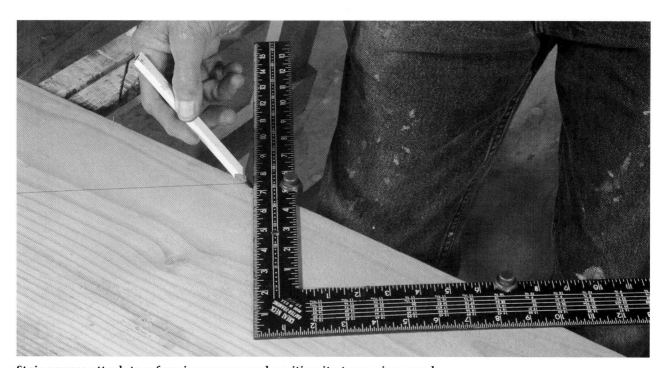

Stair gauges attach to a framing square and position it at any given angle.

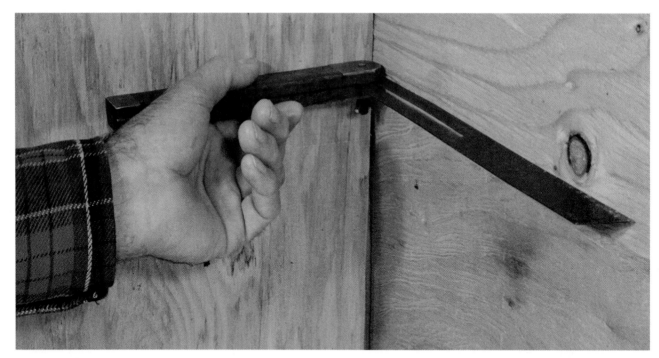

When you have a corner that's out of square, you can check it with a T-bevel square. Place the square in the corner, adjust the handle until it fits flat against the wall, then tighten the wing nut. Transfer this angle to the material to be cut.

of the square, making it possible to mark the same angles on a stair stringer repeatedly.

Combination square

Most combination squares have a 12-in. blade marked off like a ruler with a sliding head. One side of the head is used to lay out a 90° angle, and the other side is used to lay out a 45° angle.

I often use my combination square to mark stock for ripping. To make a 2½-in. rip cut, for example, set the head at 2½ in. on the blade. Now set the square on the stock, and you can quickly mark a cut line 2½ in. from the edge. Place a pencil at the blade end and pull the square down the stock to mark the cut line.

T-bevel square

A T-bevel square has a blade that pivots and slides on a handle and can be locked in any position by a wing nut. I have one with an 8-in. blade, but many lengths are available.

This is an effective tool for fitting material to an odd angle. For example, you can use it to fit a shelf into a corner that is not 90° (see the photo above). First place the square in the corner with the blade against one wall. Then adjust the handle until it fits flat against the wall and tighten the wing nut. Now you can transfer this angle to the shelving, marking a precise cut. What makes the T-bevel square especially handy is that you can bring it right over to the chopsaw and use it to help adjust the angle of the blade exactly (unplug your saw before doing this).

Tape measures are available in a wide variety of sizes. Most carpenters use either a 16-ft. or 25-ft. tape.

Drywaller's T-square

A drywaller's T-square is shaped like a "T" with a 22-in. tongue and a 48-in. blade that are both marked with inch scales. While usually used to mark sheets of drywall, this square is also a good tool to use when marking other sheet goods (like plywood) or doors for cutting. Just press the tongue along a square edge and mark along the long blade.

Treat the T-square with kindness. If you drop it, you can easily knock it out of square. To check for square, lay it across a sheet of plywood and mark along the blade side. Then turn the square over and mark again. If the blade is not on the line, the tool is not square.

TAPE MEASURES

Taking measurements has radically changed since I started building. My everyday measuring tool used to be a 6-ft. folding ruler. Imagine the time it took to measure and cut a board to length, especially one over 6 ft. long. First I had to unfold the ruler, section by section, then measure out the distance on the board. Then I had to fold up the ruler and put it away. It's no wonder that steel tape measures are now much more common on job sites everywhere.

TAKING CARE OF TAPE MEASURES

Tape measures get used a lot and so require special care. Here are some maintenance tips to ensure that your tapes continue to work smoothly for a long time.

• Don't leave an extended tape lying around on the floor. If someone steps on the tape, it will be creased and will never work properly again.

• Don't let a tape reel in too fast. If the hook on the end hits the case at full speed, the hook can break off. Slow the tape down with your fingers.

• Keep the tape clean, or it will be difficult to pull out and reel in. Tapes gummed with wood pitch, tar, or caulk can be cleaned with a soft rag and some mineral spirits (paint thinner).

• When working in wet conditions, wipe the tape dry with a cloth before reeling it back into the case.

A good tape measure for carpentry work will be highlighted or marked at 16-in. intervals (16 in., 32 in., 48. in., etc.), which makes it easy to lay out walls, floors, ceilings, and roofs on 16-in. centers.

A tape measure has a hook on the end of a flexible steel blade that grabs the edge of a workpiece. The blade can be locked in place so that measuring becomes a one-person job.

Many sizes are available, but the two most commonly found on a job site are 16 ft. and 25 ft. Longer tape measures (up to 100 ft. or more) made of steel or cloth are also available. They work well to lay out long distances like the foundation of a new house or when measuring the exact location of a building when siting it on a lot.

Most tape measures used for general construction have an extra mark at 16-in. intervals (see the photo at left). Because this spacing is often standard for studs in a wall, joists in a ceiling, or rafters in a roof, these marks are helpful when laying out a house frame. Some tapes have decimal equivalents and metric conversion charts on the back.

To snap a chalkline for a short distance, hold one end of the line with one hand and the other end with the little finger of the second hand. Pick up the taut line with the thumb and forefinger of your second hand and snap it.

MARKING TOOLS

A carpenter uses many different tools to mark all kinds of materials: wood, Formica, drywall, concrete, tile, you name it. Most of this can be done with a few basic marking tools, such as pencils, keel, pens, chalklines, and dryline.

Pencils, keel, and pens

While many lumberyards give away standard pencils, flat-sided carpenter's pencils are more durable, easier to sharpen with a utility knife, and won't roll away when set down on a board.

Keel (commonly known as a lumber crayon) is easier to see than a pencil on some surfaces, making it better for some kinds of layout work. Blue and red keel show up well on rough lumber and concrete; white works best on new concrete.

A few specialty pens are also useful on the job site. I use mechanical pens for laying out fine cuts on finish work, no-blot pens on wet wood, and felt-tip pens on dry wood.

Chalklines

Chalklines have been around about as long as carpenters and are used about as often as a saw. Anytime you want to mark from one point to another—if you wanted to rip 1 ft. from an 8-ft. piece of plywood, for instance—you can do it with a chalkline.

Chalklines are available in lengths of 50 ft. or 100 ft. and are wound inside a box filled with powdered chalk. I buy chalk by the gallon and refill the box as needed. Years ago I used a teaspoon to fill the box with chalk, but now I use a plastic squeeze bottle with a nozzle, making the process easier and quicker.

Using a chalkline is pretty simple. To ensure that the snapped line will be straight, stretch the line taut before pulling it up and snapping it. Also, snap perpendicular to the surface to be marked, or you may leave a curved line.

For short distances, hold one end of the line with your foot, stretch out the line to the measuring point, and snap it. Or you can hold one end of the line with one hand and the other end with the little finger of your other hand. Pick up the taut line with the thumb and forefinger of your second hand and snap it (see the photo on p. 33).

On long runs, secure the line at both ends, go to the center of the line, hold down the line at that point, and snap each side individually.

Dryline

A dryline is simply a stringline without chalk. It is often made of yellow or orange nylon for visibility. I buy dryline in 250-ft. lengths and use it for laying out house foundations.

I also use dryline to check and straighten framing. Stretched from one end of a wall to the other along the top plate, for example, a dryline can quickly indicate where the wall might need to be straightened.

TOOLS FOR CHECKING LEVEL AND PLUMB

Checking for level and plumb are jobs a carpenter has to do every day. You don't want floors running downhill or walls that lean. The tools used to check for level and plumb are levels and the plumb bob.

Levels

Although today there are many high-tech leveling devices that rely on lasers or microchips, the old standbys work quite well for most carpentry work. Many carpenters carry at least two or three different sizes of spirit levels, and some still swear by water levels.

Spirit level The spirit, or carpenter's, level is the best known of all. It is a simple tool consisting of a straight length of wood or metal with two or three glass vials located on it. Each vial is filled with spirit (like alcohol) so it won't freeze, has a bubble in it, and is usually protected by a glass lens.

I have two spirit levels: a 2-ft. one and a 6-ft. one. If I need to check a surface that is larger than 6 ft. for plumb or level, I simply attach my 2-ft. level to a long straightedge with duct tape to make a plumbstick (see the sidebar on the facing page). I use an 8-ft. piece of aluminum from an old sliding door, but a 2x4 could be used too, provided that it is straight.

A spirit level needs a bit of loving care. Don't leave this tool leaning against a wall or on the floor of a work area. Instead, hang it from a nail or place it flat on the ground, away from the work area. I carry each of my spirit levels in a carrying case made from a length of 3-in.-dia. plastic plumbing pipe cut to fit. I simply cap one end of the

Carpenters often make a plumb-stick for checking that walls are straight up and down. What's great about making a plumbstick is that you can use your old, battered level, even if it's inaccurate.

Take an 8-ft. 2x4 stud and nail a 16-in. 1x2 strip on each end. Let the 1x overhang the stud ends 3 in. or 4 in. Attach a 2-ft. level to the opposite edge with rubber bands or duct tape. Now you have a long level.

To check this tool for accuracy, hold it flat against a wall. Move the top of the stick back and forth until the bubble is centered exactly in the tube and make a pencil mark on the wall along the 1x extensions. Now turn the plumbstick side for side—not end for end—so that the same edge is on the opposite side of the line flat against the wall. Line the extensions up with the marks on the plates. If the bubble returns to the exact center of the vial, the plumbstick is accurate.

If the bubble is not centered in the tube, the level needs to be adjusted. Stick a wooden shim, a folded piece of paper, or even an 8d nail under one end of the level and check the plumbstick again. Keep adjusting the shim until the bubble is centered both ways.

A plumbstick is useful for checking a wall for plumb. It is made of a straight 2x4 and a 2-ft. level.

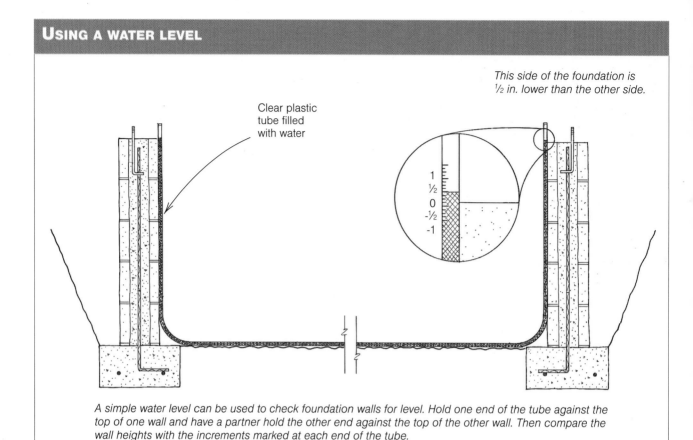

This side of the foundation is ¹/₂ in. lower than the other side.

Clear plastic tube filled with water

1
¹/₂
0
-¹/₂
-1

A simple water level can be used to check foundation walls for level. Hold one end of the tube against the top of one wall and have a partner hold the other end against the top of the other wall. Then compare the wall heights with the increments marked at each end of the tube.

pipe with duct tape and slide the level in. You can also buy carrying cases at most tool centers.

Water level One of the easiest and least expensive ways to determine level over long distances or around corners is with a water level (see the drawing above). This tool, which is simply a plastic tube filled with water, relies on the fact that water seeks its own level. I used to make my own, but now I find it's easier to buy them. Water levels are available from Zircon (see Sources on p. 198).

Plumb bob
As its name implies, a plumb bob is used to check a vertical surface—such as a door, wall, or window—for plumb, or to find a spot directly below any given point. It is a simple but very accurate tool consisting of a tapered weight attached to a string. It's really easy to use, too. To find plumb below a spot on a ceiling joist, for example, hold the string to a point on a joist and extend the string so that the weight is close to the floor (see the photo on the facing page). Plumb is directly below the point of the weight.

A plumb bob is a very accurate tool for finding the location of a point that is directly above or below another point.

2
POWER TOOLS

Power tools have revolutionized the way houses are built. Some of the tools common on the job site include (clockwise from bottom) ⅜-in. drills, miter saws, belt sanders, cordless drills, reciprocating saws, ½-in. drills, trim saws, and circular saws (worm drive left, sidewinder right).

Tools aren't like stretch socks where one size fits all. A saw that has the right combination of power, weight, and feel for one carpenter may be the wrong choice for another. But here are a few tips that should help you make an educated choice when it comes time to invest in a power tool.

• The tool should be comfortable to use, so (if possible) try before you buy. Do some homework, and try out a few to see how each one feels.

An 18-volt cordless circular saw can make short work of 2x stock.

• I also recommend asking people who use tools daily—like other carpenters or contractors—which models and makes they prefer. For these folks, durability is a big issue, and they won't mind telling you which tools have lasted and which ones haven't. It also helps to read magazines that research and evaluate different tools (*Fine Homebuilding* magazine is a good place to start).

• Buy the best quality you can afford. In general, steer away from homeowner-grade tools, which won't stand up to heavy-duty job site use. Professional-grade tools cost more, but they are more durable, more powerful, and easier and safer to use than homeowner grade.

• Many portable power tools are available in cordless versions with rechargeable batteries. The first cordless tools I used years ago were actually playthings for those who loved gadgets. This is no longer true. Today's cordless tools are used by professional workers in every trade. These tools have plenty of power and allow carpenters to move around the job site without the frustration of having to pull an extension cord around behind them.

• Almost every carpenter I know uses a cordless drill/screwdriver daily. In addition, now there are cordless jigsaws, reciprocating saws, and circular saws that have enough power for daily professional use. The new 18-volt systems have enough juice to power a cordless saw through 2x stock, and with a spare battery and charger on site, the only break you'll have to take is for lunch.

The first time I had my hands on a circular saw was in 1951, when power tools were first becoming readily available. What a sense of wonder it gave me. That stack of framing lumber that used to take me hours to cut with a handsaw could now be cut in minutes with the circular saw I was holding.

In my lifetime, carpenters have gone from building an entire house in a few months using hand tools to building the same house in a matter of weeks—even days in some cases—using power tools. The power-tool revolution has changed how carpenters work. Today, power tools are used in every aspect of carpentry, so one of the tasks of a beginning carpenter is to learn a little bit about these tools, including how to choose them and how to use them safely.

In this chapter I'll focus on the most common tools used on the job: circular saws, portable table saws, miter saws, reciprocating saws, jigsaws, drills, pneumatic nailers, routers, and sanders. Because practice is essential to gaining familiarity with any tool, at the end of the chapter I'll give you plans and instructions for building a workbench using some of the power tools discussed in the chapter.

SAWS

Old-time carpenters needed many hand tools to cut and shape raw wood, such as the handsaw, keyhole saw, and miter box. Today's carpenters use power tools, such as the circular saw, reciprocating saw, jigsaw, and miter saw.

Circular saw

The portable circular saw is as indispensable to a carpenter as a word processor or computer is to a writer. It is the one tool that you will use over and over again every day.

Circular saws come in two basic styles (see the photo below). One is a worm-drive saw with the blade on the left side. Direct-drive saws (also called sidewinders) have the blade on either the right or left side. Like many framers I know, I prefer the worm drive because it's heavier, more durable, and delivers more power to the blade than the sidewinder.

For most carpenters, the average job can be handled by a heavy-duty 7¼-in. circular saw. For big work, such as timber framing, carpenters use a larger circular saw, called a beam saw. Beam saws are available with blade diameters of up to

The circular saw is the workhorse of the building industry. Shown here are (from left) a 7¼-in. direct-drive sidewinder, a 5⅜-in. cordless trim saw, a 7¼-in. direct drive, and a 7¼-in. worm drive. (Photo by Joe Haun.)

When using power tools at home or on the job, make sure you plug them into quality extension cords. A good cord ensures that adequate electricity will be delivered to the tool you are using. So when shopping for an extension cord, don't just buy the cheapest one on the shelf. A cheap cord can be dangerous.

In 1948, the year I first helped build a house, I was helping to finish a concrete slab in a basement. It was getting dark, so I asked for a light, and someone handed me a trouble light. It was trouble all right! I was standing with wet shoes on wet concrete. The extension cord supplying electricity to the light was frayed and ungrounded. The shock that went through me knocked me over backwards, and as I fell, I pulled the plug out of the outlet. Sometimes you get lucky!

BUYING GUIDELINES

When shopping for an extension cord, pay attention to the gauge (the diameter) of the wire. The smaller the gauge number, the larger the diameter of the wire. A 12-gauge wire is larger in diameter (or heavier) than a 14-gauge wire.

A corded power tool needs an extension cord with wires heavy enough to deliver adequate power to the tool. Imagine trying to water a lawn with a hose the diameter of a toothpick. Not much water will pass. When using a light-gauge extension cord, a power tool doesn't get enough electricity. That means the motor will work harder, causing it to overheat and possibly burn out.

In general, a long cord requires a heavy-gauge wire to deliver the electricity with a minimal drop in voltage. As a rule of thumb, use 16-gauge wire for a 25-ft. cord. A 50-ft. cord needs at least 14-gauge wire, and a 100-ft. cord needs 12-gauge wire.

For protection against electrical shock while using a power tool, buy an extension cord equipped with a ground-fault circuit interrupter (GFCI). In the event of a short, or ground fault, the GFCI automatically shuts off power—and fast. (Many localities require GFCI protection on all job sites, so check your local codes.)

CARE AND STORAGE

Proper care of an extension cord is critical to making it last. Like a water hose with a hole in it, an extension cord (or a cord on a tool) with exposed wires can allow electricity to leak out, possibly into you. Take time to temporarily repair any cord that is frayed or cut by wrapping the area with electrical tape and by replacing the cord as soon as possible.

Another thing that will help an extension cord last—and remain tangle free—is proper storage. You can simply loop it into a circle and hang it on a hook. Or you can loop it into a daisy chain—which is a simple crochet stitch—and hang it on a hook.

Hang extension cords from hooks when not in use. To help ensure tangle-free cords, loop them into a circle (right) or a daisy-chain (left).

16 in. and are capable of cutting through 6-in.-thick stock. Smaller circular saws for trimwork are available with blade diameters as small as 4½ in.

While most circular saws come equipped with a steel blade, I recommend replacing it as soon as possible with a carbide-tipped blade. These blades stay sharp longer than standard steel blades, which makes cutting faster and safer. Most carpenters use a thin combination blade, which allows you to crosscut and rip wood easily. While not indestructible, most carbide-tipped blades will cut through the occasional nail without too much damage. But be sure to sharpen or replace a dull blade. A dull blade requires more pressure to make a cut, making the saw harder to control and creating more opportunities for accidents. Special blades for cutting materials like plastic, masonry, ceramics, tile, and even metal are also available.

Portable table saw

When I first started framing back in the 1950s, the only power tool we had on the job was a table saw. It was a heavy monster with more iron in it than a John Deere tractor. It definitely was *not* portable. These days, table saws aren't used much in framing, but they're still very useful on the job site. Fortunately, these new machines are now so portable that they can be lifted with one hand. I find the table saw especially useful when it's time for finish work. With it, I can easily and quickly cut siding and interior and exterior trim to size.

While these saws are convenient, they—like any tool—can be hazardous if used improperly. They're light, so they should be secured to a work table at a comfortable working height. Once secured, the saw won't move around during a cut, which decreases the possibility of kickback. For safety, always stand to one side of the workpiece so you're out of the line of fire in case the material kicks back.

As with any power tool, familiarize yourself with the manual before using it, and make sure the blade guard is in place and functioning properly before plugging the saw in. Also, raise the blade so that it projects only about ⅛ in. above the material being cut. Hold the stock securely against the fence when ripping, but, of course, keep your fingers away from the blade area. If the stock is longer than the table, set up a makeshift out-feed table or have someone support the opposite end as it comes off the table. Use a push stick to keep your hands clear of the blade as you finish the cut.

Power miter saw

What the circular saw did for rough frame carpentry, the power miter saw did for finish trimwork. Just as the circular saw replaced the handsaw, the power miter saw replaced the miter box. The miter saw (often called a chopsaw) can make fast, accurate cuts in framing lumber, door and window casings, baseboard, and crown moldings.

The first miter saws I recall were used almost exclusively by plumbers to cut plastic pipe. Basically a circular saw mounted on a short table, a power miter saw is used to make square and angled cuts and has evolved into a tool that's used daily by both frame and finish carpenters. Unlike a radial-arm saw, which slides along a track and is notoriously difficult to keep aligned, a power miter saw lowers into the cut with a chopping action from a fixed pivot point. The saw is rugged and easy to use and, when equipped with a high-quality blade, can make glass-smooth cuts. Blade diameters range from 8 in. to 16 in. Most carpenters prefer the 10-in. model,

A kickback occurs when the sawblade gets pinched in the kerf (the saw cut) and the power of the motor forces the saw backward. This can be a bit scary, and it is bound to happen to you if you use a circular saw all day.

There are two keys to preventing a kickback. First, always cut in a straight line. Don't try to force or twist the saw as you cut, which will cause the blade to bind in the kerf, kicking the saw out. Second, provide solid support for the stock on both sides of the cut. Without proper support, the stock will sag and pinch the blade, as shown in the drawing below.

If a kickback occurs, release the trigger on the saw immediately and allow the saw to stop. As long as the blade guard is working properly, there is little danger of injury.

Not enough support

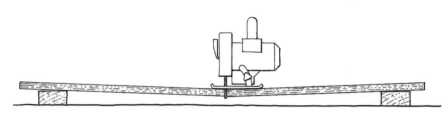

The stock sags in the middle, pinching the blade.

Not enough support

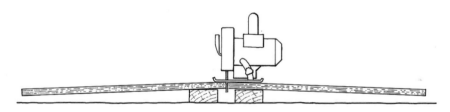

The stock sags on the end, pinching the blade.

Proper support

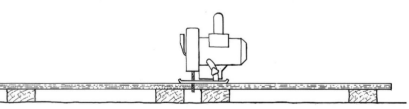

The stock is supported on both sides of the cut.

Before using a circular saw, or any power tool, first study its manual, familiarize yourself with its parts, and follow the instructions on using and caring for the tool.

The blade guard of the saw should always move freely. If the guard is stiff, it could have a buildup of wood pitch on it. To remove the pitch, use bleach on the guard and brush off the pitch with a wire brush. Or better yet, try a common cleaner called Oxi-Solve on both (see Sources on p. 198). Before cleaning or testing the guard, be sure the tool is unplugged.

When you're sure the guard is working properly, set the sawblade to the proper depth. In general, the blade should be set about 1/8 in. deeper than the thickness of the stock. Again, be sure to unplug the cord when setting the blade depth so that you don't accidentally start the saw.

The three basic saw cuts used by carpenters are the crosscut, rip cut, and plunge cut. The key to making any of these cuts with a circular saw is being able to make straight cuts. With practice, this will become second nature, so grab some scrap wood—2x4 stock or plywood—and start cutting.

CROSSCUTTING

A cut across the grain is called a crosscut. To make one, first scribe a cut line on the stock using a square to draw the line straight. Make sure that the stock is adequately supported either by sawhorses or by 2x blocks placed on the floor so that the cutoff can fall free. Then place the saw base on the stock with the blade about 1 in. from the edge of the wood and align the blade with the cut line. Hold the saw with both hands, pull the switch, and slowly push the blade into the wood, following the cut line. Going slowly and cutting straight helps prevent kickback (for more on preventing kickbacks, see the sidebar on p. 43).

To make a square cut without scribing a cut line in 2x4s and other narrow stock, align the front edge of the saw base parallel to the edge of the stock and make the cut. Try this a few times on scrap, checking each cut with a square to see how you're doing.

A straightedge ensures a straight crosscut.

To make a long, straight crosscut, say on finish-grade plywood or across a door, clamp a good straightedge to the workpiece and slide the saw base along it as you cut (see the photo above). You can make your own straightedge, but I use a commercial one from Griset Industries (see Sources on p. 198) that is arrow-straight and easy to clamp to the workpiece.

Another way to make a straight crosscut is to use a shootboard, which is simply a straightedge with a fence (saw guide) screwed to it. You can buy a shootboard (Olive Knot Products makes an adjustable one—see Sources on p. 198), but it's pretty easy to make one.

Just cut two pieces of 1/2-in. plywood—one 8 in. wide and one 1 1/2 in. wide—as long as the material you wish to cut. Glue or screw the 1 1/2-in. piece to one edge of the 8-in. piece. The wider piece will be the base, and the thinner piece will serve as the fence. Place the circular saw on the base against the fence and cut off any excess material.

To use a shootboard, clamp it to the workpiece with the front edge of the base right on the cut line. Place the saw on the shootboard against the fence, reset the blade so that it extends 1/8 in. below the stock, and cut. The base will also keep the wood fibers from tearing out at the end grain (for more on preventing tearout, see the sidebar on p. 47).

RIPPING

A cut along the length of a board is called a rip cut, and it can be done in several ways. Most ripping is done simply by cutting freehand along a pencil mark or chalkline that has been laid out on a board. Again, make sure the stock is adequately supported and that the saw isn't forced or twisted during the cut.

When you need an accurate rip cut, use a ripping-guide attachment. A good one is available from Prazi-USA (see Sources on p. 198). Another type of guide fits into the slots on the front of the saw base. Both guides work like a table-saw fence and can be adjusted to various widths (see the photo below). Both have a flange on one end that you hold against the edge of a board as you make the cut. If you have a flat saw base, you can attach a stair gauge to the front edge and use it as a ripping guide (see the photo at right).

PLUNGE CUTTING

A plunge cut is made in the middle of a board and is used, for instance, to cut a window opening in the center of a piece of plywood sheathing.

To make a plunge cut, lean the saw forward over the cut line so that it is resting on the front edge of the saw base with the blade about 1 in. from the wood (see the bottom right photo). Use the lever to raise

the guard and expose the blade, then start the saw and, using the front edge as the hinge point, slowly lower the blade into the wood. Hold the saw with both hands and continue the cut, following the cut line. When you get to the end of the cut, turn the saw off and let the blade stop spinning before pulling it out.

If you need to finish a cut near where you started, don't try to back the saw into the cut. Instead, turn the saw around and finish from the opposite direction.

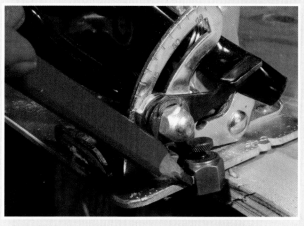

A stair gauge attached to a saw base makes a simple but effective ripping guide.

A ripping-guide attachment makes it easy to cut on a straight line, even on long stock. (Photo by Roe A. Osborn.)

To start a plunge cut, lean the front edge of the saw base over the cut line, and start the saw with the blade about 1 in. from the wood.

When cutting long stock with a miter saw (also called a chopsaw), support one end on an extension table, on a sawhorse, or on blocking, as shown here.

which can crosscut a 2x6, because of its versatility. Smaller models work well for cutting trim, while larger ones can cut through 4x stock.

There are now a variety of power miter saws that offer even greater capacity and versatility than the simple version just described. Some of the newest sliding compound miter saws have the capacity to crosscut up to a 4x12. They also tilt from side to side to allow you to make a compound (double-angle) miter cut. These saws are rugged enough for daily use by framers, yet are plenty accurate for finish work.

Some power miter saws come equipped with extension wings for the table, which can be useful for cutting relatively short stock. For longer stock, you may need extra support so that the stock

doesn't lift and pinch the blade. Extension tables for miter saws are available, but I usually support long stock with a block set to the side of a job-made table (see the photo above).

Reciprocating saw

Years ago, every carpenter had a key-hole saw for cutting in tight places. Nowadays carpenters use a reciprocating saw, which is basically a keyhole saw with a motor. It's the tool of choice for remodeling work, such as tearing out walls, replacing doors and windows, or removing old cabinets, because it cuts through wood, metal (including nails and pipes), plaster, and plastic. It can also get into places you can't reach with a circular saw: for instance, when you need to cut a hole in a subfloor right against a wall.

PREVENTING TEAROUT

Tearout of wood fibers is a common occurrence when cutting wood, especially during crosscutting. This is okay for framing but not for finish work. One way to prevent tearout is to lay a straightedge directly on the cut line and run a utility knife or a pocketknife along the line to score the wood fibers on the cutoff side of the line. This will prevent them from lifting up as the saw makes the cut.

Another way to prevent tearout is to lay a strip of masking tape over the area to be cut. The tape will hold the wood fibers in place during the cut. To prevent the tape from lifting any loose fibers from the wood when removing it, pull it toward the edge of the board.

To prevent tearout, place masking tape over the cutting area, draw the cut line on it, and make the cut slowly.

The first reciprocating saws had only one speed, but most of them now have either a two-speed or a variable-speed switch. While wood can be cut at high speed, hard materials—such as metal pipe—need a lower speed to minimize the heat generated by friction. The variable-speed mechanism also makes it easier to do plunge cuts and precision work. When using a reciprocating saw (say, for cutting into an existing wall), be careful not to cut through plumbing or wires. It's a good idea to shut off power to any nearby electrical circuits when making blind cuts, but it's an even better idea to avoid making blind cuts whenever you can. Use both hands when using this saw, and hold the shoe against the material being cut to make the cut faster and safer (see the top photo on p. 49).

Reciprocating saw blades are available in lengths from 2½ in. to 12 in. A good all-purpose size is 6 in., which is large enough for most jobs and easier to control than longer blades. In general, use the shortest blade that will do the job. I prefer to use bimetal blades, which are more expensive than standard blades but can cut both wood and metal. If you bend a blade while cutting, don't worry. Blades can usually be straightened and reused, and you usually don't even have to take them out of the saw to do it.

• Stay alert at all times. Accidents happen not so much when we are still learning but when we think we have mastered a tool. As a beginner, your mind is focused and you are careful. But once you gain experience, you may feel so confident that you pay less attention to what you are doing.

• Keep small children away from power saws (and other tools).

• Use sharp blades. Dull blades don't cut well and can cause accidents.

• When changing blades, unplug the saw.

• If the saw has a blade guard, make sure it's working properly, and use it. Cut scrap wood to practice working with the guard in place so you can get used to it.

• Don't force a saw. Let it work at its own pace. Forcing a saw can overload the motor, causing it to overheat.

• When you feel the blade bind in the kerf, stop and start over.

• Wear safety glasses or goggles.

• Wear a mask if you are sensitive to sawdust.

• Use hearing protection.

• Don't use a power saw—or any power tool—when you are fatigued.

• Remove anything that might distract you, such as a loud radio.

• Keep your fingers away from the blade! Blow—don't brush—sawdust away from the cut line to clear the line as you cut.

However, the blade can get quite hot when cutting, so be sure to use pliers, not your fingers, to straighten it.

Jigsaw

The first carpenter I learned from was a master with a coping saw, which he used to cut intricate patterns. I think he would have loved a power jigsaw (also called a sabersaw), which can literally cut circles around a coping saw. It's a versatile tool used for cutting circles, curves, and irregular patterns, as well as for making sink cutouts in countertops.

Most jigsaws have an adjustable base plate that allows you to make angled cuts. And I recommend getting a jigsaw with a variable-speed control, which gives more control over the cut through various types of materials. Like its cousin the reciprocating saw, a jigsaw can cut through wood, ceramic tile, plastic, fiberglass, and metal—when equipped with the proper blade.

Jigsaw blades are designed to cut either on the upstroke or on the downstroke, depending on the blade. To avoid tearout on the finish side of a workpiece, keep the finish side down if your

When using a reciprocating saw, place one hand on the handle to control the switch and the other on the rubber boot at the front end of the tool.

To start a plunge cut with a jigsaw, rest the front edge of the base plate on the workpiece with the blade clear of the wood. Start the saw and ease the blade into the wood.

blade cuts on the upstroke. Keep the finish side up if your blade cuts on the down stroke. To reduce vibration and chipping, hold the base plate firmly against the surface of the material when making your cut, letting the saw work at its own pace. If you push it too hard, especially through a knot, the blade could break. On a tight curve, cut very slowly so as not to bind or break the blade. And don't brush sawdust away from the cut line with your hand; instead, blow the dust away and save your fingers.

Both jigsaws and reciprocating saws can cut an opening in thinner material, such as plywood paneling, without drilling an initial pilot hole. To make a plunge cut with a jigsaw, tilt the saw forward and rest the front edge of the base plate on the workpiece with the blade clear of the wood (see the bottom photo on p. 49). Then start the saw and ease the blade slowly into the wood. Once the blade penetrates all the way through, the saw can be placed in its normal vertical position and the cut completed.

DRILLS

I remember making hole after hole with a hand-powered brace and bit in the early '50s. I still have one hanging on the wall of my shop. Drilling bolt holes by hand in 2x6 sill plates was easy. But drilling a 1-in. bolt hole in a thick, solid beam took effort. Even with sharp bits, hand drilling was time-consuming. Today, a power drill fitted with the proper bit can drill the toughest hole in seconds. The power drill is a versatile tool. It makes holes in all sorts of material and can even be used for driving screws and for mixing paint and drywall compound.

Every carpenter owns a power drill or two. Shown here are (from left to right) two ⅜-in. pistol-grip drills and a ½-in. right-angle drill.

- For clean, easy cuts, use sharp bits.

- Don't force the drill. Let it cut at its own pace. When drilling into hard wood, coat the bit with wax or soap to make drilling easier. Use low speeds for drilling into steel and lubricate the bit with oil to reduce friction and heat buildup.

- Treat any drill with respect, just as you would a circular saw. Drills have a lot of torque (turning power). If a bit gets hung up on a hard knot or a nail, all the power of the drill is transferred to its handle, which will give your arm a powerful (and potentially wrist-breaking) twist.

- When drilling into heavy or thick material, use two hands to hold the drill steady. When drilling with an auger bit or with a powerful drill, use the side handle. The torque can be so great that it is hard to hold these tools with one hand.

- Work with your feet apart and your body in a well-balanced position. Be especially careful when drilling from a ladder. Make sure the ladder is stable and that you are not in an awkward position.

- Make sure what you are drilling is secure. If it is not stationary, clamp the workpiece to a sawhorse or to a workbench. Don't try to hold the piece to be drilled with your hands. It's too easy to lose control of the piece and injure yourself.

There are three basic things you should consider when buying a drill: its size, type, and chuck style. Drill sizes are dictated by the largest bit shank (the shaft of the bit) that will fit into the chuck (the jaws that hold bits). Common drill sizes are ¼ in., ⅜ in., and ½ in., and most carpenters own both ⅜-in. and ½-in. drills. My ⅜-in. drill is reversible (meaning I can change the direction the bit rotates) and has a variable-speed switch. These two qualities allow me to use the drill for both driving and removing screws. Even better, when a bit gets stuck, I can switch to reverse and back it out of the hole. I use my powerful ½-in. drill when I need to drill larger holes (for example, for bolts or locksets). A handy accessory for a ½-in. drill is a side handle, which allows you to hold the drill securely with two hands when drilling large holes.

There are different types of drills. Some have a pistol grip, while others have two handles. Some drill straight on, while others drill at a right angle (see the photo on the facing page). The type of drill you need depends on the work you do.

I use my ½-in. right-angle drill in tight places (for example, in stud and joist bays) and hold on tight when I'm using it. This tool has a lot of power. The hammer drill is a variation of the standard drill. This tool moves a drill bit in a circular and up and down motion at the same time. You can drill through concrete or other masonry materials like magic.

Although many drills have chucks that are tightened around a bit's shank using a key, most carpenters now prefer drills with keyless chucks. That means the chuck is tightened by hand. Keyless chucks are fine for most work and allow for quick bit changing. But for heavy-duty drilling, you'll still need a keyed chuck to keep the bit from slipping.

Having a variety of drill bits adds versatility to a power drill. Shown here are (clockwise from top right): hole saws, a Forstner bit, auger bits, spade bits, an expansion bit, carbide-tipped twist bits, and a set of standard twist bits.

Bits

In general, buying drill bits in sets is less expensive than buying them individually. I use standard twist bits (from $\frac{1}{64}$ in. to $\frac{1}{2}$ in.) to drill holes in wood, and hardened or carbide-tipped bits to drill holes in metal, masonry, tile, and glass.

I use spade bits or Forstner bits for drilling large-diameter ($\frac{3}{8}$ in. to 2 in.) holes. Sharp spade bits cut right through wood but leave a fairly rough hole, while Forstner bits leave holes with flat bottoms, smooth sides, and a clean top edge that can later be filled with a wood plug.

Holes for door locksets (which are typically $2\frac{1}{8}$ in. dia.) can be drilled with a hole saw. Available in sizes ranging up to 6 in., hole saws (which are bits that have teeth around the perimeter like a saw) can have bimetal teeth for cutting large holes, not only in wood but also in light metals, plastics, and fiberglass.

A magnetic bit holder that fits into the chuck allows you to drive screws with one hand and hold the material with the other.

Auger bits are handy for cutting holes through thick material, such as 6x6 beams. They are self-feeding, meaning that they pull themselves into the hole, and don't require a lot of force on the part of the drill operator. Adjustable expansion bits can cut holes of varying size.

For finish work, it's often a good idea to countersink screws (putting the screw head below the finish surface) using a countersink bit. This type of bit has a beveled face that makes the screw hole larger at the top to fit the head of a wood screw.

For driving screws, every carpenter carries different screwdriver bits. While you'll still occasionally come up against a slotted screw, most screws on a construction site have a Phillips head. This configuration keeps the bit centered on the screw and provides better purchase, perfect for setting screws with a drill or screw gun. A useful accessory for driving screws is a magnetic bit holder, which fits into the drill chuck to hold screw-driver bits (see the photo on p. 53). This setup makes it easier to drive screws with one hand and change bits quickly.

PNEUMATIC NAILERS

My first pneumatic tool drove only sta-ples, and I used it to nail subfloor and roof sheathing. Today, pneumatic nailers drive many types of fastener. In some areas of the country, they are almost as common on job sites as hammers.

What makes a pneumatic nailer so appealing is its speed. The nails are automatically fed into the nailer from a clip or coil (which can hold 200 nails or more), so you don't have to keep reach-ing into your toolbelt for nails.

Today, there's a nailer for every job, from rough framing to roofing to the finest finish work. I own two framing nailers, a finish nailer, and a palm nailer. Both framing nailers drive 8d or 16d nails (see the photo below)—one feeds the nails from a clip, and the other feeds them from a coil. Both fit well in my hand,

A framing nailer can be used for rough framing, as well as for nailing a ply-wood subfloor to joists. (Photo by Roe A. Osborn.)

A finish nailer works well for trimwork, such as nailing in the stool for a window. (Photo by Roe A. Osborn.)

seldom jam, and require very little maintenance. They take a drop of oil twice a day and need to be cleaned with a wire brush now and then, but that's about it.

The same is true with my finish nailer, which drives nails from 1 in. (brads) to 2½ in. (8d) long (see the photo above). Finish nailers not only drive the nails but can also set them below the surface of the wood, which saves a lot of nail-setting time. I use my palm nailer to drive nails in hard-to-get-at places, where it's not easy to swing a hammer. It's a

great tool for nailing in hurricane ties and joist hangers (see the photo on p. 56).

Most nailers operate off compressed air, though there are also electrically powered brad nailers and staplers and propane-powered framing and finish nailers. Buying a nailer and the necessary air compressor, gauges, and air hoses represents a substantial investment, though these items can pay for themselves in short order due to increased productivity.

• A pneumatic nailer is as dangerous as a gun and needs to be treated with respect.

• Read and carefully follow the instruction manual regarding maintenance and use.

• Don't point a nailer at yourself or at others.

• Don't walk around with your finger on the trigger. You might bump the nailer against your leg, release the safety, and fire a nail accidentally.

• Adjust the air pressure as needed (larger nails require more pressure). But don't exceed the recommended amount of air pressure.

• Wear safety glasses or goggles.

• Don't nail with the gun in front of your face, especially if you are working on a vertical surface. If you hit a hard knot or metal strap, the gun can bounce back and strike you.

• Disconnect the gun from the air compressor when clearing a jammed nail.

• When nailing studs to a plate, drive the low nail first. Then remove the hand holding the stud and drive the high nail. If you drive the high nail first, sooner or later you will miss the wood plate and drive a nail through your hand.

• Take a break now and then to stay focused. An unfocused mind can cause you to shoot a nail into your body, which will bring you back to reality like an early morning alarm clock, sudden and unpleasant.

A palm nailer can drive nails in tight places, as when installing a joist hanger. (Photo by Roe A. Osborn.)

OTHER USEFUL POWER TOOLS

Although not often used by frame carpenters, two other power tools worth mentioning are routers and sanders. These tools are typically used for finish work, like preparing a bookcase for stain or paint, which makes them more suitable for trim and finish carpenters.

Routers

Routers are classified according to the largest-diameter bit shank that the collet (or chuck) can handle. Common sizes are ¼ in., ⅜ in., and ½ in. The most powerful routers have 3-plus HP motors and can make big cuts through heavy stock in a single pass.

Equipped with the right bit, the router can be adapted to a number of carpentry jobs. You can cut grooves and notches, round over edges, trim materials (like plastic laminate), and make moldings with a router. With the right attachment, you can cut perfect circles and even mortise doors for hinges.

For all its usefulness, though, a router can be a frightening tool. Its motor is directly connected to an unguarded bit, which protrudes from a base plate. The motor can spin the bit up to 25,000 revolutions per minute (rpm) or faster and makes more noise than a roomful of rock musicians. Because of the noise and the fact that the bit is exposed, I always wear ear protection and safety glasses

The belt sander (left) can remove a lot of stock quickly. The pad sander (right) is more suited to finish work.

Carpenters learn to work without sawhorses, but there are times when a good pair of horses can save your back or help you work overhead. Stock placed on sawhorses allows you to cut, drill, or shape materials without having to bend over. For a temporary workstation, top a pair of horses with a sheet of plywood. Planks placed across horses make a good scaffold.

There are many different styles of sawhorses. Some are works of art suitable for a living room, and others are simple structures. Here are plans and instructions for a strong sawhorse that can be made in just a few minutes.

Measure and cut the 8-ft. 2x4 into two 48-in.-long pieces. Then measure and cut four 30-in.-long legs from the 12-ft. 1x6.

Begin assembly with the crosspiece of the sawhorse. Turn one 2x4 on edge, center another 2x4 flat on the first so that they form a T, and nail them together with four 16d nails.

Next, position the end of a 1x6 leg flush with the top of the crosspiece (see the drawing on the facing page) and about 2 in. from the end. Nail the legs (or use 1½-in. drywall screws) with two 8d nails into both pieces of the T. Do the same with the remaining three legs, then set the sawhorse upright.

Nail the 48-in.-long 1x4 to the top of the crosspiece with two or three 8d nails. Countersink these nail heads with a nailset so you won't hit them with a saw blade when you are cutting on the sawhorse.

Now take a plywood square and hold it against the legs on one side of the sawhorse. Make sure the top of the plywood is flush to the bottom of the crosspiece, then trace the outline of the legs onto the plywood. Repeat with the other piece of plywood on the other side of the sawhorse. These pieces brace the legs of the sawhorse.

Cut both plywood pieces along the lines you traced. Use several 8d nails or 1½-in. drywall screws to attach the plywood pieces to the legs, one on each end and flush with the bottom of the crosspiece. (You may have to predrill small pilot holes to keep the nails or screws from splitting the wood.)

when I'm working with a router. And I'm always extremely aware of where my hands are.

Portable sanders

Any carpenter who builds something that will be exposed to view probably has some type of portable sander. I own three: a belt sander, a pad sander (see the photo on p. 57), and a random-orbit sander.

A belt sander is useful for heavy, rough jobs like sanding down a cutting board that needs to be refinished. It can remove a lot of stock rapidly, so use this tool with care. Common belt sizes range from 3 in. by 18 in. to 4 in. by 24 in. (The small number refers to the width of the belt, while the large number indicates the length of the loop.)

My pad sander (also called a finish sander) has a base pad to which the sandpaper is attached and is powerful

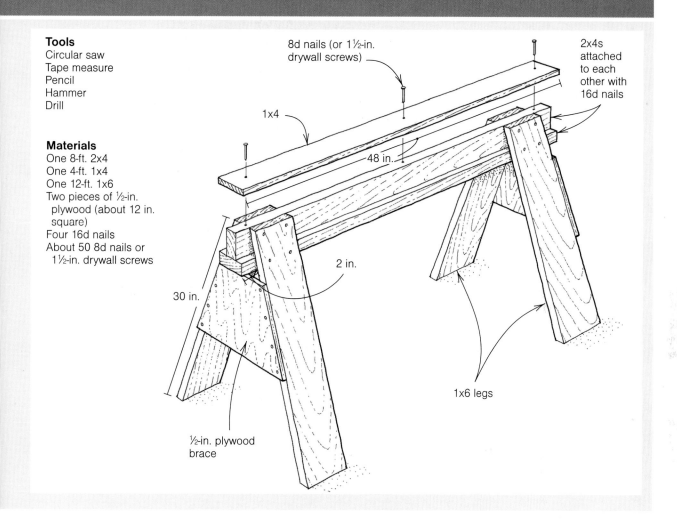

Tools
Circular saw
Tape measure
Pencil
Hammer
Drill

Materials
One 8-ft. 2x4
One 4-ft. 1x4
One 12-ft. 1x6
Two pieces of ½-in.
  plywood (about 12 in.
  square)
Four 16d nails
About 50 8d nails or
  1½-in. drywall screws

8d nails (or 1½-in.
drywall screws)

2x4s
attached
to each
other with
16d nails

1x4

48 in.

2 in.

30 in.

1x6 legs

½-in. plywood
brace

enough to remove substantial stock when fitted with coarse-grit sandpaper. However, I use it mostly for finish work, including prepping trimwork for paint.

I love my random-orbit sander. It's small enough to be held with one hand. It has a circular base pad that moves in both circular and back-and-forth motions, which enables it to remove stock quickly yet not leave swirl marks. It is easy to use and is quite powerful for its size.

Sanders create a lot of dust, so choose one with a dust bag and an efficient dust-collection system to help reduce the amount of sawdust that gets airborne. Whether your sander has a dust bag or not, it's also a good idea to always wear a dust mask or respirator when using a sander to help keep fine dust from getting into your lungs.

A workbench is a handy item to have on the job site. Here are plans and instructions for building a sturdy 2-ft.-long by 20-in.-high workbench that can be used to carry tools, to support wood that needs cutting, and even to stand on when working overhead.

CUTTING THE PARTS

Begin by cutting the top, the shelf, and the ends. Lay the 8-ft. 1x12 on the floor over a piece of 2x so the cutoff end can fall free, then measure down 24 in. for the bench top. Using a square, mark a line across the wood at this point. Cut just beside the mark so that the top will be a full 24 in. long. Carpenters sometimes call this "leaving the line." Don't worry if the cut isn't quite perfect.

Now measure 20½ in. down the 1x12 for the shelf and draw a cut line across it using the square. Make the cut, but remember to leave the line. Lay the shelf and top aside and cut the two end pieces to a length of 19¼ in. from the remaining 1x12.

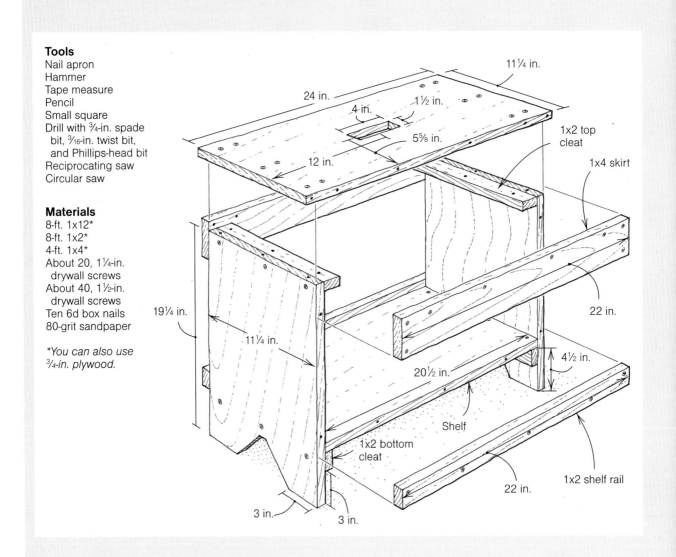

Tools
Nail apron
Hammer
Tape measure
Pencil
Small square
Drill with ¾-in. spade
  bit, ³⁄₁₆-in. twist bit,
  and Phillips-head bit
Reciprocating saw
Circular saw

Materials
8-ft. 1x12*
8-ft. 1x2*
4-ft. 1x4*
About 20, 1¼-in.
  drywall screws
About 40, 1½-in.
  drywall screws
Ten 6d box nails
80-grit sandpaper

*You can also use
¾-in. plywood.

24 in.
11¼ in.
1½ in.
4 in.
5⅝ in.
12 in.
1x2 top cleat
1x4 skirt
19¼ in.
11¼ in.
22 in.
4½ in.
20½ in.
Shelf
1x2 bottom cleat
1x2 shelf rail
22 in.
3 in.
3 in.

To lay out the feet, place one side on top of the other. Measure in 3 in. from each side and use a small square to mark a 45° line to the center.

Lay out the "feet" on the end pieces next. To make the feet identical on both end pieces, place one on top of the other. Measure in 3 in. from the end, hold the small square to this point, and mark a 45° line to the center, creating a V (see the photo above). The top of the V should be about 3 in. from the bottom of each piece. Cut out this V section.

Next, cut two 22-in. skirts from the 4-ft. 1x4. The skirts will help strengthen the bench top. Now grab the 8-ft. 1x2 and cut two 22-in. shelf rails and four 11¼-in. cleats.

ASSEMBLING THE WORKBENCH

Start the assembly by attaching the cleats to the end pieces. The top cleats help tie the ends and top together. The bottom cleats help support and tie the shelf to the end pieces.

Lay one of the end pieces on top of the other, but place them on some 2xs so you don't drill into the floor. From the top, measure down ⅜ in., draw a square line across, and drill three ³⁄₁₆-in. holes across the line, spaced evenly. From the bottom, measure up 3¾ in., draw a square line across, and drill three more holes.

Attach the bottom cleats to the sides using 1¼-in. drywall screws.

Attach the shelf to the bottom cleats with 1½-in. drywall screws.

Place a cleat on edge on the floor and place an end piece on the cleat flush with the top. Join the two with three 1½-in. drywall screws. Drive the screws slowly and with care using a Phillips-head screwdriver. If you drive them too fast or too deep, you could strip the screws. If you make a mistake, drill another hole through the side and try again. Repeat for the other side.

Now attach the bottom cleats. To help ensure that the cleats will be level and straight, use a square to draw a line across the side just on top of the V (3 in. from the bottom). The bottom of the cleat should sit flat on that line. Now drive three 1¼-in. drywall screws through the holes in the side and into the cleat (see the left photo above). Repeat for the other side.

Next comes the top, which overhangs the end pieces 1 in. on both sides. On the underside of the top, draw a line 1 in. from each end to mark the outside edge of the end pieces. Hold an end piece to the 1-in. line. Drill three $^3/_{16}$-in. holes through the top and drive three 1$^1/_4$-in. drywall screws or three 6d nails through the top and into each cleat. Repeat for the other side. Now stand the workbench up. Take a look to see if everything is in proportion. Trust your eye; if it looks good, it is good.

The shelf comes next. Measure in $^3/_8$ in. from one end of the shelf, draw a line across with the help of a square, and drill three $^3/_{16}$-in. holes along the line, one about 1 in. from each end and one in the center. Repeat on the other end. Set the shelf between the ends and rest it on the bottom cleats. Attach it to the cleats with three 1$^1/_2$-in. drywall screws on each end (see the right photo on the facing page).

Next come the 1x4 skirts. Drill two $^3/_{16}$-in. holes $^3/_8$ in. from each end of a skirt. Then drill four $^3/_{16}$-in. holes along the length about $^3/_8$ in. from the edge. Repeat for the other skirt. Attach the skirts flush with the top of the bench using 1$^1/_2$-in. drywall screws.

Now grab a 1x2 shelf rail and drill one $^3/_{16}$-in. hole $^3/_8$ in. from each end and three more along the length $^3/_8$ in. from the edge. Repeat for the other rail. Attach the bottom of each rail flush to the bottom of the shelf using 1$^1/_2$-in. drywall screws.

It's nice to have a handhold in the top so that you can move the bench around. In the center of the top, lay out a handhold so that it's 1$^1/_2$ in. wide and 4 in. long. Drill a $^3/_4$-in. hole in opposite corners using a spade bit. Use a reciprocating saw or jigsaw to cut out the wood between the holes (see the photo at right). Sand the edges of the hole with 80-grit sandpaper. Then round the corners of the top with sandpaper. Now you're ready to go to work.

Cut out the handhold using a reciprocating saw (as shown) or a jigsaw.

3

ON THE JOB SITE

There's more to carpentry than the ability to drive a nail with a hammer. A big part of being a good carpenter is knowing not only the names of tools and how to use them but also the parts and materials that make up a house. Whether it's a 6d finish nail or a frieze board, you need to know what your co-workers are talking about.

In this chapter, I'll discuss briefly the parts of a typical house and how they go together. Then I'll talk about the various materials (lumber, fasteners, hardware) that make up a house. Knowing the parts and how they go together will help you read plans and learn how to estimate and order the amount of materials needed.

THE HOUSE STRUCTURE
When I was a child, I thought that houses just *were*. They existed like the hills, the trees, and the wind. It was only when I saw houses actually being built that I realized they are put together board by board and nail by nail. The construction starts at ground level, with the foundation.

The foundation of a house can be a full concrete basement, concrete stemwalls (short walls) with a crawl space under the house (see the left photo on p. 66), a concrete slab, concrete piers on footings, or pressure-treated wood on solid ground. Local codes and soil conditions generally dictate the type of foundation that a house will have.

Pressure-treated mudsills installed on the top of foundation walls help tie the floor system to the foundation and support the floor joists. Pressure-treated wood is impregnated with a preservative that inhibits dry rot (a fungus that can destroy wood) and helps repel termites, which can otherwise make a meal of your house and cause a lot of damage.

Pressure-treated wood is usually easily identified by its greenish color, and, because of the chemicals used in it, you should handle it and cut it with care. I wear gloves and a long-sleeve shirt when working with it to keep the chemicals off my body; I also wear a mask to help avoid breathing the dust.

Girders are often needed to support floor joists with long spans. The size of the girders will vary, depending on the load they carry. The house plans will indicate the size, based on local codes.

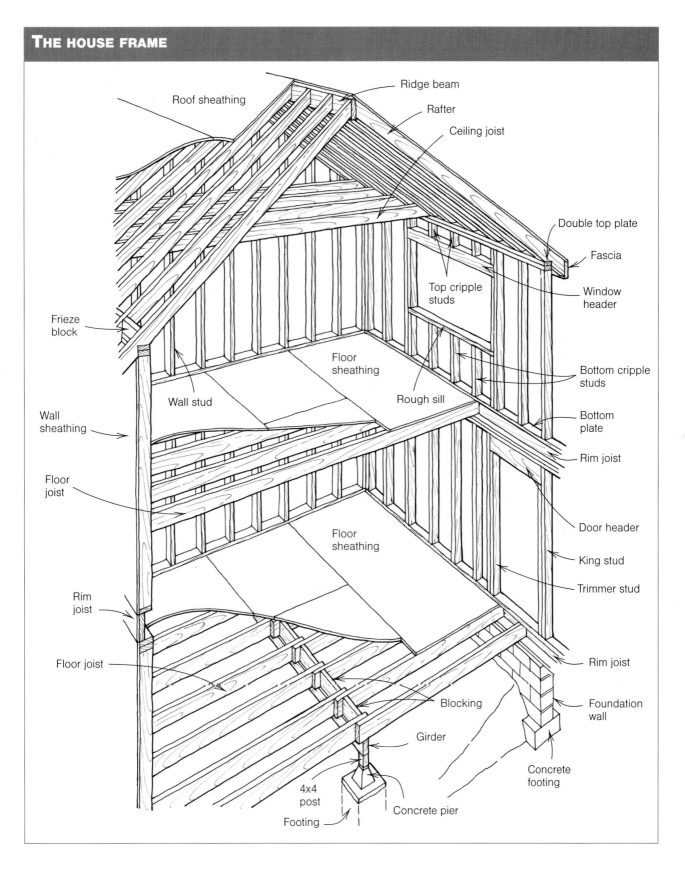

Roof sheathing

Ridge beam

Rafter

Ceiling joist

Double top plate

Fascia

Top cripple studs

Window header

Frieze block

Bottom cripple studs

Wall stud

Floor sheathing

Rough sill

Bottom plate

Wall sheathing

Rim joist

Floor joist

Door header

King stud

Floor sheathing

Trimmer stud

Rim joist

Floor joist

Rim joist

Blocking

Foundation wall

Girder

4x4 post

Concrete pier

Concrete footing

Footing

A house foundation can be a combination of full concrete basement and concrete stemwalls enclosing a crawl space, such as shown here, or just stemwalls with a crawl space, a concrete slab, or concrete piers on footings. (Photo by Roe A. Osborn.)

Floor joists form the platform, or floor, of the house and usually are spaced 16 in. or 24 in. on center.

Floor joists are placed horizontally over and perpendicular to the girders and form the platform, or floor, of a house (see the right photo above). Joists are usually spaced 16 in. or 24 in. on center (o.c.). Today, many builders use manufactured joists (such as Trus-Joists) rather than regular 2x lumber because these joists are straight, can span long distances, and don't shrink much (see the photo on the facing page).

Floor sheathing—generally 4x8 sheets of ⅝-in. or ¾-in. tongue-and-groove plywood or oriented strand board (OSB)—comes next. To help eliminate floor squeaks, the sheathing should be glued to the joists with construction adhesive and then nailed in place.

Wall plates are the horizontal members that hold together the pieces in a wall. Each wall has three plates—one on the bottom and two on top (called a top plate and a double top plate, respectively). The plates are usually made from long, straight 2x stock. The width of the plate stock depends on the width of the walls. Exterior walls often are built with 2x6s to accommodate the extra insulation required by many building codes. Interior walls (both studs and plates) are typically built from 2x4s. If you are framing on a concrete slab, the bottom plate needs to be pressure-treated wood to resist rot and insect damage.

Studs are the vertical wall members nailed to the wall plates. Typical spacing is either 16 in. o.c. or 24 in. o.c. The studs are the same width as the plates. If you are building a house with 8-ft. ceilings, you can save time and avoid waste by purchasing studs precut to 92¼ in. This length, plus the three horizontal 2x plates—which are actually 1½ in. thick (for more on lumber dimensions, see the sidebar on p. 68)—gives you a wall height of 96¾ in. After putting ½-in. drywall on the ceiling, you'll have a ceiling height of roughly 8 ft.

Where there are openings in walls, whether for doors or windows, the load (or weight) from the upper stories or roof must be transferred around the opening and down to the foundation. Otherwise, the weight from above may not allow a door or window to open and close properly and could cause other, more serious, structural problems like a sagging roof. This load transfer is accomplished with a header and a pair of wall studs. A header is a horizontal member that is sized according to the width of the opening and the load bearing on it. For example, a garage-door header has to be much larger than a standard window header because the garage opening is larger.

Wall studs are nailed into the header on each end. The header is supported by a trimmer stud (the same width as the wall studs) placed underneath on both ends. A trimmer stud runs from the bottom plate to the header on a door and from the rough sill to the header on a window. The space between the header and the double top plate or the windowsill and the bottom plate is filled with cripple studs (also called jack studs).

After all the walls have been framed straight and plumb, the ceiling is covered with joists, just like the floor, and the roof is built. The traditional method of building a roof is to connect a series of rafters to a ridge beam that runs the length of the building. These days, how-

Wooden I-beam joists like these are being seen more often on house building sites. Made with a plywood web glued into flanges at top and bottom, I-beams are light and strong. (Photo by Roe A. Osborn.)

ever, many houses are built with roof trusses delivered fully assembled to the job site. Trusses consist of a rafter chord, a joist chord, and posts and webbing between the chords to give them structural strength (see the photo on p. 69). Trusses are strong, make building a roof fast and easy, and are available just about everywhere in the country.

Once all the walls and roof have been framed, the house can be sheathed (though sometimes walls are sheathed

Studs are the vertical members that make up the frame of a wall and usually are spaced 16 in. o.c. or 24 in. o.c. (Photo by Roger Turk.)

before being raised). Exterior walls are most often sheathed with 4x8 sheets of ½-in. plywood or OSB. Roofs are usually sheathed with ½-in. to ⅝-in. plywood or OSB (depending on the span between rafters).

Once the house has been sheathed and roofed, windows and doors are installed, the house is sided, and the interior is fin-ished and trimmed out. That's the basics. I'll explain the process in detail in Chapters 4 through 8.

LUMBER

Now that we've covered the basic parts of a house, let's look at the specific materials that go into it. Lumber is graded for both strength and appear-ance. Construction-grade lumber used in

LUMBER DIMENSIONS

When ordering lumber or making plans for anything built with wood, it's important to remember that the lumber designation (2x4, 4x4, 1x8, etc.) is not the actual lumber size. For instance, a 2x4 is not really 2 in. by 4 in., and a 1x8 is not really 1 in. by 8 in. (this is called the nominal dimension).

In general, rough lumber stock (2xs, 4xs, 6xs, etc.) is ½ in. under the nominal size (all lumber lengths are actual, however). For instance, a 2x4 is actually 1½ in. thick and 3½ in. wide. For 1x stock, however,

the actual dimensions are a bit different. A 1x8, for example, is ¾ in. thick (¼ in. under the nominal size) and 7½ in. wide (½ in. under the nominal size).

Manufactured lumber can be designated by the ac-tual dimensions. A ¾-in.-thick 4x8 sheet of OSB is just that: ¾ in. thick and 4 ft. wide by 8 ft. long. A 6x12 laminated beam, on the other hand, will usual-ly measure 5½ in. by 11½ in. When buying these items, check their dimensions to see if they meet your actual needs.

Roof trusses, which are delivered to the site fully assembled, simplify roof construction. Notice the frieze blocks (on right) between these king-post trusses, which help tie the whole roof together. (Photo by Roe A. Osborn.)

the frame of a house has to be structurally strong, but it doesn't have to be free of knots. Clear, knot-free lumber is desirable for finish work because it looks the best. Unfortunately, clear lumber has become increasingly expensive because of the depletion of our old-growth forests, so choosing finish lumber often involves sorting through stacks of boards.

In the western part of the country, construction-grade Douglas fir and hemlock are the preferred framing woods. In other parts of the country, selected species of pine or spruce are strong enough to support a house frame.

Clear-grade finish lumber in almost any species is available at a premium price. Popular species such as redwood, pine, and oak are available in more economical grades. I prefer the No. 2 stock over

clear grades. The cheaper grade may be harder to work, but knots add character and interest to a board.

I am a carpenter, so I love the feel of real wood. It's sad that the old-growth trees are gone, because the new, fast-growing trees have little structural strength. Many are cut into chips to make manufactured lumber.

Manufactured lumber

Manufactured lumber products are being used for sheathing, joists, and beams. Manufactured sheathing products include plywood, OSB, and medium-density fiberboard (MDF). These sheet goods are available in various thicknesses, from 1/4 in. to 3/4 in. and thicker.

Plywood is made by gluing and pressing thin layers of veneer together. Construction-grade exterior plywood

Construction-grade lumber used in house framing, such as the 2x12 I'm marking in this photo, must be structurally strong, but it's not necessarily free of knots. (Photo by Larry Hammerness.)

(CDX) is made from thin layers of fir or other common softwoods glued together with a waterproof glue so it can be used on the building exterior.

OSB and MDF are made by compressing and gluing strands or particles of wood fiber to create panels. Structurally rated OSB is used for exterior sheathing, while MDF makes a good substrate for things like countertops and closet shelves. Be careful when working with MDF. The substance bonding the wood fibers may contain formaldehyde, and the dust from cutting it is fine, like flour. It's a good idea to wear a respirator (which is much more effective than a dust mask) when cutting this material, unless you are working outside in a stiff wind.

Becoming more common in house construction are wooden I-beam joists (see Sources on p. 198) made with a ply-

CARRYING LUMBER

Much of the lumber used in frame carpentry is heavy. To avoid hurting your back, learn to lift with your legs and arms, and learn how to carry lumber around properly.

If you carry lumber with your hands at your waist, you may strain your lower back. It's better to carry boards on your shoulder, where the backbone, rather than the back muscles, supports the weight. When you need to carry a long, heavy 2x rafter or joist, grab it at its balance point near the center and lift it in one easy motion, flipping it so that it lands gently on your shoulder. Then it's simply a matter of balancing the board as you walk, rather than wrestling with it.

Don't get into a strength contest. If something is too heavy to carry by yourself comfortably, ask another person for help, or make more trips with smaller loads. A strained back is no joke.

When carrying lumber around the job site, it's easier on your back if you balance it on your shoulders.

wood strip (called a web) glued into flanges at top and bottom (see the photo on p. 67). These joists are light-weight and can span long distances, making it possible to create very large rooms. Also, they are always straight and don't shrink as much as 2x joists, so floors tend to remain flat, level, and relatively squeak free.

Engineered beams are typically made from laminated strips of lumber. These are available in several widths and depths and can span distances upwards of 60 ft. without support. A 3½-in.-wide beam can be used as a header in a 2x4 wall. Engineered beams are stable, which means they won't twist and split the way regular 2x or 4x lumber does.

Siding

A builder friend of mine here in wet, coastal Oregon was showing me a new house that was lap-sided with new-growth cedar clapboards. He told me that 25 years ago the old-growth cedar trees had 20 growth rings to the inch, while today the new-growth trees have around three rings to the inch. Almost every board on the house he showed me was cupped.

Quality wood siding that will stay flat on a building is expensive and hard to find. Because of this, wood clapboards —though still popular—face stiff competition from alternative siding products. Today, builders are siding houses with aluminum and vinyl, composite materials like plywood, boards made of pressed wood fibers (OSB), or even material with a cement-fiber content.

While some of these materials—like synthetic or natural stucco—are applied by specialty subcontractors, cutting and fitting siding is typically a job for a carpenter. Siding must protect the building from sun and rain and make the house look good, so I'll devote more time to installing it later on in Chapter 8.

Despite increasing cost, wood clapboards remain a popular siding option. Use stainless-steel, aluminum, or galvanized nails to fasten siding and exterior trim. (Photo by Roe A. Osborn.)

Windows, doors, and trim

When I was growing up, we forced strips of cloth around all the window sash with a kitchen knife when the weather got cold to plug the cracks around the loose-fitting windows. What a pleasure it is now to have tight-fitting, insulated windows and doors to keep out the cold.

When carpenters talk about windows and doors, you'll hear them say "a three-oh by four-oh unit" (3/0 x 4/0). They are talking about a window that is 3 ft. wide by 4 ft. high. The width is given first and the height second. A 2/8 x 6/8 ("two-eight by six-eight") door is 32 in. wide by 80 in. high.

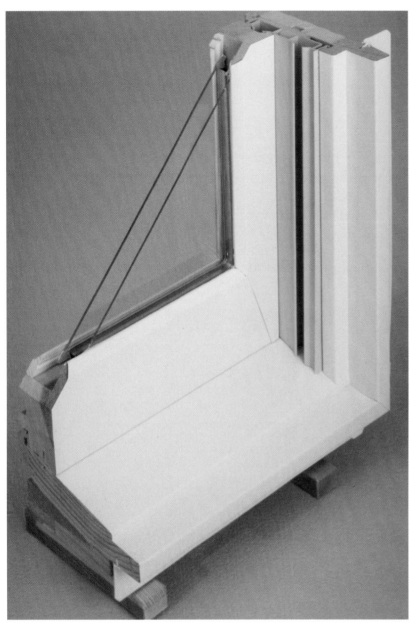

Insulating glass is made by sealing air or some other inert gas between two or three glass panes. The insulating glass in this photo is separated by a stainless-steel spacer that's thermally isolated by polyisobutylene, which reduces conductive losses of heat and cold. (Photo courtesy Kolbe & Kolbe Millwork Co., Inc.)

climates. Both frames are basically maintenance free, requiring just an occasional washing. Aluminum-framed windows are less expensive than vinyl and come in different colors (most vinyl-framed windows are white).

Windows with double glazing (called insulated glass) have two or three panes of glass with a sealed airspace between them (see the photo at left). The airspace keeps the window free from condensation and cuts down on heat loss in the winter, helping to keep the cold—and the noise—outside.

Among the dozens of window styles, the most commonly used are fixed, sliding, double hung, and single hung. A fixed window is just a frame with glass. Sliding windows have fixed glass on one side and a frame that slides back and forth on the other side. A double-hung unit has a bottom and top sash, both of which can be moved up or down. A single-hung unit also has a bottom and top sash, but only the bottom sash can be opened.

Windows When I first started building, we had basically one choice for windows: wood framed. Although wood-framed windows are still around, other options are available now in a wide variety of styles.

Vinyl- and aluminum-framed windows are sold everywhere. Vinyl frames cut down on condensation in cold or humid

Doors Doors have also changed a lot since I first started building. Now there are molded wood-product interior doors with a hollow core, genuine frame-and-panel interior and exterior doors, doors sheathed with metal or fiberglass over a wood frame and an energy-efficient foam core, and elaborate hardwood doors with etched glass, often with a solid core. Doors come in a wide range of prices and quality and are available either individually or as prehung units.

Prehung doors come already mounted in their jambs, have a threshold and weatherstripping (if it's an exterior door), and often even have holes bored for the lockset and dead bolt. These units radically simplify door installation because you don't have to make the jambs or mount the door on its hinges, a time-consuming process that takes a high

- Take a course in basic first aid.

- Watch out for your fellow worker. Be aware of who is nearby so you don't hit someone with a piece of lumber or with your hammer.

- Try to have a good, positive attitude.

- Keep your work area clean. It's easy to trip over scrap wood, lumber, tools, and trash.

- Pull or bend over nails that are sticking out of boards so nobody gets injured.

- Spread sand on ice in winter to provide traction.

- Don't turn the radio up so loud that you can't hear other workers. Concentration and communication on the job site are critical to avoiding accidents.

- Concentrate on the task at hand.

- Work at a steady, careful pace.

- Back injuries are very common on the job. To preserve your back, remember to lift with your legs, not with your back.

- Take care of your body by eating good food and exercising. And don't forget to rest. Getting enough sleep is important to keeping your concentration and to avoiding fatigue.

- Take a break when you feel tired. Don't overwork yourself. Exhaustion leads to carelessness.

- Don't drink or take drugs while working. Operating power tools under the influence is as dangerous as driving under the influence.

- Watch where you walk, especially when working on scaffolds or on the frame of the house. Many injuries on the job are the result of falls.

- Follow your instinct. If something you are about to do feels unsafe, it probably is. Pay attention to the voice inside your head when it says, "Be careful."

---

degree of skill. Still, installing a prehung door requires attention to detail, which is why I'll discuss the process more in Chapter 8. I'll also talk about how to install a lockset.

Exterior and interior trim
Trimming out a house is like adding the frosting to a birthday cake. Whether you are installing exterior or interior casing, sills, aprons, or baseboard, there's a wide variety of styles and profiles from which to choose—from simple 1x4 trim to ornate crown moldings.

Clear stock is pricey, but it's ideal for trim because it can be stained, left unfinished, or painted with little preparation. Finger-jointed stock (short pieces glued together) is less expensive than clear stock but needs to be painted to

cover the joints (that's why it's called paint-grade trim). Knots aren't an insurmountable problem as long as they are sound and won't fall out, and trim can be preprimed so that the knots won't bleed pitch through the paint.

Exterior casing around doors and windows not only serves a functional purpose but also adds beauty and character. Look at houses as you drive around your neighborhood and note all of the different kinds of trim. Check out the vertical boards nailed to the corners. See the casings that go around doors and windows. Fascia boards are nailed to rafter tails to give them a finished look. Frieze boards are nailed between rafters to seal them off. All of this exterior trim can be as simple as a plain 1x4 or as elaborate as the filigree that you

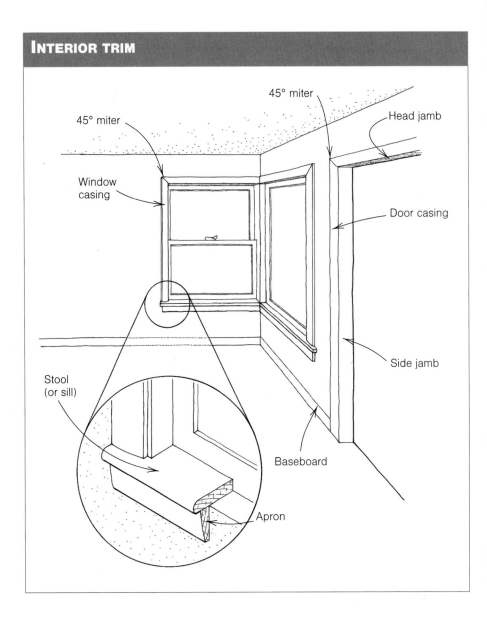

45° miter

45° miter

Head jamb

Window casing

Door casing

Side jamb

Stool (or sill)

Baseboard

Apron

might see on a Victorian-style house. Because I want the trim to look good, I use hot-dipped galvanized, stainless-steel, or aluminum finish nails when installing exterior casing so that the nails won't rust and stain the wood.

Interior casing goes around interior doors and windows and hides the gap between the drywall and door jambs or window frame (see the drawing above). The joint where the side piece meets the casing at the top is usually a 45° miter.

Flat, rectangular casings that are wider and more affected by shrinking/swelling cycles are often cut square and butted together. Use finish nails to attach casing so they can be set below the surface and covered with wood putty.

The stool (sometimes called a sill) is the flat piece of trim installed at the bottom of a window (a perfect place to set flowers). Some windows have a stool built in as part of the frame, but more often than not the stool needs to be installed separately. A piece of trim called an apron covers the joint between the stool and the drywall below the window.

Baseboard runs horizontally and covers the joint between the wall and the floor. It is usually joined at outside corners with a 45° miter joint and is nailed to the wall with finish nails after the finish floor is installed. Interior corners can be joined with a 45° miter or with a coped joint (where one piece of trim is cut to match the profile of the mating piece).

Even though there are literally thousands of different styles of trim today, the ones used most often are still quite simple (some common profiles are shown in the drawing at right).

FASTENERS AND HARDWARE

Carpenters don't just use wood, nails, and screws for building. Many other types of metal hardware go into a house as well, and knowing what to use and when to use it can be baffling. Fortunately, most of the time we use only a few varieties on a regular basis. Here's an overview of the basic types of hardware used by carpenters.

Nails

Nails are the most common fasteners used by carpenters because they are inexpensive and quick and easy to use.

Nail sizes When choosing nails, you have to think about the size you need, whether it's for interior or exterior use, and how many you'll need.

Nail sizes are dictated by the penny-weight system (abbreviated with a "d"). In general, a nail with a lower penny designation will be shorter and will have a thinner shank than a nail with a higher penny designation. For instance, an 8d nail is thinner and shorter than a 16d nail.

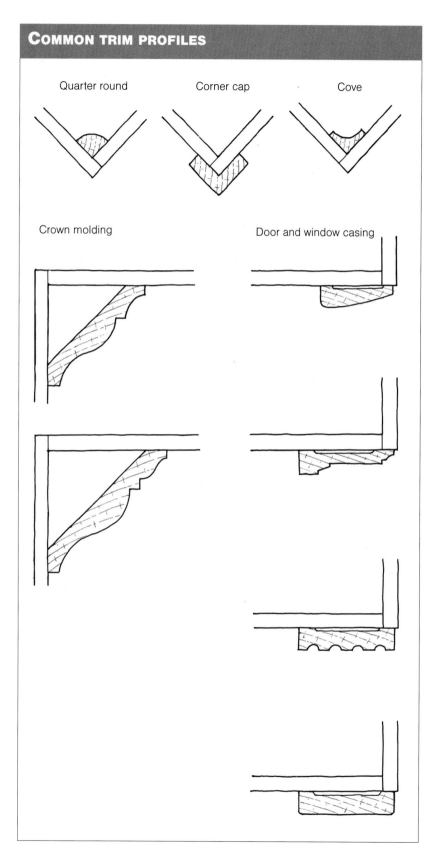

COMMON TRIM PROFILES

Quarter round   Corner cap   Cove

Crown molding   Door and window casing

Nails used inside the house aren't exposed to the weather, so they usually don't require coatings or treatment to withstand rusting. On the exterior, however, nails have to stand up to whatever Mother Nature throws at them. When nailing exterior siding, for instance, use nails that won't rust and stain the wood, like hot-dipped galvanized (zinc-coated), stainless-steel, or aluminum nails. For holding power, choose ring-shank nails (nails with ridges) or screw nails.

Nails are purchased by the pound, so carpenters typically buy large quantities to save money. It's cheaper to buy one 50-lb. box than it would be to buy five 10-lb. sacks. A typical 1,200-sq.-ft. wood-framed house can be nailed together with about 10,000 16d nails (200 lb.) and 5,000 8d nails (50 lb.).

Types of nails The type of nail you buy depends on the job at hand, and whether you're framing or doing finish work. The nails a carpenter uses often are designated common, box, or finish.

Common and box nails are used mainly for framing. Box nails are thinner than common nails and are preferred for framing because they're easier to drive. Many framers use what are called sinkers, which are nails coated with resin or vinyl. These nails drive easily and have good holding power.

The two most common framing nails are 8ds (2½ in. long) and 16ds (3½ in. long). The 8ds are used to nail sheathing to floors or walls and cripple studs to headers, for example, while 16ds are used to nail together 2x stock, such as plates to studs.

Finish nails are used to nail trim boards like door casing and baseboard. These nails have small heads and can be driven below the surface of the wood with a nailset and the holes covered with putty. There are many different finish-nail sizes,

Carpenters use 16d nails for most rough framing, such as nailing top plates together. (Photo by Roe A. Osborn.)

There's no reason to drive larger nails than needed. I've seen carpenters nail door jambs to studs with 8d nails when 6ds would have sufficed. If you are in doubt about the size nail needed, check with your building department. Many codes specify the minimum size nail needed for a particular job, how many to use, and where to drive them (this is typically called a nailing schedule).

the most common being 4d, 6d, and 8d. Brads are short (less than 1 in. long) finish nails. If nailing trim on the exterior, use aluminum, stainless-steel, or galvanized nails.

There are also a number of different specialty nails. Double-headed (or duplex) nails are used in concrete formwork and for temporary scaffolding. The top head remains above the surface, making the nail easy to pull out. Hanger nails are short, hardened nails used to attach metal framing anchors (such as joist hangers) to wood. Masonry nails are used for nailing into concrete.

There are even plastic nails that can be used with pneumatic nailers (Utility Composites; see Sources on p. 198). Plastic nails have good holding power, won't rust, can be cut with a saw, and can even be sanded with a belt sander.

Screws

The advent of the cordless screw gun has made screws the fastener of choice for many carpenters. Screws are used for everything from fastening sheet goods to installing trim and hardware. As with nails, don't use a larger-size screw than you need, and if the screw is installed outside, choose a type that will stand up to the weather.

Wood screws can be used for all sorts of home-building jobs. Stores stock many types of wood screws, such as slotted, Phillips head, and square drive (see the drawing above). Standard lengths range from ¼ in. to 6 in., and common gauges are 8 through 14 (the lower the gauge number, the thinner the screw shank). Head shapes are flat, round, and oval, and some are designed to be driven below the surface of the wood (called countersink heads). Most screws are made of steel, but aluminum, brass, and stainless steel are available. A standard

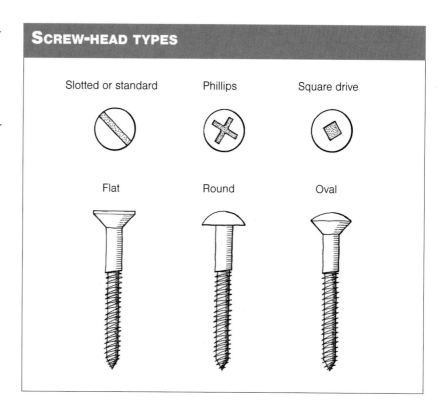

SCREW-HEAD TYPES

Slotted or standard   Phillips   Square drive

Flat   Round   Oval

wood screw often requires a pilot hole so you don't split the wood as you drive the screw.

For better or worse, drywall screws have replaced wood screws on today's building sites. Although they were originally designed just to attach drywall to wood or metal, carpenters discovered that they have other uses. They are used so often that, when people ask for screws on a job site, they are usually talking about drywall screws.

Drywall screws (sometimes called bugle-head screws) have a Phillips head, range from ¾ in. to 3 in. long, and usually have a flat black finish. With their thin shanks, deep threads, and sharp points, they can often be driven without a pilot hole. Drywall screws hold well and usually won't split the wood, and their bugle-shaped, flat head countersinks itself in drywall or soft wood.

COMMONLY USED BOLTS

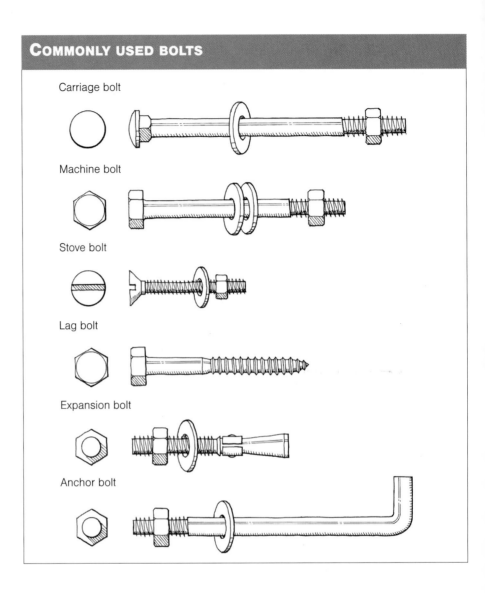

Carriage bolt

Machine bolt

Stove bolt

Lag bolt

Expansion bolt

Anchor bolt

Drywall screws love plywood—they zip through a ¾-in.-thick sheet in nothing flat—so they're great for attaching sheathing or flooring. But drywall screws are somewhat brittle, so don't use them in shear walls (which are built to resist the shear forces of earthquakes and high winds) without first getting approval from an engineer or your building department. Drywall screws can also break when being driven into thick stock or hardwoods. I have driven a 3-in. screw through 2x6 decking into a joist only to hear a snap right before the screw sets. A new, hard-to-break line of interior and exterior drywall screws is now available from Faspac, Inc. (see Sources on p. 198). These screws have self-drilling tips that make them easy to use in thick wood or hardwood.

Deck screws are drywall-type screws that have been coated, galvanized, or made of stainless steel for corrosion resistance. Use these for exterior jobs such as attaching deck boards or fence slats.

Heavy-gauge lag screws (¼ in. dia. and up) are typically used to attach a 2x ledger (a horizontal wood member) to the house framing. They are usually driven into the wood with a wrench. Lag screws are smaller than lag bolts.

Bolts

Bolts have many applications, from holding a house to the foundation to securing a deck to a wall to uniting a row of kitchen cabinets. When buying bolts, you have to specify the thickness and length you need (⅜ in. thick by 6 in. long, for example). A carpenter often uses carriage, machine, stove, lag, expansion, and anchor bolts (see the drawing on the facing page).

Carriage bolts have round heads, sometimes with a screwdriver slot on top, and are fitted with a washer and nut on the threaded end. I like to use carriage bolts when building deck railings.

Machine bolts have square or hexagonal heads. When using machine bolts to join two pieces of wood, place a washer on both ends before tightening; otherwise, you could tear into the wood. Machine bolts are often used to connect beams in post-and-beam construction and to attach metal plates to the house framing to stabilize it in case of an earthquake or hurricane. Stove bolts are small machine bolts.

Lag bolts are similar to lag screws but go clear through the wood. Lag bolts can be used to fasten a deck ledger to a house (just make sure that you are attaching the ledger to good, solid wood). Because lag bolts are driven into wood like screws, you need to drill pilot holes about ⅛ in. smaller in diameter than the bolt (a ⅜-in. hole for a ½-in. bolt, for example).

Expansion bolts are fitted in holes drilled in existing concrete. They expand in the concrete to ensure a secure hold and are used to attach wood to a foundation or other concrete surface.

Anchor bolts are shaped like a J. They are normally embedded in a concrete foundation to secure wood sills to the foundation, which helps hold a house in place.

Framing anchors

There are a wide range of framing anchors (Simpson Strong-Tie Co. is a good source—see Sources on p. 198) that help increase the structural stability of a house (see the drawing on p. 80). Carpenters use joist hangers, right-angle and hurricane clips, plate straps, hold-downs, post caps, and T-straps. Anchors are often required by local building codes, particularly in areas of seismic activity or high wind. In other cases, they just make framing faster, easier, and more efficient.

Joist hangers can be nailed to beams or rim joists to support joists for a floor or ceiling. These hangers come in various sizes to fit the joist size and are nailed into the beam through side flanges. The joist is placed in the hanger and nailed in. A tool made by Ator Tool Works, called a Joister, holds the hanger in place so both your hands can be free for nailing.

Right-angle clips and hurricane clips are widely used to attach one wood member to another. A commonly used right-angle clip is 4½ in. long with six nail holes in each side. A hurricane clip is a metal device that can be nailed to both rafter and wall plates to hold them securely together. Both types of clips help keep a house in place in earthquake and hurricane country.

FRAMING ANCHORS

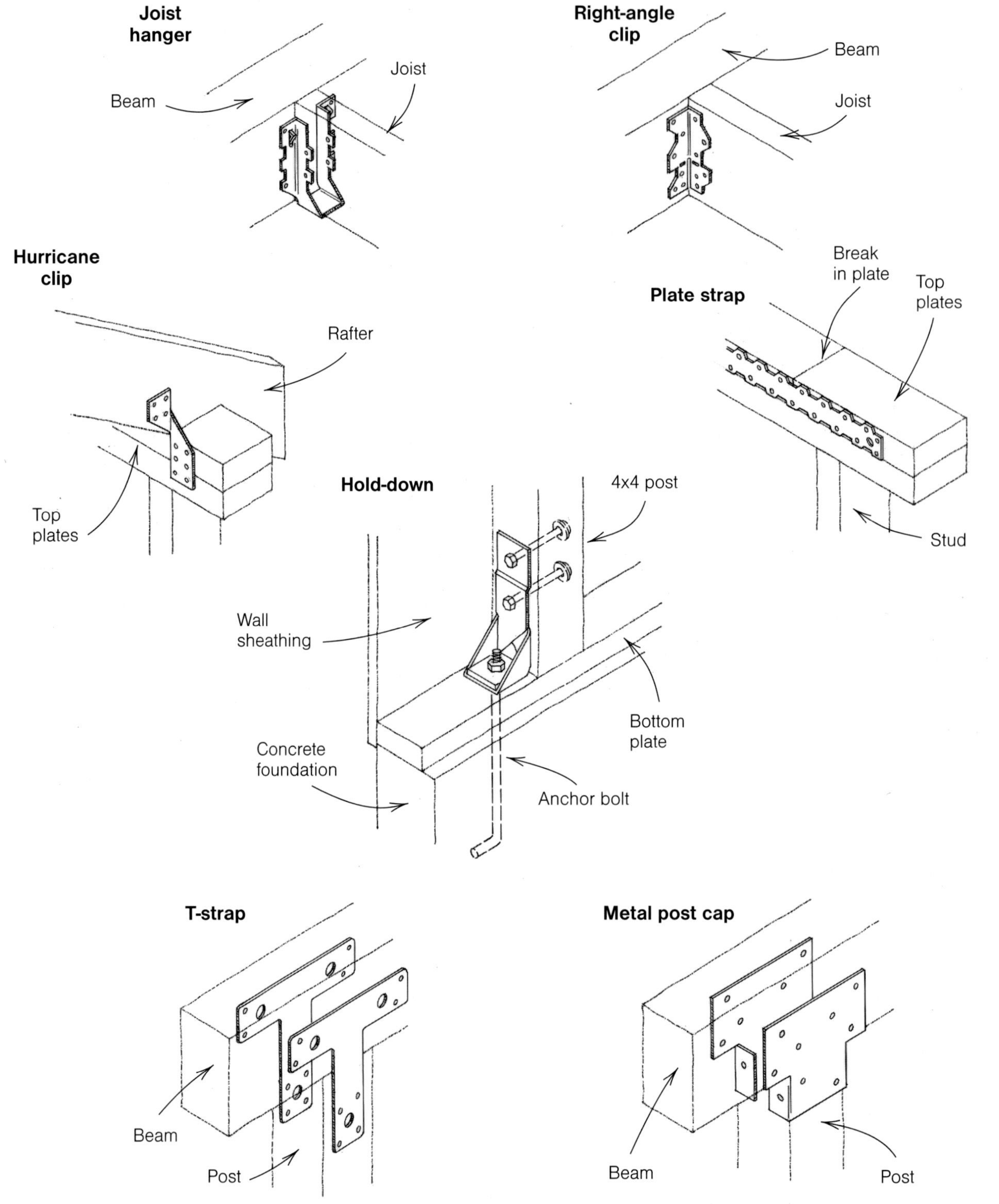
Joist hanger
Beam
Joist
Right-angle clip
Beam
Joist
Hurricane clip
Rafter
Top plates
Plate strap
Break in plate
Top plates
Stud
Hold-down
4x4 post
Wall sheathing
Bottom plate
Concrete foundation
Anchor bolt
T-strap
Beam
Post
Metal post cap
Beam
Post

- Keep a first-aid kit on the job site at all times.

- Keep the sun off your body. It may be okay to wear tank tops, shorts, and sandals to the beach, but these are not okay to wear on a construction site day in and day out. You won't stay cooler by letting the hot sun beat directly on you. Wear long-sleeve shirts, jeans, good shoes, and a wide-brim hat when the sun is shining. If you are especially sensitive to the sun, keep a bottle of sunblock handy. (If you aren't convinced of the value of protecting yourself from the harsh sun, ask an old carpenter with skin cancer to find out what he thinks about it.)

- Don't wear loose-fitting clothing or jewelry that can get caught in a power tool. If you have long hair, tie it up for the same reason.

- Drink lots of water. It's easy for the body to become dehydrated on a hot day. Dehydration can lead to heat exhaustion, which can lead to accidents.

- Keep a hard hat handy. Many carpenters resist wearing hard hats, but when someone is working overhead, wearing a hard hat below is a good idea. You may have a hard head, but it won't be hard enough to protect you from falling tools or lumber.

- Eyes are fragile. Always protect them with safety glasses or goggles when using a power tool or when nailing. Buy a pair that feels comfortable. And so you won't forget them at home, stuff your safety glasses in a sock and carry them with you. If you wear prescription glasses, don't think they protect your eyes. Standard prescription lenses are not rated to shield your eyes from flying objects. You need lenses that are made specifically for safety. I wear safety glasses with plastic prescription lenses and side protectors.

- Use ear protection whenever operating a loud power tool like a router or circular saw. Otherwise, make "huh?" part of your vocabulary. I keep a few sponge ear plugs in a 35-mm film canister and store them in my toolbucket so that I have them with me at all times.

- Wear knee pads to protect your knees—for example, when putting down roofing or nailing down flooring.

- Lungs need protection, too. A dust mask helps keep large particles out of your lungs. I use one when sanding or when working in an enclosed area with poor ventilation. With toxic materials, wear a respirator. I have often worn a respirator during remodeling jobs in which I've ripped out old plaster and insulation. When ripping out these materials, the dust particles may be small enough to penetrate a dust mask (and some older plaster may even contain asbestos).

- Protect your hands with gloves when necessary. Wear light rubber gloves when painting or staining to prevent harmful materials from entering your body through your pores. Use heavy work gloves to protect your hands from wood slivers when handling rough lumber.

Flat plate straps are another type of anchor used to tie wooden members together. They are made from heavy-gauge metal, contain numerous fastener holes, and come in many different widths and lengths (up to 4 ft. long).

Hold-downs are heavy-gauge, L-shaped metal anchors that help prevent house uplift by connecting the building to the foundation. They often attach near the mudsill with an anchor bolt set in the concrete foundation and are bolted to posts in the wood frame.

Post caps attach larger posts, like 4x4s, to beams or to concrete. L- or T-straps connect two members that meet in a right-angle or T configuration, such as when a beam rests on a post.

MISCELLANEOUS MATERIALS

Work is not complete when the house frame is standing or when all of the trim and siding are nailed in place. From sandpaper to tape, from adhesive to caulk, other important materials are available to help carpenters put the finishing touches on our work.

Sandpaper

The simplest thing to do when buying sandpaper is to pay attention to the grit. Look on the back of the sheet for the number of the grit. The higher the number, the finer the sandpaper grit, and the smoother the finished surface will be. So, for example, 40 grit is coarse paper, 80 grit is medium, and 120 grit is fine. I try to buy sandpaper in bulk rather than in expensive precut pieces. Cut larger sheets of sandpaper grit-side down using a straightedge and a utility knife.

Wherever there's a danger of water getting into the house, such as under a door threshold, a bead of caulk can help seal the gap. (Photo by Roe A. Osborn.)

Tape

The two tapes I keep in my toolbucket are duct tape and electrical tape. I never go to the job without my roll of duct tape. Carpenters use it for a variety of jobs, such as holding plastic in place, patching torn building plans, protecting sharp sawblades and chisels, and even for mending ripped jeans. The original gray roll of duct tape is cloth backed and strong.

It's always good to have a roll of electrical tape on hand. I use it to wrap my hammer handle near the head (to protect it) and to repair damaged power cords. Like duct tape, it can be used to protect the tip of a sharp chisel or to seal a tube of caulk.

Adhesives

As a child, I mixed flour and water to make the paste for my kites and art projects. This paste held about as well as anything I could buy in the store. Not so today. Now there are many types of super-strong adhesives available. The most common used by carpenters are construction adhesive and yellow glue.

Construction adhesive unites wood to wood and is used extensively by carpenters. It comes in small or large tubes that fit into a caulking gun. A bead of this adhesive is often spread on floor joists before laying down plywood sheathing or under stair treads.

Yellow glue is also used to join wood. Smear it on two edges, hold them together with clamps until the glue dries, and you have a joint as strong as the wood itself.

Polyurethane glue is a fairly new waterproof glue that can be used inside or outside (Gorilla Glue; see Sources on p. 198). It bonds to stone, metal, ceramics and plastic, and even works well on wood that has a high water content. It foams as it bonds, so it fills small gaps, and the foam is easy to scrape off and sand after it sets. While it costs a bit more, it's a versatile glue I use often.

Caulk

If they make a mistake, carpenters joke that they can leave it for the painters to fix with caulk. While there is no excuse for poor work, many minor problems can be solved with a long-lasting, flexible caulk. For instance, a gap between a door and the subfloor can be closed with a good waterproof caulk (see the photo on the facing page). Caulk is flexible, so it allows for wood expansion without cracking and creating holes where rain can enter. Cracks between wood trim and a wall can also be filled with caulk.

There are a number of different types and colors of caulk on the market, and the type you choose depends on the job you need it to do. The one most of us use is a latex caulk with acrylic or silicone added.

READING PLANS

Anything a carpenter builds—a workbench, a sawhorse, a house—comes to life because someone had a plan. Once

Carpenters use plans to figure out how the parts of a building will go together and to order all of the building materials.

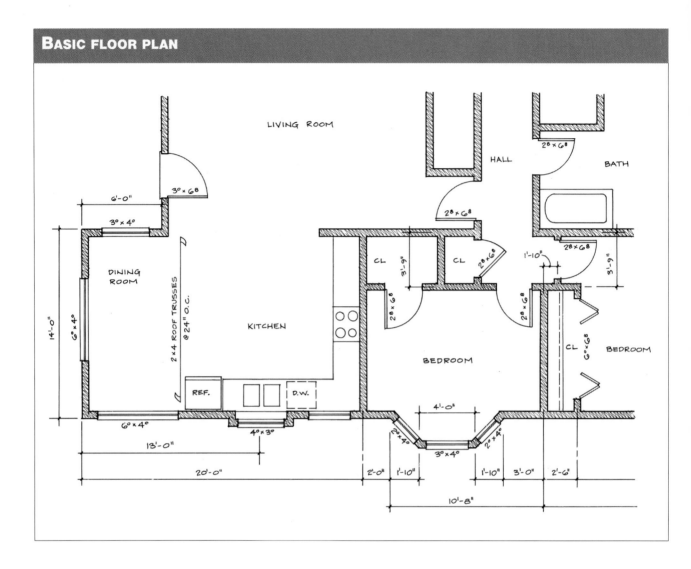

this plan is on paper, you can start to figure out how to build the project and calculate what materials you will need.

House plans are like road maps. If you want to drive from Oregon to New York, for example, you look at a map. You know you can't visualize everything you will see along the way, but if you follow the lines and symbols properly, you will arrive at your destination. The same goes for building: Learn to follow the plans step-by-step, and you will complete the project.

Scale and dimensions

When reading plans or doing layout on a building, pay attention to the scale of the drawings and how the dimensions are marked. These are critical to making a good estimate of materials and to building the structure.

If house plans were drawn full size, you would need very large paper—and a lot of it. That's why maps and plans are scaled down (called a scale drawing). To make a scale drawing, designers and architects assign a smaller dimension to the real-life dimensions. For instance, the most common house-plan scale is ¼ in. = 1 ft. (on the plans this would read ¼" = 1' 0"). This means that each ¼ in. of line on a plan represents 1 ft. of actual house. So if you measure 1 in. on the plans, the real-life dimension would be 4 ft.

Types of plans

A typical set of house plans tells you everything you need to know to build a house, from where to site it on the lot to how the finished house will look. In addition to site plans and elevations (which provide a horizontal look at the house from all angles), house plans also typically include floor-framing plans, sections, and detail drawings. While all of these plans are useful, the plan that is used most often is the floor plan.

The floor plan (see the drawing on the facing page) gives a bird's-eye view of a horizontal surface. A lot of information can be crammed onto this plan, including the size of the rooms; the size and location of doors and windows; the location of electrical, plumbing, heating, and structural elements; the size of lumber needed for headers, posts, and beams; and the size, spacing, and direction of ceiling joists and roof rafters.

Section views give yet another perspective. Slice down through the house or part of the house, just as you would through an apple, remove one half, stand back, and look at the other to get a section view. Section views give carpenters a close look at the different elements that will be put in the floors, walls, and ceilings (see the drawing at right).

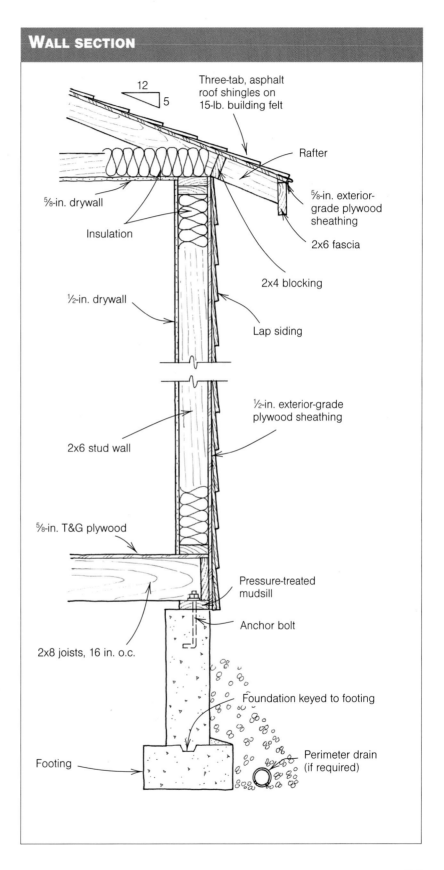

WALL SECTION

Three-tab, asphalt roof shingles on 15-lb. building felt

12
5

Rafter

⅝-in. exterior-grade plywood sheathing

⅝-in. drywall

2x6 fascia

Insulation

2x4 blocking

½-in. drywall

Lap siding

½-in. exterior-grade plywood sheathing

2x6 stud wall

⅝-in. T&G plywood

Pressure-treated mudsill

Anchor bolt

2x8 joists, 16 in. o.c.

Foundation keyed to footing

Footing

Perimeter drain (if required)

4

FRAMING FLOORS

When a carpenter first arrives at the job site, the foundation is often poured and ready for sill plates, joists, and floor sheathing. Just make sure you're building on the right foundation. I once started building on the wrong lot in a tract of houses. My crew was well under way when the owner of the property arrived and said he appreciated our efforts but wasn't intending to build just yet.

CHECKING THE FOUNDATION

Like most things in life—from cooking to marriage—if you get started right, things just seem to go better the whole way. This is certainly true in construction. So before attaching the wooden sill plates to the foundation, you must be sure that the foundation itself is accurate. Problems get worse by the day unless you get started square, plumb, and level.

Begin with a visual on-site check. Get down and sight along the foundation. The concrete wall should sight straight and true, with no dips or waves. Next, use your tape measure and level to check for foundation accuracy (see the sidebar on the facing page).

Walls that are out of parallel can be corrected by adjusting the sill-plate chalklines. Say, for example, that the

Chalklines on top of the concrete foundation indicate the position of the sill plates. (Photo by Roe A. Osborn.)

walls are out of parallel ½ in. and the sill plates are 5½ in. wide. Go to the narrow end of the foundation and measure in from the outside 3⅝ in. on each corner. Then go to the wide end and measure in 3⅜ in. at each corner. By making a small, ⅛-in. change at each corner, you

CHECKING A FOUNDATION FOR SQUARE AND PARALLEL

Most things carpenters build—including foundations, walls, and cabinets—have square (90°) corners. So it's important to know how to check that corners are really square and that the opposite sides are parallel to one another. Out-of-square houses, or walls that are not parallel, make it hard to set cabinets and to do fine finish work later.

A square or rectangle can be checked for square (all corners are 90°) by measuring it diagonally from corner to corner with a tape measure (see the bottom drawing at right). If each measurement is the same, the building is square.

Another way to check for square is to use the Pythagorean theorem: $a^2 + b^2 = c^2$ (see the top drawing at right). On the job this is called the 6-8-10 rule. To check a foundation for square, measure 6 ft. from a corner along one side of the foundation, 8 ft. along the other side, and then check the length of the diagonal. If it is 10 ft., the corner is square. You can use other divisibles or multiples of 6-8-10, such as 3-4-5 or 12-16-20. On a big building with long walls, use as large a multiple as possible to avoid error.

To see if walls are parallel, measure the distance from wall to wall at one end. Then move to the other end and measure the distance again. If the measurements are the same, the walls are parallel. Some error can be okay, depending on the size of the building. For instance, walls that are out of parallel ½ in. in 10 ft. are worse than walls out of parallel ½ in. in 100 ft.

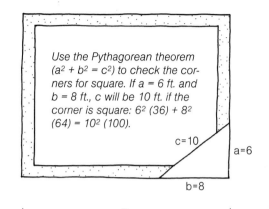

Use the Pythagorean theorem ($a^2 + b^2 = c^2$) to check the corners for square. If a = 6 ft. and b = 8 ft., c will be 10 ft. if the corner is square: 6^2 (36) + 8^2 (64) = 10^2 (100).

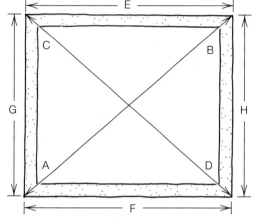

The foundation is square if the two diagonal measurements (A to B and C to D) are equal.

Walls are parallel if they measure the same distance across each end (E = F and G = H).

gain ½ in. overall, and the walls are now parallel. Pressure-treated shims can be put under the sill plates to bring everything up to level.

Once you know the condition of the foundation, take the time to sweep any debris from the concrete walls and to straighten the anchor bolts. Bolts can be straightened by placing a 3-ft. length of ½-in. pipe over a tipped bolt and bending it upright. The next step is to snap chalklines on the concrete to mark where the sill plates will be bolted (see the photo on the facing page). Be sure to use straight pressure-treated stock for the sill plates. Set the crooked ones aside to cut up for short walls later.

CUTTING, MARKING, AND DRILLING SILL PLATES

Just as you must follow rules when playing sports, there are rules—or building codes—to follow when building a house. Most codes require that every sill plate have a bolt about 1 ft. from each end and every 4 ft. to 6 ft. between to connect the house frame securely to the foundation. So the edges of the foundation and the location of the bolts let you know where cuts in the sill plates should be made.

These cuts can be made by eye if you're feeling confident in your ability to make a square cut with a power saw.

Remember, sill plates must be placed on the foundation accurately, not perfectly. This is frame carpentry, not finish work.

Sill plates normally are bolted flush to the outside of the foundation. Place the plate directly on the inside of the chalkline and use a tape measure or a bolt marker to locate where the bolt holes are to be drilled (see the photo below). You can make a simple measuring device to mark bolt holes or buy one from Pairis Enterprises (see Sources on p. 198).

As you become more experienced, try placing the sill plate on top of the bolts and eyeball the edge of the sill flush

A simple measuring device called a bolt marker can be used to locate the bolt holes. With the sill plate lined up on the inside of the chalkline, hold the end of the marker against the bolt and mark the bolt hole. (Photo by Roe A. Osborn.)

with the chalkline or the outside of the building. Hit the sill with a hammer right over each bolt to leave a mark for drilling.

Many tasks you do in carpentry can be done by trusting the eye. Marking bolt holes in a sill plate is an example of this. Carpenters call this "eyeball carpentry." Basically, all it takes to train the eye to see accurately is practice.

With the bolt locations marked, set the sill plates on a block of wood and drill the holes. Use a ⁵⁄₈-in. or ¹¹⁄₁₆-in. bit with a power drill to make holes for ½-in. bolts. Place the sill plates over the bolts, using your hammer to drive boards onto tight-fitting bolts. Put a washer and a nut on each bolt. Now is the time, if needed, to put pressure-treated shims under the sill plates to make sure they are level. Finish by tightening the nuts with a crescent wrench.

In colder parts of the country, you may want to lay down a thin layer of insulation between the sill plates and the foundation. This helps prevent air leaks.

SUPPORTING FLOOR JOISTS

It's common in many regions to build houses directly on a concrete slab. When this is the case, wall building can begin once the sill plates are down. Other builders use a system of posts and girders to support joists so that a floor can be nailed to them. Still others use manufactured joists (called I-joists) that span a basement from sill plate to sill plate without any interior support, leaving a room large enough for a dance hall.

I just helped finish a Habitat for Humanity house that used smaller I-joists supported on the ends by the concrete foundation and midspan by a single bearing wall. This wall was built on a concrete footing that ran the entire

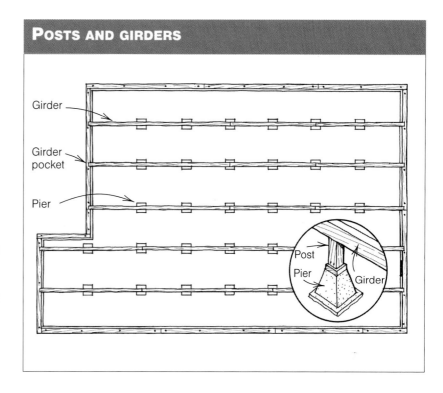

length of the building. Houses frequently have an exterior stemwall foundation with girders supported by piers set on concrete footings (see the drawing above).

Post length

Posts in a basement will be quite long, while posts in a crawl space will be shorter—only about 1 ft. to 2 ft. But to keep wood dry and away from termites, make sure that no wood is within 6 in. of the ground. To determine the exact length of each post, pull a chalkline directly over the tops of the concrete piers that will support them, from foundation wall to foundation wall (see the top drawing on p. 91). Then place a scrap piece of girder stock (like a 4x6) on a pier. The distance between the string and the top of the girder stock is the length of the post for that pier. Make a list and note the length of every post before beginning to cut them.

Posts are usually cut from 4x4 stock. In some areas, they may need to be pressure treated. They can be cut to length with a circular saw or with a chopsaw. Leave the string in place to help align the posts as you nail them to the top of the piers. Toenail three 16d nails (two on one side, one on the opposite side)—or four 8d nails—down through the post into the wooden block on top of the pier (for more on toenailing, see the sidebar below).

Girders

Once the posts are nailed in place, it's time to cut and nail on girders. Again, use straight stock that isn't twisted. Pier posts are often 6 ft. apart, so cut the girders to break in the middle of a post, which will ensure solid bearing for all girders. Secure the girders to the posts with three 16d or four 8d nails. Take some simple steps to strengthen the girder frame structurally, especially if you live in earthquake country: If the posts are over 3 ft. long, nail a 1x brace diagonally (45°) from the bottom of the post to the girder with five 8d nails in each end (see the bottom drawing on the facing page). Unite the joints with a metal strap or a plywood gusset. I prefer the gusset because it ties girder to girder and girders to the post.

INSTALLING JOISTS

Joists are placed on edge across the sill plates to provide support and a nailing surface for the subfloor and a platform for the walls (see the drawing on p. 92). The joists need to be strong enough to support your grand piano without having it wind up in the basement.

Joist systems are made from either standard 2x lumber or from manufactured joists. The weight these members can

TOENAILING

Carpenters need to know how to drive a nail at an angle. This technique is called toenailing and is often used to join pieces of wood that meet at a right angle.

When toenailing, you have to be careful not to split the wood, which is easy to do when you're nailing so close to the end of a board. You can often avoid splitting the wood by dulling the point of the nail. Place the nail head on a hard surface and tap the point several times with your hammer. Instead of spreading the wood fibers and splitting the wood, the blunt point will simply break the wood grain as it penetrates.

To toenail two boards, hold the nail at a 60° angle and start it about ¾ in. from the end of the board that's perpendicular to the other (or you can start the nail straight in, then pull it up to the correct angle). Then drive it home into the adjoining piece of wood.

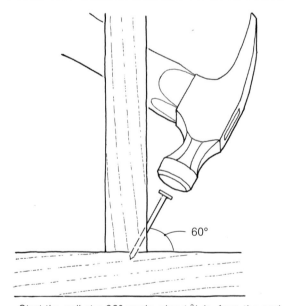

Start the nail at a 60° angle, about ¾ in. from the end of the board.

MEASURING POST LENGTHS

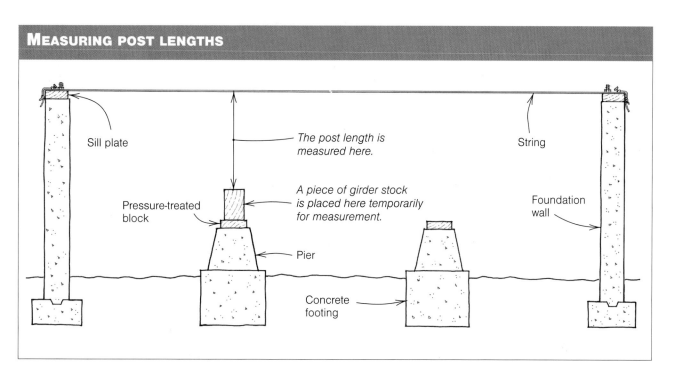

Sill plate

The post length is measured here.

A piece of girder stock is placed here temporarily for measurement.

Pressure-treated block

Pier

Concrete footing

String

Foundation wall

BRACING AND SPLICING GIRDERS

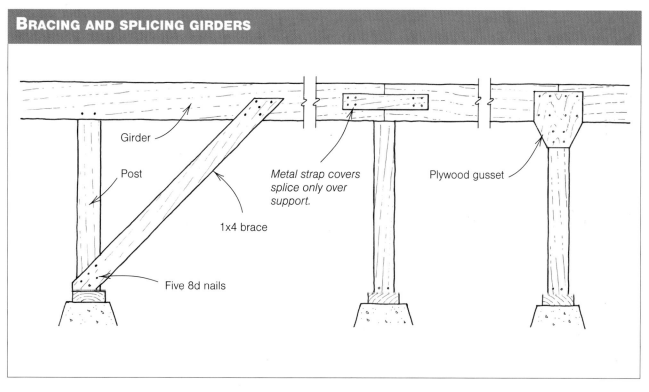

Girder

Post

1x4 brace

Five 8d nails

Metal strap covers splice only over support.

Plywood gusset

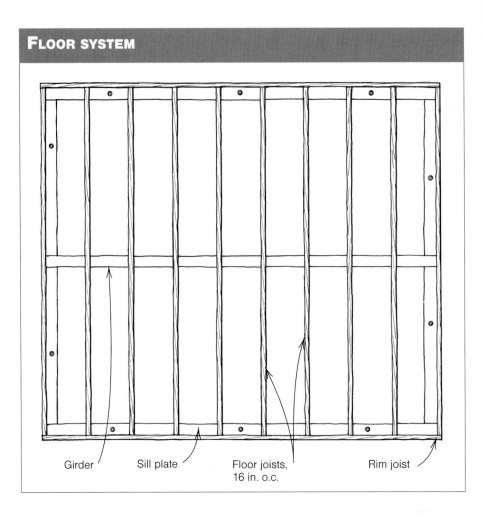

Girder   Sill plate   Floor joists,   Rim joist
                                    16 in. o.c.

support has been determined by tests and incorporated into building codes. All you need to do is check your plans to see what type and size of joists you'll use.

Joist size is usually determined by the distance they have to span. So the larger the span, the larger the joist. When you are joisting over a basement with a single center support, you often use 2x12s. If you are joisting over a crawl space with girders every 6 ft. or so, you can usually use 2x6s. Now with I-joists, you can span from sill plate to sill plate without any support in the middle. Floor joists on the first floor may be a different size than those used on the second floor.

Whatever size or type of joist you use, nailing them in place is more or less the same for big or little.

Layout

Once the sill plates are securely in place, the next step in joisting a floor is to lay out locations where joists are actually nailed in place. I like to do my layout on the rim joists (also called band joists). Rim joists are nailed into the sill plates around the perimeter of the building and help hold the floor joists upright. I nail the rim joists onto the outer edge of the sill plate with 16d sinkers toe-nailed every 16 in. o.c. Use galvanized or stainless-steel nails in wet climates or near the ocean.

Once the rim joists have been toenailed in place, lay out the floor-joist locations on them. Joists are most often spaced 16 in. o.c. so that they can be efficiently sheathed with 4x8 sheets of plywood or oriented strand board (OSB), but check the plans to make sure. Manufactured joists are sometimes spaced at 19.2 in. This layout also fits a piece of 8-ft. sheathing. Hook a long tape measure on the end of the rim joist and make a mark on top of the rim every 16 in. (16 in., 32 in., 48 in., etc.), down its entire length. Put an X or straight line alongside each mark to show on which side of the line the joist will be nailed (see the drawing at right).

If the joists span from rim joist to rim joist, the layout will be the same on each rim joist. If the joists lap over a girder or wall, the opposing rim joists need to be laid out differently. On one rim joist, mark the 16-in. o.c. locations with an X to the right; on the opposite wall, lay out the joists with an X to the left. This will allow the joists to lap and nail at a girder, where they will be stabilized with nailed-on blocks.

Once the layout is complete, lay all of the floor joists flat across the sill plates and girders on every layout mark. Keep your eye open for joists that are badly bowed or twisted or those with large knots. These should be replaced with better stock and set aside to be cut up for blocks later. If joists need to be cut, cut them in place rather than measure each one individually (see the photo on p. 94). Just remember not to notch or cut I-joists in midspan, which compromises their structural integrity.

Once the joists are cut to length, it's time to "roll" them. Rolling means to set floor joists on edge and nail them in place with their crown (the slight bow along the bearing edge) up. Line up each joist with the layout marks on the

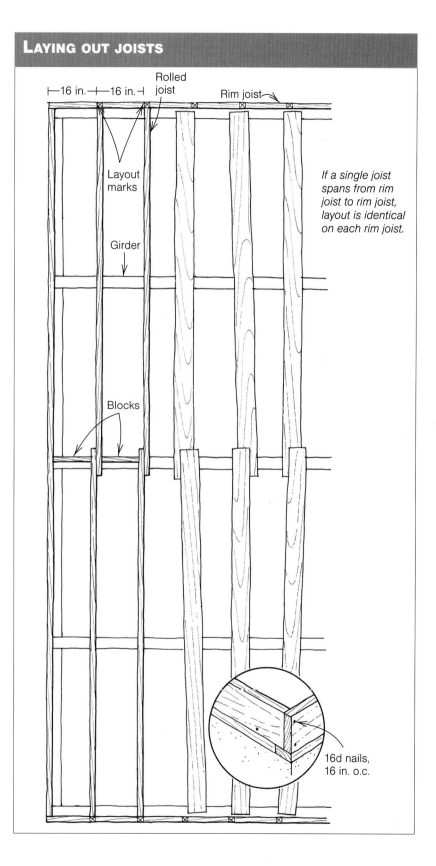

LAYING OUT JOISTS

16 in. — 16 in.

Rolled joist

Rim joist

Layout marks

Girder

Blocks

If a single joist spans from rim joist to rim joist, layout is identical on each rim joist.

16d nails, 16 in. o.c.

Butt the floor joists against one rim joist, with the opposite ends overhanging the other rim joist. Then cut each floor joist to length by eye, using the edge of the rim joist as a reference. (Photo by Roe A. Osborn.)

top of each rim joist, making sure the floor joist is snug against the rim. Then drive two 16d nails through the rim joist directly into the end of each floor joist— one nail at the top and one at the bottom (see the drawing on the facing page).

Make sure you nail all joists and blocks securely as they are installed. Someone stepping on an unnailed 2x could slip and fall. Also, don't leave nails half-driven, and don't drive nails where you might have to make a saw cut later on. Take time to do good, clean work. If

using a pneumatic nailer, drive the bottom nail first, then remove the hand holding the joist and drive the top nail. I can promise that if you drive the top nail first, sooner or later you will miss the wood and fire a nail into your hand.

Each floor joist also needs to be toe-nailed to the sill plates and supporting girders. Try walking one way, driving a 16d toenail through each joist into the sill plate or girder. When you reach the end, turn around and repeat the process on the other side of each joist.

NAILING IN FLOOR JOISTS

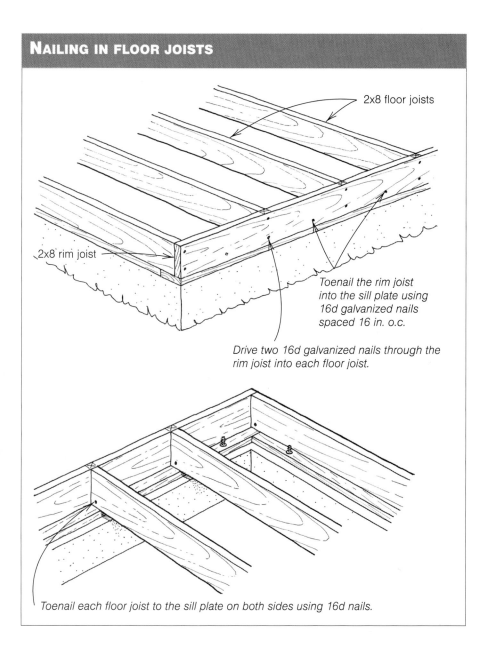

2x8 floor joists

2x8 rim joist

Toenail the rim joist into the sill plate using 16d galvanized nails spaced 16 in. o.c.

Drive two 16d galvanized nails through the rim joist into each floor joist.

Toenail each floor joist to the sill plate on both sides using 16d nails.

After nailing in the floor joists, I like to stop and look at my work. Joists on edge portray a certain symmetry and beauty. They clearly show the outline of the building.

Blocking
Blocking helps stabilize a building and keeps joists from falling like dominoes under stress, such as might happen dur-

ing an earthquake or high wind storm. If floor joists are spaced 16 in. o.c., cut blocks 14½ in. long. If you are blocking lapped joists, cut them 13 in. long (see the drawing on p. 96). I find that blocks need to be cut just a bit under their actual size (cut a 14½-in. block at 14⁷⁄₁₆ in.). I think this is because 2x lumber is frequently wet and measures just a bit more than 1½ in.

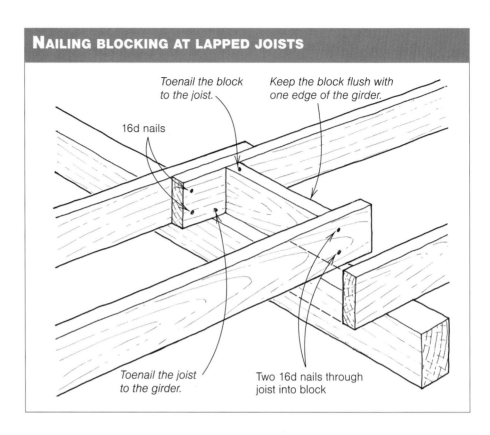

NAILING BLOCKING AT LAPPED JOISTS

Toenail the block to the joist.

Keep the block flush with one edge of the girder.

16d nails

Toenail the joist to the girder.

Two 16d nails through joist into block

When installing blocks between floor joists, set each one on edge and drive two 16d nails through the joists into the block. Offset each block to one side of the previous block. (Photo by Roe A. Osborn.)

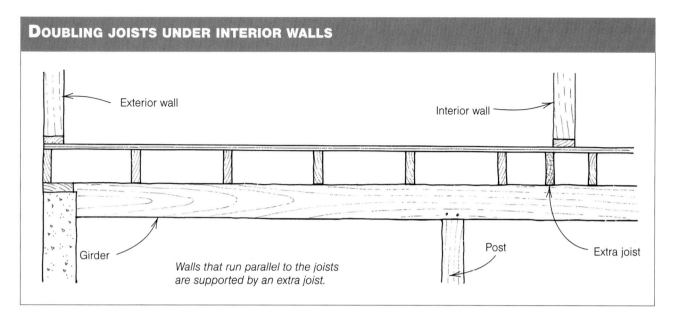

Exterior wall

Interior wall

Girder

Walls that run parallel to the joists are supported by an extra joist.

Post

Extra joist

Be careful to start correctly. Begin by setting a block on edge between the rim joist and the first floor joist over a girder or bearing wall. Nail it in place with two 16d nails through the rim joist into the block and with one 16d nail through the floor joist into the block. Next, angle a 16d toenail through both sides of the joist into the center girder. Grab another block, offset it to one side of the previous block, and repeat the nailing process (see the photo on the facing page). Once you have a few blocks nailed in place, use your tape measure to check for accuracy. The floor joists will be straight if they maintain the same on-center layout (16 in., 32 in., 48 in.) over the girder as they do at the rim joist. If the blocks are too long or too short, the floor joists will be curved rather than straight.

Extra joists and headouts

Extra joists are needed under parallel walls (walls that aren't perpendicular to the floor joists) to carry the added weight that gets transferred down through these walls. Move the extra joists away from the center of each

parallel wall about 3 in. to allow room for pipes and conduit to be run up into the walls from below (see the drawing above).

Sometimes joists must be cut to allow room for a stairway, access to an attic, a place to install a skylight, or even for a heater vent in a wall or a tub trap in a bathroom. Carpenters call these openings headouts (see the drawing on p. 98). Regular 2x joists (not I-joists) can be cut as long as they are supported by a header joist and fastened to parallel joists. Here are some basic rules for headouts:

• If more than one joist is cut, double the header joist and side joists.

• Support cut joists temporarily by nailing a flat 2x across their tops.

• Nail 16ds through the header joists into the cutoff joists.

• Support both header and cutoff joists with metal joist hangers at intersecting points.

Double trimmer joist

Double header joist

Stairwell opening

2x4 stabilizes cut joists.

Metal joist hanger

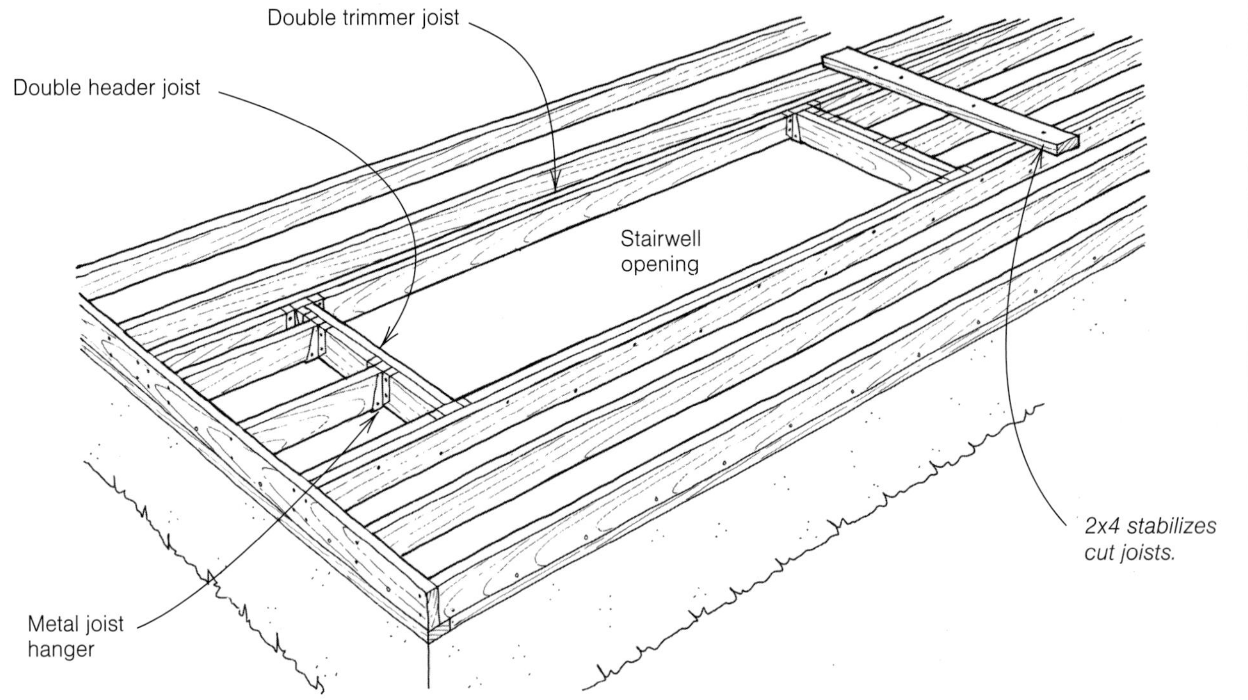

• Nail double joists together with 16ds at 16 in. o.c.

• Keep all wood at least 1 in from heating vents.

• A common mistake made by carpenters framing a headout is to forget to leave room for the header joists. If, for example, a 6-ft.-long floor opening is needed, cut it 6 ft. 6 in. This leaves room for a double header joist at each end.

SHEATHING THE FLOOR

Once floor framing is complete, it's time to cover it with sheathing. Although it's easier to install rough plumbing and heating ductwork now, this can be done after the subfloor has been laid. After the sheathing is nailed in place, you'll have a level platform, perfect for building a house or for having a dance!

Normally floors are sheathed with 4x8 sheets of $5/8$-in. or $3/4$-in. tongue-and-groove (T&G) plywood or OSB. The sheathing should be exterior grade so that it won't come unglued when exposed to moisture. While square-edged sheathing can be used, codes often require it to be supported by edge blocking between joists. The edges of T&G sheathing are self-supporting and don't require blocking.

Floor sheathing is bulky and awkward and in windy conditions can act like the sail of a windsurfer. So be mindful when handling it. Also, T&G plywood should be handled with care so you don't wind up with damaged edges, which can make it hard to fit two sheets together. When I carry sheathing, I grasp it with one hand underneath and one on top for balance, allowing much of the weight to rest against my upper body. Or I get a helper.

Sheathing is installed so that the 8-ft. edges are perpendicular to the floor joists. Before laying any sheathing down, though, first measure in 48¼ in. from each end and snap a chalkline across the joists between these two marks. This line acts as a control, or reference, line for the first row of sheathing, and the extra ¼ in. allows for any slight variation in the rim-joist alignment. With the first row of sheathing straight, the rest of the job will be easier.

Fastening down the sheathing

It's a good idea to lay down a bead of construction adhesive on each joist before installing the sheathing. The adhesive secures the sheathing tight to the floor joists and helps prevent or reduce floor squeaks, which happen when joists dry out and shrink away from the subfloor. Apply a ¼-in. bead to each joist over a section large enough to lay down a 4x8 piece of sheathing (see the top photo at right).

Lay the first sheet with the grooved edge right along the control line with each end hitting along the center of a joist. If the plywood edge doesn't fall on a joist, snap a chalkline and cut the sheet to length so that it breaks on the center of the joist. Set the circular saw to the proper depth (⅞ in.) and make the cut. Don't leave the cutoffs under the floor, or you'll give termites an easy meal.

Tack down the sheet to the joists with one 8d nail near each corner. On large floors, nail off the sheets after you have laid four or five; otherwise, the adhesive could set up (especially in hot weather). Be careful not to drive nails within 6 in. of the leading edge, because you'll need

Construction adhesive helps secure sheathing tight to the joists and reduce floor squeaks. Place a ¼-in. bead on each joist. (Photo by Roe A. Osborn.)

After each row of sheathing has been installed, mark the joist location on top at the leading edge so you will know where to drive the nails. (Photo by Roe A. Osborn.)

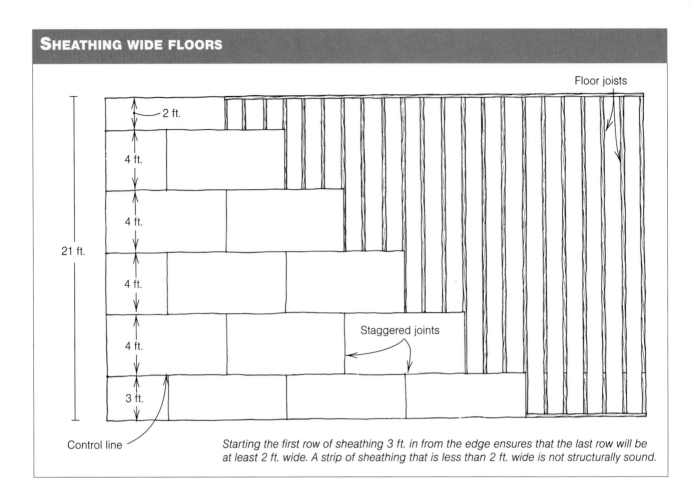

Starting the first row of sheathing 3 ft. in from the edge ensures that the last row will be at least 2 ft. wide. A strip of sheathing that is less than 2 ft. wide is not structurally sound.

a little flexibility here to make it easier to mate the groove of the first row with the tongue of the next.

After placing a row of sheathing, mark the location of every joist with a pencil or keel on the leading edge of the sheathing (see the bottom photo on p. 99). This will make it easy to find the joists when you start nailing all the sheets down.

If you live in a wet climate, leave about 1/8 in. between the ends and edges of the sheets to allow for expansion. This gap can be gauged by eye or by using an 8d nail as a spacer.

Don't install sheets so that four corners meet at the same point. Instead, stagger the plywood joints, as a bricklayer would do when building a chimney, to add strength to the floor (see the drawing above). Begin the second row with a 4-ft. by 4-ft. sheet, and install it adjacent to the 8-ft. sheet in the first row. Then complete the row with 8-ft. sheets.

Sometimes a little extra persuasion is needed to unite T&G plywood. One way to do this is for one person to stand on the sheet, holding it flat and snug against the previous row of sheathing. The second person places a scrap 2x against the edge (to protect the edge

A nail buggy is a good tool when you have to nail subfloor by hand. Better to nail sitting on your bottom than crawling on your knees. Cut a 20-in. circle or square from ¾-in. plywood. Buy three or four good wheels at least 2 in. in diameter and screw them to the bottom of the plywood. Attach a bread pan to the side to hold nails. Now, like an Olympic swimmer doing laps, you can sit on the buggy and push yourself backward as you nail down subfloor. Just don't roll off the edge of the floor.

Sitting on a nail buggy makes it easier to nail floor sheathing. (Photo by Roe A. Osborn.)

from damage) and hits it with a sledge-hammer (see the photo at right). A couple of licks should bring the two sheets together.

Once you have all the sheets tacked in place, you can move around the floor driving nails to secure the sheathing to the joists firmly. (A nail buggy will make this job easier; see the sidebar above.) A typical nailing schedule would be to drive 8d nails 4 in. o.c. on the perimeter (around the outside), 6 in. o.c. near joints, and 12 in. o.c. in the field (in the middle of the sheets). You may want to use ring-shank nails for better holding power.

Drive the nails straight into the center of the joists. While some carpenters snap a chalkline as a nailing guide across each sheet, try nailing by eye. When you feel that you have missed a joist, stop, pull the nail, and drive another.

Sometimes T&G plywood needs some not-so-gentle persuasion. Have one person stand on the sheet to hold it flat and snug against the previous row while another hits it with a sledgehammer. The 2x placed in front of the sheet protects the plywood edge from damage. (Photo by Roe A. Osborn.)

5

WALLS AND CEILINGS

The first house I helped build was in 1948, on the high plains of western Nebraska. It was a precut house, shipped by rail and brought to the job site on a large wagon pulled by a team of horses. Every piece of wood—wall plates, studs, headers, cripple studs, sills, braces, and joists—was wrapped and labeled in color-coded bundles. Putting the house together was like putting together a three-dimensional jigsaw puzzle.

Houses are still puzzles. All the different pieces have to be laid out, cut, and nailed together to create the frame. The sheathed floor or concrete slab acts as the "table" on which all the puzzle pieces are assembled. But puzzles go together easier when you have an idea of what the finished product will look like. So before pounding the first nail, study the plans thoroughly and develop a picture of the house in your mind.

LAYING OUT WALLS

Framing walls is a challenging task for a beginning carpenter (see the photo on the facing page). The first steps—laying out the location of every wall and snapping chalklines to transfer the floor-plan dimensions to the slab or subfloor—are critical (see the drawing on p. 104). Once the house is framed, these wall-layout lines become bedrooms, bath-

rooms, and kitchens. If walls are out of square or not parallel, cabinets won't fit properly, floor tiles will have to be cut, and even the roof ridge may run downhill. At this point, accuracy is more important than speed.

Exterior walls

Before you get out your tape measure or chalkline, sweep the floor to get the deck clean for the layout. Start by snapping the location of two long exterior walls that are at right angles to each other. Get these two long walls laid out right, and you can measure the location of all the other walls off them. Once you pick a wall, measure in 3½ in. for 2x4 construction or 5½ in. for 2x6 construction. Then mark the slab or subfloor with a carpenter's pencil or keel exactly where the wall will stand. Or you can lay a short piece of 2x4 or 2x6 at both ends and mark the inside (see the photo on p. 105). Connect these two marks with a chalkline. Keep it all clear and simple; don't complicate the puzzle.

After snapping a chalkline for the first wall, lay out the perpendicular wall. Be sure to check that the walls are perpendicular, especially if you're working on concrete. Don't trust that a slab is square. Instead, use the 6-8-10 method (see p. 87) to check for accuracy.

Once walls are laid out and plated, they are assembled piece by piece on the floor. Sometimes the studs are marked and cut to length in place. (Photo by Roger Turk.)

As you lay out the remaining exterior walls, note that their dimensions are often given from outside to outside. Look closely to see whether a measurement is from outside to outside, outside to center, center to center, or wall to wall.

You don't have to strive for total perfection when building the house frame. It's okay to leave walls a tiny bit out of parallel (like ¼ in. in 12 ft.). But walls out of parallel by ½ in. in 12 ft., for example, need adjusting. To do this, go to one end of the floor or slab and measure in

LAYING OUT WALLS

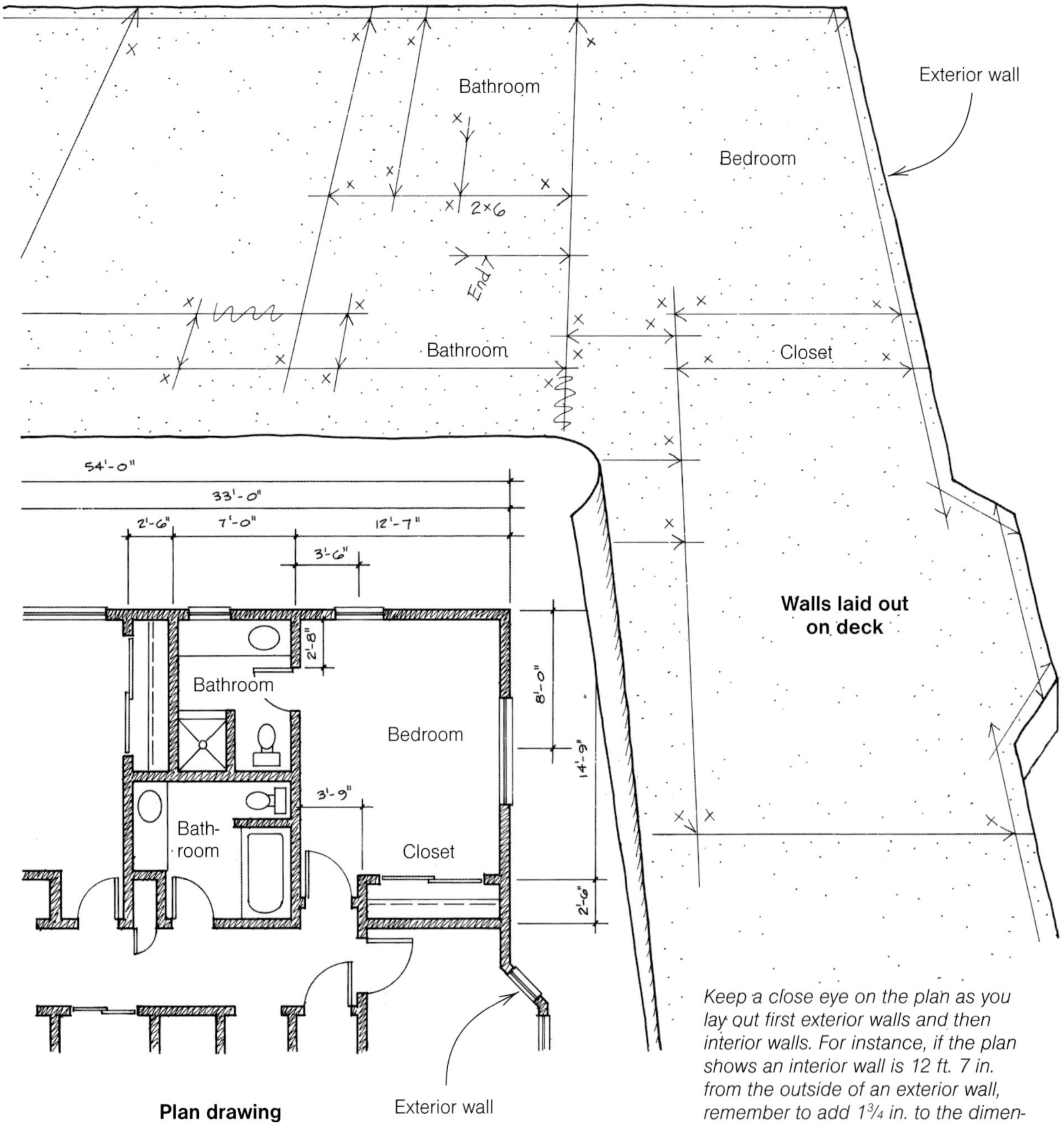

Exterior wall
Bathroom
Bedroom
2×6
End
Bathroom
Closet
54'-0"
33'-0"
2'-6"
7'-0"
12'-7"
3'-6"
2'-8"
8'-0"
14'-9"
3'-9"
2'-6"
Walls laid out on deck
Bathroom
Bedroom
Bath-room
Closet
Plan drawing
Exterior wall

Keep a close eye on the plan as you lay out first exterior walls and then interior walls. For instance, if the plan shows an interior wall is 12 ft. 7 in. from the outside of an exterior wall, remember to add 1¾ in. to the dimension of the interior walls, which will be 12 ft. 8¾ in. from outside to outside.

3⅝ in. at both corners. This increases the width by ¼ in. Then go to the other end and measure in 3⅜ in. at each corner. This narrows the width by ¼ in. The walls are now parallel. At this point, there is no need to pay attention to door or window locations.

Interior walls
Once the exterior wall lines are accurately in place, you can measure off them to get the location of interior walls. Just keep an eye on the plans to get the dimensions right.

Laying out the long interior walls next makes it easier to locate and mark all the short, 2x4 walls that make up closets and bathrooms. Watch the floor plan. It may show that an interior bedroom wall is 12 ft. 7 in. from the outside of the building to the center of the 2x4 wall. Because half of 3½ in. is 1¾ in., add 1¾ in. to 12 ft. 7 in. to get the overall dimension of this wall, which is 12 ft. 8¾ in. from outside to outside.

Measure in this distance from the outside of the exterior wall of the slab or floor deck, mark it, and place an X to the inside of the mark, as shown in the drawing on the facing page. Do this at both ends of the wall and connect the marks with a chalkline. The location of the X is important because it indicates the exact location of the wall. Placing the X on the wrong side of the mark can be disastrous. Imagine the excitement of a plumber, for example, trying to install a bathtub in a room that is 3½ in. too narrow.

You might find that plans don't always have the exact measurements you need. For example, floor plans might show a 60-in. dimension in a bathroom to accommodate a standard-size bathtub. In reality, what is needed is 60¼ in. so that the tub will actually fit without having to carve up the walls. And because

To lay out the wall locations at a corner, place a 2x4 or 2x6 block flush with the outside of the building and mark on the inside with a pencil. (Photo by Roe A. Osborn.)

of the size of plumbing drains and vents, it's best to build bathroom walls out of 2x6s to accommodate the plumbing.

PLATING
Once you're finished with the wall-layout chalklines, you can begin to lay down the top and bottom plates. Eventually, when you frame the wall, a third plate will be nailed to the top plate to hold the walls together. At times, when doing remodeling work, I have opened up a wall to find that only a single top plate was used. This allowed the walls to separate, opening up cracks in the plaster and siding, because they were not tied together with the double top plate.

Pick long, straight stock for plates, which makes it easier to keep walls straight once they're raised upright. Plate the long outside walls (called

Once the wall layout is complete, it's time to lay down top and bottom plates. Eventually, when you frame the wall, a third plate will be nailed to the top plate. Here I'm cutting a bottom plate to length. (Photo by Roe A. Osborn.)

and tack it in place with two or three 8d nails. Run your plates continuously, ignoring door and window openings. The bottom plate in doorways will be cut out later.

Plating on a slab
Plating on a concrete slab requires a slightly different approach than plating on a wooden floor system. Slabs normally have anchor bolts located around the perimeter to hold the exterior walls in place. On interior walls, the plates are held in position by a hardened screw or nail or by actually shooting a steel pin through them into the concrete. However you do it, you can't easily tack the plates in place like you can on a wooden deck. Just position the bottom plate on the line and tack the top plate to it.

Don't forget to use pressure-treated wood for plates that are in direct contact with concrete. Anyone who has done remodeling work can tell stories of termite-ridden sills or plates made of untreated lumber. If termites get by the sills or plates, they start eating toward the attic. That's why, in Hawaii (home to the mother of all termites), entire frames are often made of treated wood.

Where there are anchor bolts, their location can be marked on the plate in the same manner as with sill plates (see Chapter 4).

HEADERS, CRIPPLES, ROUGH SILLS, AND TRIMMERS
Now it's time to cut some of the parts that make up the wall, beginning with the window and door headers and the rough sills. Recall from Chapter 3 that headers are needed at window and door openings to transfer the load of the building around these elements to the foundation. This wasn't always done in old houses, so walls often

through walls) first. Shorter walls that intersect the through walls are called butt walls. These can be plated once the through walls are in place. Get the long borders of a house in place, and the shorter inside pieces fit together easier.

Placing and securing plates
Remember that top and bottom wall plates are placed flush with the chalklines on the X side of the marks made on the deck. But these plates need to be cut accurately or the walls won't end up square and plumb. Again, begin with the outside walls. Lay down a long 2x plate on the chalkline, cut it to length,

HEADERS, CRIPPLES, ROUGH SILLS, AND TRIMMERS

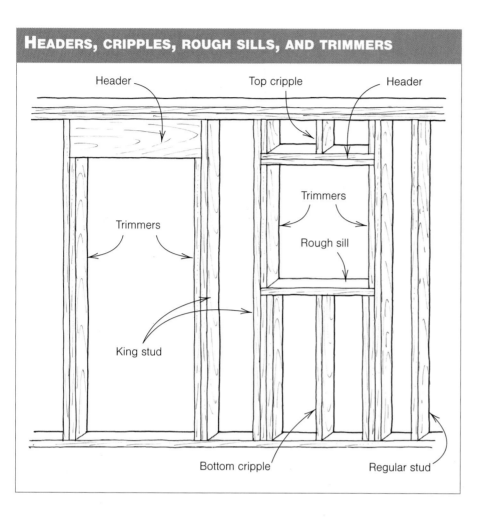

Header

Top cripple

Header

Trimmers

Trimmers

Rough sill

King stud

Bottom cripple

Regular stud

sagged and doors and windows became hard to open because of all the weight put on them. Frequently, part of a remodeler's job is to open up old walls and cut in solid headers over every door and window.

Ordinarily, the distance from the floor to the bottom of the door or window header is 6 ft. 10 in. Cripple studs (called cripples) are used to fill in the short space between the top of the header and the top plate, or between the bottom of a window opening and the bottom plate. Trimmer studs (called trimmers), nailed to the inside of the studs that border each end of headers, support the headers at the correct height (see the drawing above).

Cutting headers and rough sills

There are different types of headers for different applications. Solid headers (typically a 4x4 or a 4x6) are sometimes used, but more often than not, the headers are built up by sandwiching ½-in. plywood between a couple of 2xs. Flat 2x headers can be used for openings in nonbearing walls. Some builders like to put in double flat headers to make sure they have solid nailing for door and window trim. Or you can make a box header that can be filled with insulation to guard against heat loss (see the drawing on p. 108).

Outside walls are normally considered to be weight-bearing walls. Interior walls can be bearing or nonbearing, depend-

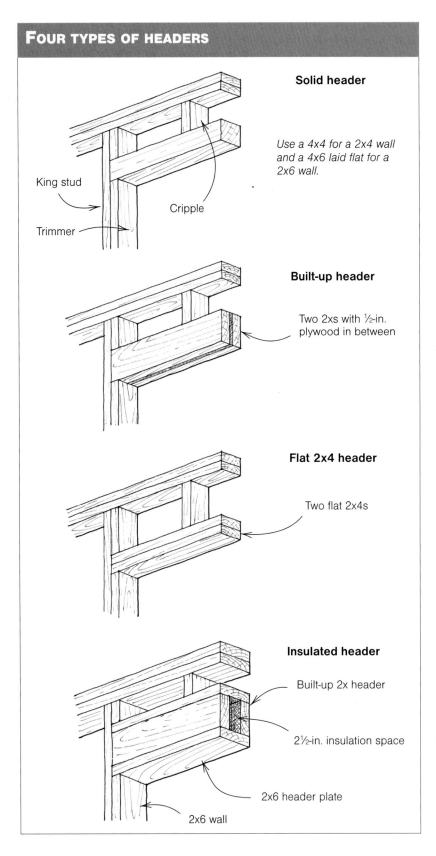

FOUR TYPES OF HEADERS

Solid header

Use a 4x4 for a 2x4 wall and a 4x6 laid flat for a 2x6 wall.

King stud

Cripple

Trimmer

Built-up header

Two 2xs with ½-in. plywood in between

Flat 2x4 header

Two flat 2x4s

Insulated header

Built-up 2x header

2½-in. insulation space

2x6 header plate

2x6 wall

ing on whether they carry weight from above. If you are using manufactured trusses for the roof, all interior walls are usually nonbearing, which makes it possible to use the flat 2x for interior headers. In houses without roof trusses, joists and even roofs might be supported by an interior wall. Such walls are bearing walls and need larger headers to support the weight.

I'm often called on to remove a wall to make a room larger, so it's important to know about bearing walls. The easiest way to check if a wall is bearing weight is to look in the attic to see whether joists or roof rafters are supported by it. Most walls can be removed, but a bearing wall must be replaced with a beam to support the weight. Of course, another owner may come along later who wants smaller rooms, making work for the next generation of carpenters.

The standard length of a header for doors and windows is 5 in. over the rough-opening size. Thus the header for a 3-ft. opening is 41 in. The extra 5 in. leaves 3 in. for a 1½-in. trimmer on each side, 1½ in. for a ¾-in. jamb on each side, plus ½ in. to plumb the trimmers. When using prehung doors, cut the headers 5½ in. longer for greater ease in installing the jamb.

Rough-opening sizes for aluminum and vinyl-clad window frames generally are 3 in. wider than the rough-opening size of the window. So, for a 3/6 window, cut the header 45 in. long. The extra 3 in. leaves space for a 1½-in. trimmer on each side plus enough room to set the window. Window frames are actually ½ in. smaller than their nominal size. So a 3/6 window, for example, is usually 3 ft. 5½ in. wide. Once set in the rough opening, the frame is nailed on with a ¼-in. clearance on all sides. This gap is closed in by drywall or wood trim. Rough windowsills are cut to the same length as the corresponding header.

Cutting cripples and trimmers

Keep your mind focused when measuring and cutting cripples and trimmers. A mistake here can cause you big headaches and lots of extra work later on. I recall cutting all the top window cripples 1 in. too long for the first floor of an apartment house we were building. I didn't catch the mistake until after the walls were framed and raised. Every window and door header had to be removed and the cripples shortened. Not a good way to start your week.

To make the job of cutting cripples and trimmers easier, I usually make a story pole. As the name suggests, this is a pole—actually a 2x4—that tells a story, and it's used to mark multiple measurements or to transfer measurements from one place to another. A story pole can be used to show the locations of headers and sills or the lengths of cripples and trimmers (see the photo at right) or to locate the height of rows of siding (see Chapter 8).

To make a story pole for a 96¾-in. wall, take a 92¼-in.-long 2x4 and tack a short piece of 2x4 to one end to act as the bottom plate. Since the height of both the door and window headers from the floor is generally 6 ft. 10 in., measure up this distance from the bottom of the bottom plate and mark the location of the bottom of the headers. Then measure up from this mark another 3½ in. for a 4x4 header and 5½ in. for a 4x6 header. Measure up 1½ in. for a single flat header, or 3 in. for a double flat header.

A story pole shows locations of headers and sills and the lengths of cripples and trimmers. (Photo by Roe A. Osborn.)

Left over on the pole are the lengths of the top cripples: 6¼ in. for the 4x6 header, 8¼ in. for the 4x4 header, 10¼ in. for the 2x flat header, and 8¾ in. for a double flat header. Cut enough top cripples to nail one on each end of every header and one every 16 in. on center (o.c.) between.

To determine the length of the door trimmers, measure down from the bottom of the header to the top of the bottom plate. This distance is 6 ft. 8½ in. To make the trimmers fit snug, add about 1/16 in. to this length, which you usually can do by leaving the line when you cut.

Window trimmers for aluminum- or vinyl-clad frames are the rough-opening size of the window. If you have a window that is 5/0 high, the trimmer will be 60 in. For wood-frame windows, add 3 in. to make room for the wood sill.

To find the lengths of the cripples under a 5/0 window, measure down 60 in. and make a mark. Measure down another 1½ in. for a single 2x rough sill. The amount left over on the stud—19 in.—is the length of the bottom cripples.

MARKING THE PLATES

Once all the parts have been cut, you have to figure out where to nail them. When I first began as a carpenter, I used to plate, lay out, and build one wall at a time. Now I start by laying out (detailing) where every piece nails into every wall plate. I indicate on the plates the locations of corners, doors, windows, and every stud. It's best to keep these detail marks on wall plates simple. Extra marks tend to be confusing.

Start by marking the corners and channels (the T-intersection where one wall meets another). Corners and channels require extra studs so that walls can be properly nailed together once they are raised. These extra studs also provide backing so that the drywall can be nailed on the inside and siding on the outside. Mark the locations of these corners accurately on the plate so that raised walls will be nailed in the right place.

A bit of sloppiness is allowed in frame carpentry. Wall plates, for example, can be ⅛ in. short or long without causing major problems. But inaccuracies tend to accumulate. A small mistake made several times can add up to a headache.

MAKING CORNER AND CHANNEL MARKERS

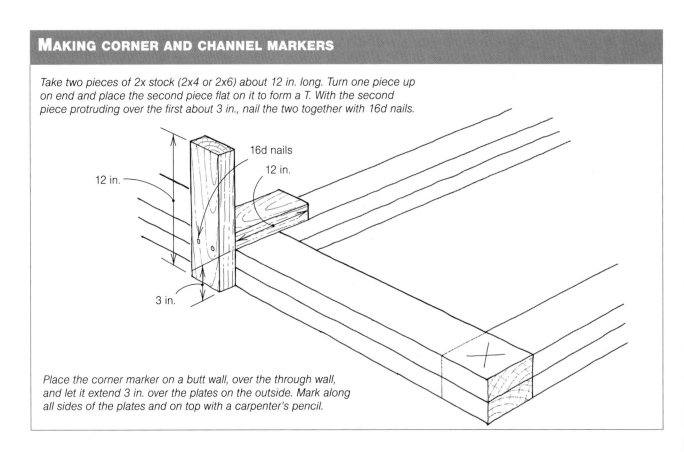

Take two pieces of 2x stock (2x4 or 2x6) about 12 in. long. Turn one piece up on end and place the second piece flat on it to form a T. With the second piece protruding over the first about 3 in., nail the two together with 16d nails.

16d nails

12 in.

12 in.

3 in.

Place the corner marker on a butt wall, over the through wall, and let it extend 3 in. over the plates on the outside. Mark along all sides of the plates and on top with a carpenter's pencil.

So a skilled craftsperson is one who learns to work quickly and, most important, with precision.

One quick and accurate way to mark corners is with a corner marker (see the drawing on the facing page). Use the corner marker as shown in the drawing to scribe layout lines for corners and channels, which will show exactly where to nail in the extra studs needed at these points. It also marks where to cut the second plate (double top plate) that is nailed to the first top plate as the walls are being framed.

Now, following the plan, find the location of each window and door. Position each header on the plates and mark down from the header ends with a piece of blue or black keel across both plates. Next to this line, mark an X on both plates on the side away from the header to indicate the location of the king stud that nails alongside the header. On the other side of the line away from the X, make a longer, straight line along both plates. This line indicates that there will be an opening for a door or window at this location (see the photo at right).

Position each header on the plates and mark down from the header ends across both plates. Mark an X on both plates to indicate the location of the king stud. On the other side of the X, mark a long, straight line to indicate that there will be an opening for a door or window. (Photo by Roe A. Osborn.)

Wall studs are usually 16 in. o.c. or 24 in. o.c., but you never know what to expect on a remodel job. I worked on an old house once in which the studs were about 5 in. o.c. Both the outside and inside were sheathed with 1x pine. Good construction, but it would be rather expensive these days. At least it was no problem to hang a picture on the wall.

I find the easiest way to mark the location of wall studs is to use a metal layout stick. The layout stick is made up of four short bars that are 1½ in. wide, or the depth of a stud, and spaced 16 in. (or 24 in.) o.c. These short bars are welded to another bar that's 49½ in. long. Forty years ago we made them from 1x2 pine, but now they are available commercially

from Pairis Enterprises (see Sources on p. 198). Laying out with this stick is certainly faster than using the 6-ft. folding rule I started with as a beginner. Most metal tape measures are clearly marked on 16-in. and 24-in. centers and can also be used for layout.

Every carpenter needs to become familiar with specialty tools like the layout stick. I seldom use a tape measure to lay out studs or plates simply because it's faster and just as accurate to use a layout stick.

Exterior walls often are sheathed with plywood or oriented strand board (OSB), materials that come in 4-ft. by 8-ft. sheets. So wall studs need to be spaced

Use a layout stick to mark stud locations on wall plates. (Photo by Roe A. Osborn.)

to fit the 4-ft. module of the sheathing. Otherwise, every piece of sheathing has to be cut to fit, a wasteful, time-consuming process. Start the stud layout at one end of the first exterior wall, being sure to detail stud layout on the same side of the plate as the door and window layout. If you are using a layout stick, set it with the legs down over both plates and scribe along both sides of the second, third, and fourth legs at the 16-in., 32-in., and 48-in. marks (as shown in the photo above). Then move the stick and scribe another set of studs until you come to the end of each wall. If you're using a tape measure, hook it over the end of the plate and pull it as far as it will extend, marking on every 16-in. or 24-in. layout mark. When you come to a window or door, transfer layout marks onto headers and rough sills to indicate where the cripples will be nailed.

FRAMING THE WALLS

Once the plates are marked up and detailed, you can begin to assemble the walls. When I first started framing walls, carpenters used to toenail a stud in each corner, string the top plate across from stud to stud, and then work off a ladder to nail in the remaining studs. Each wall took a long time to build because we had to nail in one stud, move the ladder, and nail in another. And the fact that we were working on ladders made the work unnecessarily dangerous. It wasn't long before we learned to frame walls flat on the floor, then raise them into position.

If you've done a good job marking the plates, framing walls should be easy. Simply follow the marks, nailing in studs where needed. But first, clean the floor. There's no need to have extra wood or tools around that might trip you up.

Holding the cripple in place with your foot, toenail it to the header with 8d nails. (Photo by Roe A. Osborn.)

Nailing in cripples

Now the puzzle goes together. Begin by nailing on the top and bottom cripples over and under all rough openings. Cripples are nailed on each end of every header and rough sill and at every layout mark in between. When I set out cripples, I also like to scatter 92¼-in. king studs at both ends of each window and door along with their trimmers.

To nail a cripple in place on a header, back it with your foot before starting your first two 8d toenails (see the photo above). Make sure the 2x cripple is flush with the sides of the header, then drive the nails home through the cripple and into the header. This process will become easier as you become more skilled. At first you may find that your toenail angle is too high (in which case the nail won't have enough holding power in the cripple) or too low (in

which case you'll drive the 2x4 toward your foot). I've driven toenails through a cripple and into the sole of my shoe. It's rather embarrassing to take a step dragging a cripple behind.

The nails should drive easily if you started them at the proper angle, at about 60°. After nailing off one side, toenail two more 8d nails into the other side, repeating the process until all the top cripples have been nailed to their headers.

Attaching the bottom cripples to their rough sills is easier, because it involves no toenailing. Move the rough sill to the upper ends of the cripples placed against the plates (see the photo on p. 114). Nail a cripple at both ends of the sill and at every layout mark. Drive two 16d nails in each cripple about ¾ in. from either edge of the sill.

To attach a bottom cripple to the rough sill, drive one 16d nail about ¾ in. down from the top edge of the sill and the second ¾ in. up from the bottom. (Photo by Roe A. Osborn.)

Nailing king studs and trimmers

It's best to nail king studs to the door and window headers and to the rough sills while nailing on the cripples. Assemble the studs in place, exactly as they go in the wall, but flat on the floor. First nail the king studs flush with the top of the upper cripples into the ends of the headers, driving three 16d nails through the king stud into small headers and four 16ds into larger headers.

For window openings, hold the end cripple on the rough sill flush with the bottom of the king stud and drive two 16d nails through the king stud into the end of the rough sill. Then insert a trimmer under each end of each door and window header, driving just one 16d nail through the center of every trimmer into the king stud. You'll drive in additional nails later as you prepare to set the door and window frames.

As you nail, keep all the members tight together. Take time to nail the frame together properly. Gaps left between cripples and headers, for example, can mean cracks in the drywall later on as lumber shrinks and the building settles. As you nail, keep both window and door assemblies square with themselves and with the building.

Assembling the walls

Once the door and window frames are assembled, you can start nailing walls together. Start by scattering enough 92¼-in. studs to frame one of the exterior through walls, which I always build and raise first. Later you'll frame and raise the butt walls, which are generally shorter and rise up between the through walls. Scatter the studs on the floor perpendicular to the plates, one stud per layout mark and three studs for each corner and channel.

As a beginning carpenter, one of my jobs was to set up and nail together all the corners and channels needed for an entire building. Some builders still do this, but I've found that it works better to build everything flat on the deck as you nail the wall together. Keep your eyes open for any studs that are badly bowed or twisted and put these aside to use for blocks and roof braces. A bowed stud can leave a bump in a wall once the drywall is nailed on. This can cause problems for finish carpenters who install cabinets, countertops, or interior trim. Framing carpenters need to think about the other tradespeople who will work behind them. Tilesetters like square rooms. Cabinetmakers and finish carpenters like plumb, straight walls. Always try to do work you would be proud to show to your mother or your children.

Now, using the claws of your hammer, pry apart the top and bottom wall plates that you temporarily nailed together. Be sure to bend or pull out the 8d nails used to tack the plates together so that you don't get a puncture wound as you work. (Because carpenters can't work long without getting their share of wounds and bruises, it's a good idea to keep a first-aid kit on the job site and your tetanus immunization up to date.)

Move the top plate straight up to the upper ends of the studs, keeping the layout marks aligned. I've occasionally seen framers grab the plate, turn them-selves and it around, and place it in nailing position. Switching the stud layout end for end on the top plate makes for some interesting walls, as you can imagine.

Begin nailing in studs at an outside cor-ner. You'll find that consistently working either left to right or right to left has a natural feel to you, and over time you'll develop a rhythm to nailing in studs that involves not only your arms and hands but also your entire body (see the photo at right). Even your feet can be trained to move studs into position for nailing. Framing can become like a dance, where every movement is coordinated and flows into the next. (I have had it hap-pen that my movements became so fluid that time seemed to stand still as I nailed down the plate line. Two of my children are professional dancers. They tell me the same thing often happens to them during a dance production.)

Begin nailing in studs at an outside corner, working either left to right or right to left, whichever feels the most natural to you. (Photo by Roe A. Osborn.)

Corners and channels can be built in different ways, depending on the size of the wall and local preferences (see the drawing on p. 116). A three-stud corner is the most basic configuration. If you prefer, you can save wood by building either a two-stud corner or a blocked-up corner. With a two-stud corner, the first

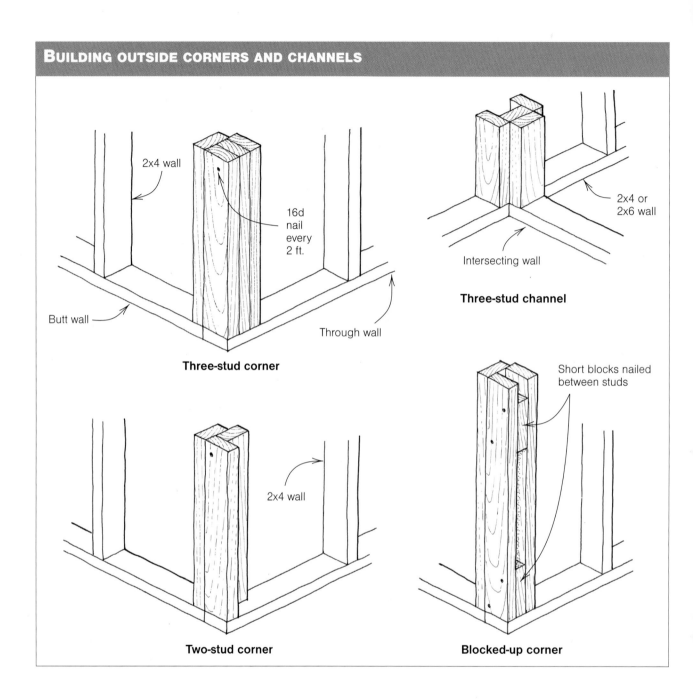

2x4 wall

16d nail every 2 ft.

Butt wall

Through wall

Three-stud corner

2x4 or 2x6 wall

Intersecting wall

Three-stud channel

2x4 wall

Two-stud corner

Short blocks nailed between studs

Blocked-up corner

stud is nailed in flush with the end of the plate. The second stud is nailed in flat alongside the first so that when the intersecting wall is raised, it can be nailed into the flat stud.

A blocked-up corner can be built by nailing three equally spaced blocks in place of the full-length center stud used in the three-stud corner. Whichever type you choose, the corner should provide adequate nailing not only for the intersecting wall but also for interior and exterior wall finishes and trim. I personally prefer the solid, three-stud corner or channel. I try to use two straight studs for the side pieces and a bowed or knotted stud for the center piece.

Use 16d nails to fasten the studs at the corner to the plate. Hold the nails apart, one high and one low, just as you nailed the rough sills to the bottom cripples, and take care that the sides of the stud are flush with the sides of the plate. After the wall has been raised, you'll nail the intersecting wall to these studs.

At channels, a stud is nailed in flat between two regular studs (see the top right drawing on the facing page). Tie channel studs together by driving three 16d nails into each side, one 2 ft. up from the bottom, one in the center, and one 2 ft. down from the top. This solidly built channel will provide adequate backing for an interior partition wall.

Once the outside corners and channels are nailed together and to the top plate, continue to nail the studs into the top plate, on the layout marks, with two 16d nails each. This is repetitive work, but you still need to pay attention. Watch the layout marks so that everything gets nailed in properly, and when you come to a door or window opening, be especially careful that you nail the king stud on the X beside the mark showing the header location. It's easy to nail the king stud on the wrong side of the layout mark, so be watchful.

When all the wall, king, and top cripple studs are nailed to the top plate, pull up the bottom plate and begin nailing it in place. Afterward, drive three 16d nails into both sides of the corner studs, 24 in. o.c., just like you did on the channel.

Nailing off the double top plate

While the wall is still flat on the floor, cut and fasten the double top plate. Structurally, the top plate is an important piece of wood because it ties the entire frame together. Without it, a building under earthquake or high wind stress can easily come apart at the joints in the single top plate. Although I still

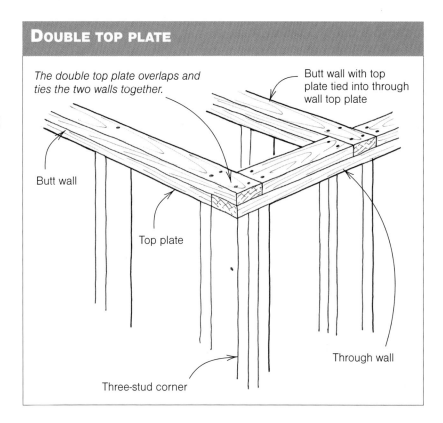

DOUBLE TOP PLATE

The double top plate overlaps and ties the two walls together.

Butt wall with top plate tied into through wall top plate

Butt wall

Top plate

Through wall

Three-stud corner

see carpenters raising the wall and then standing on ladders to nail on the double top plate, the job is much quicker and easier to do while the wall is still on the deck.

On butt walls, the double top plate laps over the top plate 3½ in. (for a 2x4 wall) so that it can tie into a through wall. On through walls, the double top plate cuts back from the end of the top plate 3½ in. to leave room for the double top plate on the butt wall to lap over and tie the two walls together (see the drawing above). There is a 3½-in. mark on the through walls left from when you located the corners with the corner-marking tool. Lay the double top plate on the wall with one end 3½ in. from the end of the top plate. Go to the other end and cut the plate at the other 3½-in. mark. At the channel marks, leave a 3½-in. cutout so that an interior butt wall can lap over and tie in at this point. Cut the double top plates a little short to leave a 3¾-in. gap (more or less) rather than 3½ in. This makes it easier for the double top plate of the butt wall to slip into the gap in the through wall. This is another one of those times when it's okay not to be totally accurate.

To start nailing on the double top plates, drive two 16d nails into the end of each plate and then one more over every stud. Avoid driving nails between studs, because electricians and plumbers run their wires and pipes through holes drilled in these locations. Hitting a nail while drilling will not only dull the bit, but it can also give your arm a nasty twist and injure your wrist. Again, skilled carpenters understand what it takes to help other tradespeople do their work well and are mindful of other workers.

Bracing walls

Before being raised, walls need to be squared and braced, either by installing structural sheathing like plywood or OSB or by using wall braces. Due to changes in the building codes, buildings are built stronger than they used to be to resist lateral forces produced by earthquakes and high winds.

As a new carpenter, I used to cut 2x braces into walls. Each piece of 2x was cut on a 45° miter to fit between the studs. Check it out on your next old-house remodel job. One brace would often take me an hour or two to finish, especially when cutting with a handsaw. Once carpenters began framing walls flat on the floor, we learned to lay a 1x6 brace diagonally across the face of the studs. Then we learned to cut slots in the studs with a circular saw to let in the brace and allow it to nail in flush.

Finally, about 25 years ago, an easy-to-install, L-shaped metal angle brace was introduced. Lay it across the framed wall diagonally from the bottom plate to the

double top plate and trace a pencil mark along one side. With a circular saw, cut a slot 1 in. deep along this line into the plates and studs. Slip one flange of the brace into the slot and nail it to the bottom plate with three 8d nails. Drive one more 8d nail through the brace and into the first stud. At the double top plate, start an 8d nail alongside the brace and bend it over to hold it in place as the wall is raised. You'll nail the brace permanently to the other studs and plates after the walls are plumbed.

Nowadays, the house frame is often held plumb by nailing on structural exterior sheathing, which eliminates the need for diagonal wall braces. Some builders like to square and sheathe walls while they are flat on the floor. I prefer sheathing walls after they are raised, especially if the house is one story. (A couple of sawhorses are all you need as scaffolding for a single-story house.) Sheathed walls are heavy and hard to raise by hand unless you use a wall jack, a device that hooks under a wall and slowly raises it upright (Qual-Craft Industries; see Sources on p. 198). Further, when building on a concrete slab, you often have pipes in exterior walls that make it impossible to sheathe some sections of a wall.

If you sheathe the walls before raising them, make sure the wall is flat on the floor and that the bottom plate is directly on the wall chalkline. Toenail this plate to the wood deck about every 48 in. or so with 16d nails to hold the plate in place as it is raised. Check the wall for square by measuring diagonally from corner to corner (see p. 87), remembering that the wall is square when the diagonals are equal.

The sheathing panels have to lap down at least 1 in. over a concrete slab. On a wooden floor, the panels have to lap down over the rim joist and 1 in. onto the foundation. So first determine how far the panels must extend below the bottom plate, and then hold your tape the proper distance below the bottom plate and measure up 8 ft. (the panel length) on the wall studs. After marking this height at both ends of the wall, snap a chalkline on the studs. Nail in a row of blocks between studs at this line to give backing for nailing panel ends (9-ft. and 10-ft. panels are available, which allow you to sheathe the entire wall without having a joint).

Raising the walls

Like barn raisings of old, it often takes a few warm bodies to raise a framed, unsheathed wall. For raising sheathed walls, it takes even more people or a wall jack. For your safety, don't try either job solo. And, as always, start with a clear deck.

With the first wall assembled, align the bottom plate with the chalkline on the floor if it hasn't already been toenailed in position. To keep the wall from slipping over the outside edge while it's being raised, nail pieces of 2x stock to the rim joist so that they stick up above the floor a few inches to catch and hold the bottom plate (see the photo at right). On a slab, bolts hold the bottom plate in place; otherwise, the bottom plate is toenailed to the deck.

To lift up an unsheathed wall, stick the claws of your hammer into the double top plate, lever the wall up a bit, and kick a 2x block beneath a member. Keeping your back straight, lift the wall to your waist using your legs, then over-head with your arms and upper body (see the photo on p. 120). Then, by pushing on the studs, continue to raise the wall until it is fully upright. Losing a newly raised wall is a common fear of beginning carpenters, but once the wall is upright, it is easy to hold in this posi-tion unless a Wyoming wind is blowing.

Nail lengths of 2x stock to the rim joist to keep an outside wall from slipping over the edge when it is raised. (Photo by Roe A. Osborn.)

With the wall in position, nail a tempo-rary 2x brace to each end, extending diagonally from about 6 ft. up on the corner stud down to the rim joist (I like to attach the brace to the wall before I raise it). Drive a 16d nail in each end of the brace. On long walls, nail other braces in the middle. Make sure that temporary wall braces are secure, espe-cially if you have to leave them over-

When raising a wall, keep your back straight and lift the wall to your waist using your legs. Then push the wall overhead with your arms and upper body until it is fully upright. (Photo by Roe A. Osborn.)

night. I've returned to a job site to find walls blown over because temporary braces weren't securely nailed.

If the wall needs to be moved end for end or aligned with the chalkline, tap the bottom plate into place with a sledgehammer. Once the wall is where it belongs, nail it to the floor, using one 16d nail between every stud and beside every king stud. Once again, drive those nails close to the studs to leave room for plumbers and electricians to drill through without hitting a nail. Don't nail in doorways because you'll be cutting out the plate when you set the door frame later.

After the first wall is done, nail together another outside through wall, raise it, and brace it. Then build and raise the butt walls (see the photo on the facing page). Remember to cut the double top plate for a 2x4 wall about 3½ in. longer at each end of the butt wall so it can lap over and tie into the through walls. Because of the top-plate overhang, the butt walls may have to be raised one end at a time. Pick up one end to clear the through wall and sort of roll the other end up into position. Remove the temporary brace on the through wall and pull the two walls together. Make sure that the plates of both walls are flat on the floor and not held up by debris,

After the first wall is done, nail together another outside through wall, raise it, and brace it. Then build and raise the butt walls. (Photo by Roe A. Osborn.)

then nail the end stud of the butt wall into each corner or channel with three evenly spaced 16d nails, just as you did on the three-stud corners. After you've nailed together and raised the remaining walls, stand back and enjoy the impressive sight of a framed-in building. Almost like magic, it's starting to look like a house.

Tying off double top plates

To tie the two double top plates together, nail the overlapping double top plate of the butt walls to the double top plates of the through walls with two 16d nails (see the photo on p. 122). Do this job accurately, and it will make it

easier to plumb and straighten the walls. When there are lots of wall plates to nail off, skilled carpenters usually hop right up on the walls to do the job. I have a gymnast daughter who once worked with me during summers. She was great at walking on plates. The plates were wider than her balance beam. But for inexperienced carpenters, it's easier—and safer—to work from a ladder (to learn about working on a ladder safely, see the sidebar on p. 123).

The corner marks you drew on the plates earlier act as guides when nailing off the top plates. Make sure that the double top plate is on these lines and

Drive two 16d nails through the overlapping double top plate of the butt wall into the top plate of the through wall. (Photo by Roe A. Osborn.)

that the top plates of both walls are touching, just as they were on the floor. If necessary, toenail a 16d nail into the top plate of the through wall up into the double top plate of the butt wall to draw everything together (see the photo on the facing page).

Plumbing and lining walls

A woman once called me after moving into a fairly new house, wondering why her pictures wouldn't hang flat against the wall. She thought she was doing

something wrong. The real problem was that her wall was leaning in 1½ in. from top to bottom! This kind of error is not acceptable. Take care not to make the same mistake. Once the walls are up and tied together, you need to plumb and line them.

Plumbing means making sure the walls are standing straight up and down. Lining means straightening the top plates from one end of a wall to the other. Neither job is difficult, but it's

WORKING SAFELY ON A LADDER

Over the years I've learned the hard way to be extremely wary of ladders. While they are often indispensable, they need to be treated with the same respect accorded a power saw. A fall from a ladder can seriously injure or kill you, and every carpenter (and many homeowners) can tell of injuries related to a ladder mishap. Here are a few safety tips to make working on a ladder safer.

• Buy a quality ladder. Check the ladder's label for a rating of 1A, which means that the ladder is a heavy-duty one.

• If working near or with electrical wiring, it's a good idea to own a nonconductive ladder. Fiberglass is a good choice, although these are typically heavy and expensive. (Aluminum and wet wood ladders can conduct electricity.)

• Don't stand on the uppermost steps of a ladder; get a longer ladder instead.

• Don't reach too far to the side of a ladder. You can lose your balance.

• Don't leave tools sitting on top of an unattended ladder.

• When using a stepladder, unfold it all the way, lock its braces, and set it on a solid surface.

• When using an extension ladder, make sure its feet are firmly and securely planted on a solid surface.

Drive a 16d toenail through the top plate into the double top plate to close any gap between plates. (Photo by Roe A. Osborn.)

Place the push stick under the top plate against a stud, parallel with the wall. Bend it down as shown, and then pull it up in the middle. As the board straightens, it will push the wall laterally. When the bubble is centered in the vial on the plumbstick, the wall is plumb. (Photo by Roe A. Osborn.)

important to do them correctly. This is one of those times when utmost accuracy is important. Straight, plumb walls leave behind a lasting story of your skills. No professional carpenter wants to leave a job with crooked walls that lean to one side. If you make sure walls are plumb and lined, all the following work by every trade will go easier, and the finished house will look better.

Plumbing is done first. You'll need a plumbstick with a level (see p. 35) and a push stick. If you don't use a plumbstick,

make doubly sure you use an accurate level. A push stick is used to push walls end for end during plumbing. To make a push stick for an 8-ft. wall, cut a 1x4 or a 1x6 about 116 in. long. Try to use stock without a lot of knots; otherwise, it may break.

You'll need a partner to plumb the walls. Start with the exterior walls. One person holds the plumbstick in a corner. Adjust this wall by pushing it in or out until the bubble is centered in the level's vial. A short wall can often be moved by giving

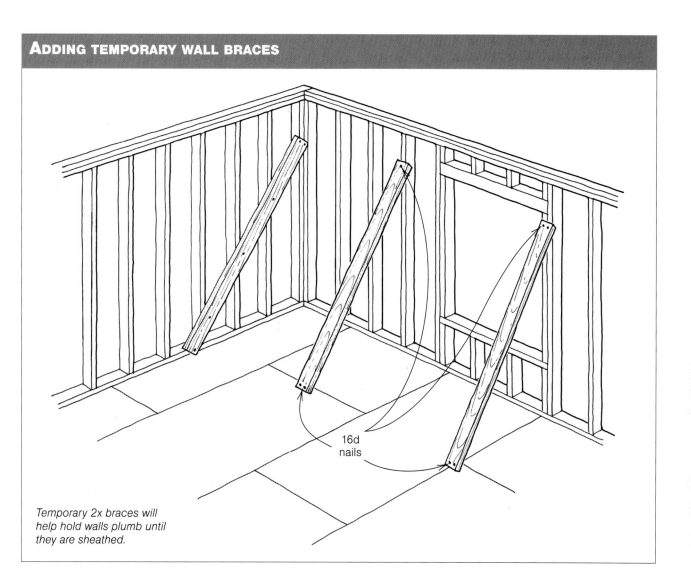

16d
nails

*Temporary 2x braces will
help hold walls plumb until
they are sheathed.*

it a shove with your body, but if you need more force, place the push stick under the top plate against a stud and running diagonally down to the floor (see the photo on the facing page). Keep the stick as close to parallel with the wall as possible. Bend the stick down, holding the bottom end against the floor with one foot. Now pull the middle of the stick up. As the board straightens, the wall will move. When the bubble in the level centers, the wall is plumb.

Once the wall is plumb, finish nailing in the metal framing braces. If you aren't using metal wall braces, nail in temporary 2x studs to hold the wall plumb (see the drawing above). Place one end of the stud about 6 ft. up in a corner and nail it with two 16d nails. Once the wall is plumb, have a partner nail the stud at the bottom with two more 16d nails.

After plumbing all the walls and nailing in all the braces, it's time to line, or straighten, the walls. Lining a wall is pretty simple. The bottom plate is

To line a wall, sight down the length of the walls and trust that your eyes can see when the top plate is straight. (Photo by Roe A. Osborn.)

straight because it has been nailed to a chalkline, and the top plates should be close to straight if you used straight stock when plating.

The easiest way to line a wall is to hop on a ladder in the corner and sight down the length of the walls (see the photo above). Trust your eye that you can see when the top plate is straight. Another method often used on long

walls is to check the walls with a dryline (see the drawing on the facing page). Nail a scrap piece of 2x to the top plates at each corner and drive an 8d nail partway into the outer ends of each block. Hook a dryline to one of the nails, pull it taut, and tie it around the nail in the other corner. Then take another scrap piece of 2x and slide it along the wall, checking for a consistent 1½-in. space between the line and the wall.

CHECKING WALLS FOR STRAIGHTNESS WITH DRYLINE

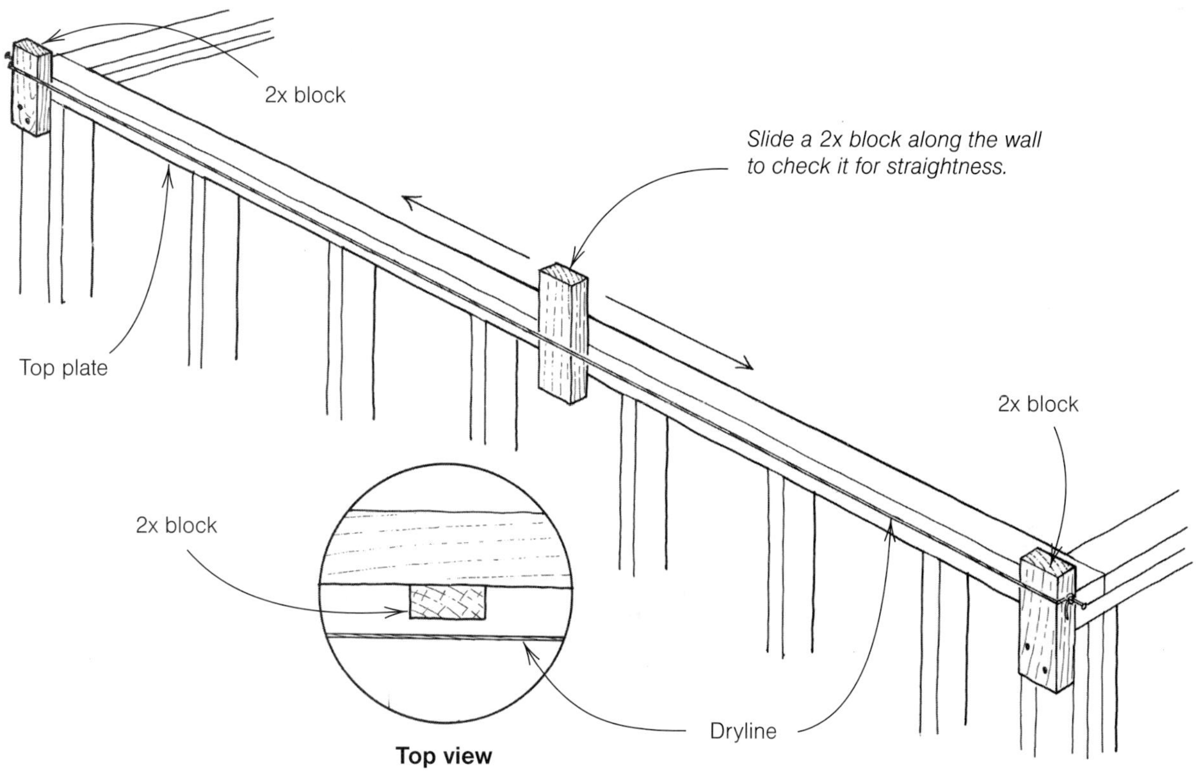

2x block

Slide a 2x block along the wall
to check it for straightness.

2x block

Top plate

2x block

Dryline

Top view

Any wall that isn't straight needs to be moved in or out. For either job, you'll need a partner. If a wall needs to be moved out, nail a 2x stud (with two 16d nails) flat against the edge of a wall stud about three-fourths of the way up on the wall (see the photo on the facing page). Hook the claws of your hammer under the stud and pry until your partner says the wall is straight. Then nail the bottom end of the stud to the floor with two 16d nails to brace the wall (see the drawing on p. 125).

If the wall needs to be moved in, nail a 2x stud on edge to the bottom of a wall stud. Let it extend to the outside, sitting on hard ground or on a short (1-ft.) 2x block resting on the ground. Nail a 2x stud in place about three-fourths of the

way up on the wall with the bottom end positioned on the horizontal 2x (see the drawing on p. 128). Now you can move the wall in the same way that was used to move the other wall out.

Don't hesitate to use plenty of temporary braces as you plumb and straighten walls. Extra braces at this point will guarantee that the building will be held plumb and straight until the rest of the framing is completed. I have worked on buildings where a temporary brace was knocked loose and the wall moved out of plumb because there were no other braces. This can cause a lot of anguish and extra work if it isn't discovered right away. It's not easy to straighten a wall once joists and rafters are nailed into it.

MOVING A WALL IN

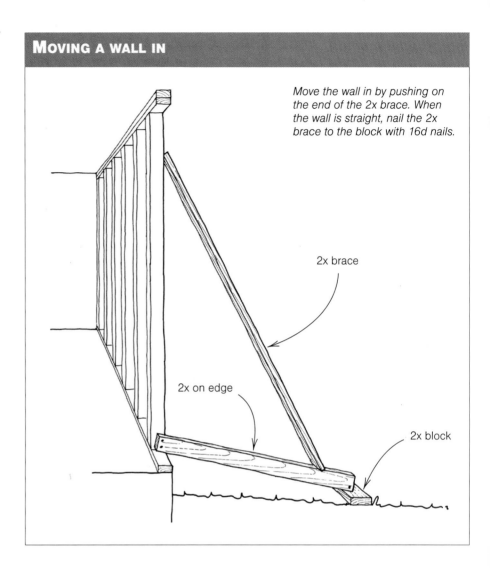

Move the wall in by pushing on the end of the 2x brace. When the wall is straight, nail the 2x brace to the block with 16d nails.

2x brace

2x on edge

2x block

SHEATHING THE WALL

Anyone who has witnessed the damage caused by an earthquake or high wind knows the importance of properly installed interior and exterior wall sheathing (shear walls). In the serious 1992 Northridge quake near Los Angeles, shear walls saved many buildings—and many lives.

Wall sheathing provides strong lateral (horizontal) and vertical strength. It helps hold buildings together. It also helps make a house windproof, which is especially important if you live where cold winds are a reality. The most common sheathing materials are exterior-grade plywood and OSB.

Most building codes allow wall sheathing to be installed vertically (see the photo on the facing page), with the long edges nailed to the wall studs. It's okay to install panels horizontally, but be sure to nail in 2x blocking between the studs at the panel joints. The shear strength of a wall panel is weakened unless it is nailed to the wall on all four sides.

Normally, shear panels aren't the final, or finish, wall covering, so they don't have to be installed perfectly. Once these rough panels are nailed in place and inspected by the building department, they'll be covered with stucco, finish plywood panels, shingles, clapboards, or even metal or vinyl siding. Before sheathing any wall, exterior or interior, check the plans to see what is required. Often, shear panels need to be longer than the standard 8 ft. so they can extend from the pressure-treated foundation sill, across the rim joist and wall studs, and nail into the plates at the top of the wall. This type of construction ties the entire frame together and gives the house added structural stability.

When sheathing the outside of a building, begin at a corner. If the stud layout is correct, the edge of the first panel should fall on a stud 4 ft. from the corner. Check to see that the corner is plumb. If the first panel is set straight and plumb, all those that follow will be easier to install.

Rough sheathing doesn't have to be absolutely flush with the corner of the framing, and in fact may be set as much as ¾ in. away from the corner, since it will be covered by housewrap, finish siding, and trim. But the sheathing does need to break on the center of a stud 4 ft. from the corner. If it doesn't break on the center of a stud, you can rip the sheet to fit, move the wall stud, or put in an extra stud so there is proper backing for edge nailing the plywood.

Remember the formula 4-6-12 when fastening sheathing, which is the typical nailing schedule using 8d nails (see the drawing on p. 131). Around door and window openings, nail only into the king studs and leave the trimmers free until it's time to set the frames. It's always a

In most areas, codes allow wall sheathing to be installed vertically, with the long edges nailed to the wall studs. (Photo by Joe Haun.)

good idea to check with your local building department if you have questions about the nailing schedule.

If you are using a pneumatic nailer, set the air pressure so that nails are driven flush with the surface of the panel. Nails driven too deep break the skin of the sheathing and weaken the shear strength of the panel. Many codes also require that you use full-headed nails rather than the clipped heads that are driven by many pneumatic nailers.

In humid climates, leave a ⅛-in. gap between panels to allow for expansion. When you come to windows and doors, you can sheathe right over them and cut

Before sheathing around windows and doors, the trimmers need to be set. Plumb a trimmer on either side of the window with a 2-ft. or 4-ft. level. The top or bottom of the trimmer may need to pull away from the king stud a bit for it to be plumb. Once the level bubble reads plumb, nail the trimmer in place with one 8d toenail on each side, top and bottom.

If the window is 4/0 wide, for example, measure over 4 ft. from the plumb trimmer and make a mark on both the header and rough sill. Pull the trimmer away from this king stud, set it on the 4-ft. marks, and toenail it to the header and to the rough sill with one 8d nail on each side—top and bottom. Measure from corner to corner and side to side to make sure the opening is square and parallel (see p. 87). Do the same for the other window openings.

Setting trimmers for a door takes a bit more time. I use a 6-ft. level or a short level attached to a straightedge. Place the level against the wide side of a trimmer. A bubble centered in the tube of the level shows if the trimmer is plumb. If it is plumb, you can toenail it to the header and to the bottom plate—one 8d toenail on each side, top and bottom.

If it is not plumb, pull one end out until it is plumb and then nail it in place.

The next step is to straighten the trimmer. Hold the level on the 3½-in. face of the trimmer and use the hammer's claws to lever the trimmer away from the king stud until the trimmer rests flush with the edge of the level (see the left photo below). The 16d nail you drove in the center of the trimmer while framing temporarily holds it straight.

Once you have the trimmer straight, hold it straight by clipping it to the king stud with two 8d nails. Begin by driving an 8d nail partway into either the trimmer or king stud. Bend this nail back onto the other upright. Then drive and bend a second nail over the head of the first (see the right photo below). Install three clips per side. This method eliminates all shims and holds the trimmer true for the life of the building.

To set the second trimmer, measure over from the first. For a prehung door, the measurement is 1¾ in. more than actual size. The extra width is for a ¾-in. jamb on each side, and the added ¼ in. gives you room for adjustment when setting the door frame in place. So for a 32-in.-wide prehung door, measure over 33¾ in. on both the header and bottom plate and toenail the second trimmer in place. Then straighten and clip it like the first.

Hold the level on the 3½-in. face of the trimmer and use the hammer's claws to lever the trimmer away from the king stud until the trimmer rests flush against the level. (Photos by Roe A. Osborn.)

A simple clip made with two 8ds will hold the trimmer to the king stud.

NAILING SCHEDULE FOR WALL SHEATHING

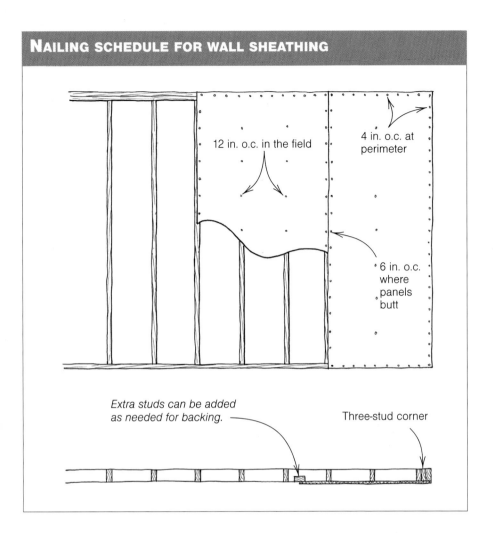

12 in. o.c. in the field

4 in. o.c. at perimeter

6 in. o.c. where panels butt

Extra studs can be added as needed for backing.

Three-stud corner

the openings out later with a reciprocating saw. However, before sheathing around these openings, you'll need to nail in the trimmers (see the sidebar on the facing page). Use scraps of sheathing to fill in any gaps around the windows and doors.

CEILING JOISTS FOR A GABLE ROOF

The saying, "They don't build them like they used to," is often true when it comes to ceiling joists. And it's just as well. I have remodeled many an old house that had ceiling joists that were sagging from the weight of time and heavy plaster. If you live in an old house,

look at your ceilings—especially in large rooms—and check to see if they sag in the center.

Once the walls have been plumbed and lined, ceiling joists can be nailed to the tops of the walls in preparation for installing roof rafters (see the drawing on p. 132). In factory-built roof trusses, joists are part of the truss (see Chapter 6 for more information on roof trusses). Joists nail to the top plates of the walls and help tie the house frame together. Roof rafters nail into both the plates and the joists, forming a truss that helps keep the roof from sagging under heavy loads like wet snow.

CEILING JOISTS FOR A GABLE ROOF

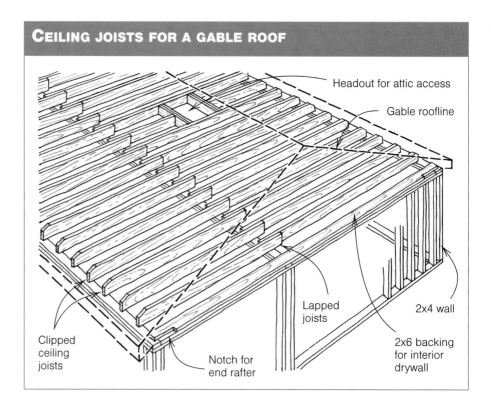

Headout for attic access

Gable roofline

Clipped ceiling joists

Notch for end rafter

Lapped joists

2x4 wall

2x6 backing for interior drywall

Laying out joists

Lay out the walls for joists just like you laid out the rim joists for the floor (for more on this, see Chapter 4). Hook a long tape on the end of an outside wall and mark 16 in. o.c. (or 24 in. o.c.) the length of the building. Just like the floor joists, make an X beside the mark to show where the joist will nail.

Joists tie into the roof rafters and sometimes need to be trimmed a bit to follow the slope of the roof. If you are using 2x8 joists and 2x6 rafters, for example, the joist ends need to be clipped, as shown in the drawing above. Otherwise, they'll stick up above the slope of the roof. Remember to mark and cut your ceiling joists with their crown up.

Use a 2x6 for the first ceiling joist, laying it flat on the end wall. If the end wall is built of 2x4s, cut notches 1½ in. wide and 20 in. long in the ends of the 2x6

and nail it flush to the outside. As shown in the drawing above, the notches leave room for the first set of rafters to be nailed to the plates. If the end wall is of 2x6 construction, nail a 2x4 flat onto the plate, 3½ in. in from the outside. This leaves room for 2x4 gable studs to be nailed under the rafter. The part of the flat 2x that hangs over the inside edge of the plate provides backing for ceiling drywall.

Installing joists

With the crown side up, start nailing the joists on edge at each layout mark with a 16d toenail in each side. Where joists lap over an interior bearing wall, nail them together with two 16d nails and toenail them to the wall with one 16d nail on each side. A joist that passes over any other wall is secured to the plate with a 16d nail on each side. This helps hold the building plumb and strengthens the entire structure.

Catwalks are seldom required by code. They are usually a 1x4 or 1x6 nailed flat to the ceiling joists in the middle of the span (see the photo on p. 140). They help keep joists upright, free from twists, and properly spaced and also make it safer to walk when stacking roof rafters. Mark a layout at either 16 in. o.c. or 24 in. o.c. on the catwalk before securing it with two 8d nails per joist.

When joisting for a second floor or any ceiling that will be covered with drywall, backing has to be nailed on all walls that run parallel to the joists. Usually this can be accomplished by nailing a 2x6 flat on the top plate of a 2x4 wall and letting 1 in. hang over on both sides. Or you can nail a 2x4 on top of the plate (see the drawing at right). This is a good place to use up shorter pieces of 2x stock, crooked studs, badly crowned joists, and lumber with large knots. Nail the backing down every 16 in. with 16d nails directly over the wall studs.

Framing headouts in ceilings

A joist or two will have to be cut to allow access to the attic. Most codes require this access to be at least 30 in. by 30 in. I like to put these access holes in an out-of-the way place, like in the ceiling of a closet.

Once the ceiling is joisted, lay out the location of the access hole right on the joists, allowing an extra 3 in. to leave room for the 2x header joists (see the drawing at right). Support the joists that will be cut by nailing a flat 2x across several joists, then make the cuts in the ceiling joists and nail in the headers. Cut 14½-in. blocks to nail to the header between the joists to help support the cut joist.

Once the walls and ceiling joists are in, you're ready to turn your attention to the roof.

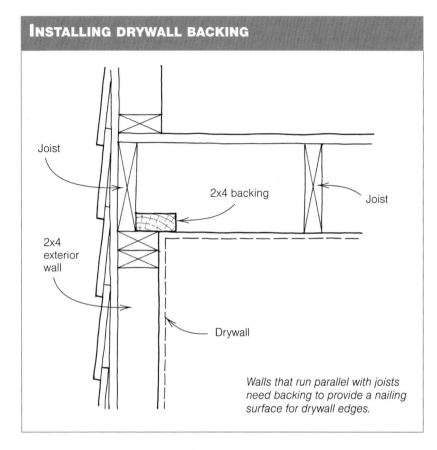

INSTALLING DRYWALL BACKING

Joist

2x4 backing

Joist

2x4 exterior wall

Drywall

Walls that run parallel with joists need backing to provide a nailing surface for drywall edges.

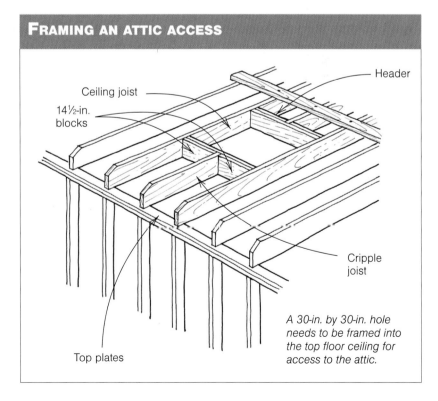

FRAMING AN ATTIC ACCESS

Header

Ceiling joist

14½-in. blocks

Cripple joist

Top plates

A 30-in. by 30-in. hole needs to be framed into the top floor ceiling for access to the attic.

6

ROOFS

I was in an office-supply house recently when a customer brought in a type-writer for repair. Folks were joking with him, wondering what he was doing with a typewriter in this time of computers. These days, in the world of roof trusses, cutting and building simple gable roofs on site has almost gone the way of the typewriter. Nevertheless, I still love the challenge of cutting and building (we call it stacking here on the West Coast) conventional stick-built roofs, whether the roof is a simple gable or a complex one with many different ridges, hips, and valleys coming together from every direction.

Now, of course, even the most compli-cated roof can usually be made by a truss company and shipped to the site ready to install. Trusses are labor-saving devices, and when you raise a truss in place, you are installing a ceiling joist and a roof rafter at the same time. Another nice part about working with trusses is that they are made from light-weight, kiln-dried lumber, so they're lighter, easier to handle, and friendlier to the back. But be careful of the metal plates or gussets that hold trusses together. These are very sharp.

The main challenge in building most truss roofs is working high off the ground. An experienced carpenter can

work off the ground like a space walker, often standing on a wall plate that is only 3½ in. wide. Most of us can also learn how to do this, but as a beginner, go slow, take your time, and be careful. With practice, it becomes easier. If being up high on a wall is scary, work off a ladder or a scaffold and follow the safety guidelines on p. 123.

Where I live on the Oregon coast, simple gable roofs are found on about 70% of the houses, including mine. Other roofs aren't quite so simple, but like learning to walk, learning to build a simple gable roof is the first step toward building those more complicated ones. What fol-lows are guidelines for building a simple gable roof, both with trusses and with conventional framing.

TRUSS ROOFS

Truss roofs are engineered structures built in a factory. They combine the roof rafters (top chord) and ceiling joists (bot-tom chord) into one unit. Wooden braces, called web members, run between the chords, adding strength to the truss. Because of this, trusses can span long distances, bearing only on the outside walls. So rooms can be larger and door headers smaller than in a stick-built roof because they are not supporting ceiling joists or rafters. Trusses can be built in many shapes and

Conventional stick-built roofs can be framed as a simple gable or a complex roof with many different ridges, hips, and valleys. (Photo by Elmer Griggs.)

designs to fit most any house (see the drawing on p. 136). In general, they require less lumber and labor to build than conventional stick-built roofs and can be installed quickly on the job site. This is especially important in areas where you want to seal off a house quickly from rain or snow.

Trusses also work well on remodel jobs. With proper planning, I have torn off an old, sagging roof and replaced it with new trusses in one day. Besides impressing the homeowners, I didn't have to worry about rain coming down and soaking their dining-room table.

Trusses are carefully engineered, so cutting them in any way may fatally weaken their structural integrity. With the exception of gable-end trusses, which have gable studs and are nailed in place directly over an end wall, trusses should not be cut without consulting the manufacturer or an engineer. Because of the web bracing in trusses, attics in most truss-roofed houses have limited storage space. Maybe this is one of the reasons public storage places have sprouted like weeds across our country.

Ordering and storing trusses

Give yourself some lead time when ordering trusses. A busy company may not be able to get to your order for a week or so. I like to deliver (or fax) the truss plans directly to the company rather than order trusses over the phone. This helps avoid costly mistakes.

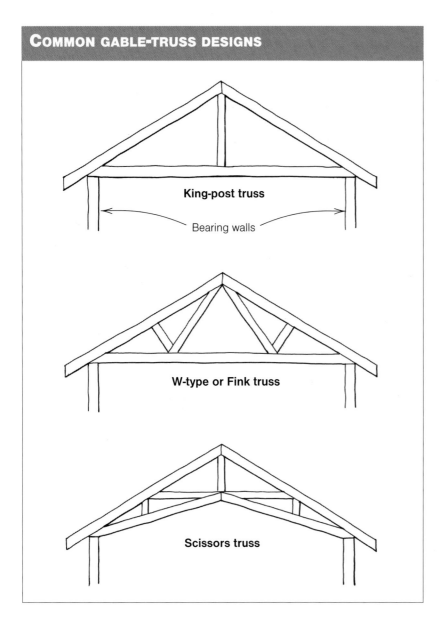

COMMON GABLE-TRUSS DESIGNS

King-post truss

Bearing walls

W-type or Fink truss

Scissors truss

Trusses usually arrive on the job site banded in bundles of a dozen or more (see the top photo on the facing page). These can often be unloaded and set right up on the wall plates with a small crane or forklift. If the walls are not yet framed and braced, be sure to stack the bundles on level ground. Trusses can withstand heavy vertical loads, but they break easily when bent too far horizontally. I recall working on a tract of houses where one set of trusses was left lying

across a gully for a couple of weeks with the ridge section bending down. By the time they were ready to be installed, half of the gussets were pulled loose from the truss members. They were beyond repair and had to be reordered, holding up the framing on one house.

Installing trusses

Most trusses are installed 24 in. on center (o.c.), so you'll need plenty of 22½-in. spacer blocks to nail between the rafters at the plate line and ridge. No truss layout is required on top of the walls because frieze blocks keep the trusses properly spaced. If these blocks aren't supplied by the truss company, they need to be cut about ⅛ in. shorter than the standard 22½-in. block to allow for the thickness of the metal gussets that join the wood members together. Have some long 1xs handy also, laid out 24 in. o.c. These nail near the ridge to hold the trusses steady and to keep them on layout. If the trusses are long, tall, or both, you will need some long 2xs to brace them as you proceed. A strong gust of wind can topple unbraced trusses.

It is not easy to move a single truss from the ground up onto an 8-ft.-high wall, let alone a higher wall. To do so usually takes three people to keep the truss from bending and causing stress to the connectors, so it's best to have the bundles set up on the walls when they are delivered. Lay the trusses flat on the walls with the ridge points sticking out over the end wall or stand them upright in the same location. Be careful when cutting the metal band that holds the bundles together. Under tension, a band can move quickly once it is cut and is sharp enough to slice a hand.

Individual trusses can now be laid flat across the walls in preparation for being nailed upright (see the bottom photo on the facing page). Experienced carpenters pull the first truss (a gable-end truss) off

In most cases, roof trusses arrive in bundles of a dozen or more, which can often be unloaded and set right up on the wall plates with a small crane or forklift. However, if the trusses are stored, be sure to stack them on level ground. (Photo by Elmer Griggs.)

In preparation for being nailed upright, individual trusses can be laid flat across the wall. The first truss has the ridge pointed outward, and subsequent trusses lay on top of the first about every 2 ft. like fallen dominoes. (Photo by Roe A. Osborn.)

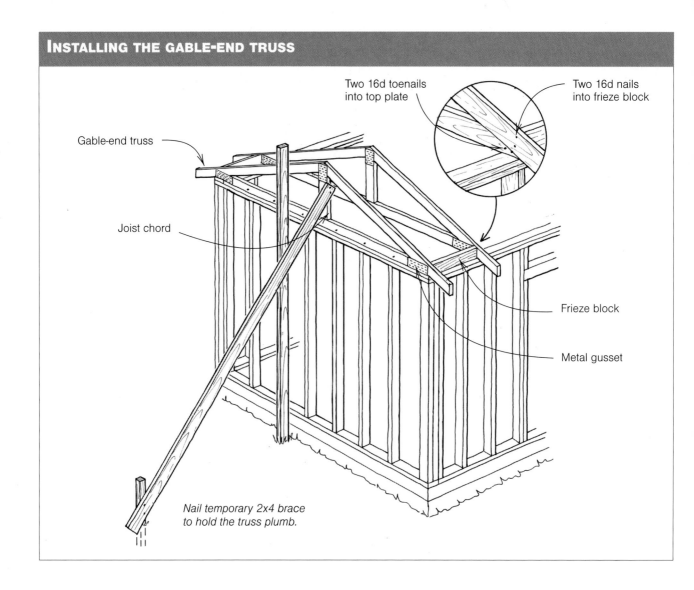

Two 16d toenails into top plate

Two 16d nails into frieze block

Gable-end truss

Joist chord

Frieze block

Metal gusset

Nail temporary 2x4 brace to hold the truss plumb.

the pile, and with the ridge point behind them, walk along the plates to the other end of the house frame. There, they flip the truss over with the ridge pointed out lying flat across the walls. Subsequent trusses lie on top of the first about every 2 ft. like fallen dominoes.

Before raising the first truss upright, nail a 2x on edge against the outside wall frame near the center of the building. The gable-end truss will be nailed to this 2x, which will help hold the truss plumb (see the drawing above). At this point, you can raise a gable-end truss upright

and move it out flush with the outside of the end wall. Make sure you have the proper roof overhang on each side of the building and toenail the truss down through the joist chord into the double top plate with 16d nails spaced 16 in. o.c. Drive a temporary nail through the rafter chord into the upright 2x brace to hold the truss plumb. Brace this truss with a long 2x reaching to the floor or to a good stake driven in the ground.

Now come the frieze blocks, which are the blocks between rafters. When a house is to be covered with stucco,

Toenail the joist chord to the top plate with two 16d nails, then drive two more through the rafter chord into the frieze block. (Photo by Roe A. Osborn.)

blocks are often nailed vertically, directly on the top plate, flush with the outside. When the wall is covered with siding, blocks can be nailed just outside the wall and square with the truss, with the back side of the block touching the wall. Frieze blocks serve as stops for the siding, eliminating the need to cut the siding around the rafters. If the rafter tails are to have a soffit (enclosed eaves and overhangs), nail the blocks directly over the walls. Remember, about every third block often contains a vent.

Nail the first frieze blocks into the gable truss at both outside walls with two 16d nails through the truss and into the block. Bring the next truss into position and set it with the rafter tails hanging over the same amount as the first.

It's important that every truss overhangs the same amount so the rafter tails and ridge will be straight. Some carpenters go to great lengths—pulling lines, checking each rafter with a spacer—to ensure absolute straightness. I think it's easier to set each truss close to right. When the entire roof structure is in place, snap a chalkline across the rafter tails and cut them to exact length. Now the fascia, which covers the ends of rafters and can be seen by the entire world, will be straight.

Toenail each truss to the top plate through the joist chord with two 16d nails on one side and one 16d nail on the other side. Then nail it to the frieze block (see the photo above). Once you set the second truss, measure to see if the block length is correct to give you

Sway braces at the gable ends and a catwalk on the joist chords help brace the roof. The 1x6 along the top of the rafters helps maintain the truss spacing until the sheathing is installed. (Photo by Roe A. Osborn.)

24-in.-o.c. spacing. Keep checking this as you set subsequent trusses. When you reach the other end of the building, make sure the second gable-end truss is nailed flush with the outside wall just like the first.

Bracing trusses

Trusses usually come with detailed information on how to brace the specific type of truss you are installing. These instructions need to be followed carefully to guarantee that the house will have a strong and stable roof in case of high wind, heavy snow, or earthquake. Don't try to guess your way through truss bracing.

Having said that, most simple gable-truss roofs are quite easy to brace. Begin by temporarily nailing a long 1x across the rafter chords of each truss, near the ridge point. (I often nail this 1x on the underside of the rafter chord so I won't have to remove it when sheathing the roof.) This 1x helps hold the trusses stable until you nail in the ridge blocks and other braces. Do the same with another 1x nailed permanently on top and near the center of the joist chords with two 8d nails into each joist. This 1x is the catwalk, like the one nailed to regular joists, and helps hold the joist chords at 24 in. o.c. and keep the roof structure steady.

Once the catwalk is in place, it's easy to walk along it and nail in the blocks at the ridge point unless the ridge is a tall one. On tall ridges, experienced carpenters walk the rafters to nail in the blocks, which is fairly easy to do with the 1x nailed alongside the ridge. Hold a block in place between the rafters at the peak. Drive two 16d nails through the rafter into the block on one side and another 16d nail in from the other side.

To help hold a gable-roof structure plumb, you also need to install a sway brace at each end of the roof. A sway brace is a 2x4 nailed in at a 45° angle from the double exterior wall plate to a ridge block nailed in at the peak of the roof. Miter-cut the sway brace at one end, set it flat on the wall running diagonally up to the top of the ridge, and mark it to length. Make the cut and nail the brace in place with three 16d nails at each end (see the photo on the facing page).

To further brace the roof and to tie it to the house frame, use hurricane clips where the joist chords meet the plates. These metal clips are not always required by code, but if you ever happen to get a serious wind, they help keep the roof attached to the house. Nail a clip on each truss with hanger nails.

STICK-BUILT ROOFS

Despite the increasingly widespread use of trusses, gable roofs are still being built stick by stick. Newcomers to the trade often think there is something magical and mysterious to cutting and building a roof and that the task is beyond their abilities. But if you can draw a right triangle, use a handheld calculator or read a book of rafter tables, use a small rafter square, and handle a circular saw, you can build a gable roof. Of course, other types of roofs are more complex and difficult to build than gable roofs, but understand-

ing how a gable roof goes together is the first step in building these more complex roofs.

You don't have to be a math genius to be a roof cutter, but the more you know about roof parts and how they go together, the easier it will be. A gable roof slopes in two directions, like two right triangles butted together (see the drawing on p. 142). It has a ridge board at the peak. Common rafters are nailed to the ridge board and slope down to the top plates of opposing outside walls. Here the rafters nail into the wall plates and ceiling joists, effectively forming a truss.

Many homeowners today seem to want more openness to their houses, with larger rooms and higher ceilings. As a remodeler, I have been asked to remove ceiling joists and change a flat ceiling to one that follows the roof pitch. This does give an open feeling, but at a cost. If you remove all the joists, the roof truss is compromised, and weight on the roof can bow exterior walls out and cause the roof to sag. In the absence of a structural ridge beam or collar ties (horizontal members that tie rafters together above the wall plate), a roof generally needs those ceiling joists.

Determining rafter length

To determine the length of the common rafters, you first need to know the pitch of the roof and the span and run of the rafters. Pitch is the amount of slope a roof has. To say a roof has a 4-in-12 pitch, for example, means that for every 12 in. a rafter runs horizontally, it rises vertically 4 in. (see the drawing on p. 143). A 12-in-12 pitch roof is fairly steep, rising at 45°, while roofs pitched at less than 3-in-12 are generally too shallow for asphalt shingles.

Span is the total distance a rafter travels horizontally (the width of the building from outside to outside). Run is one-half

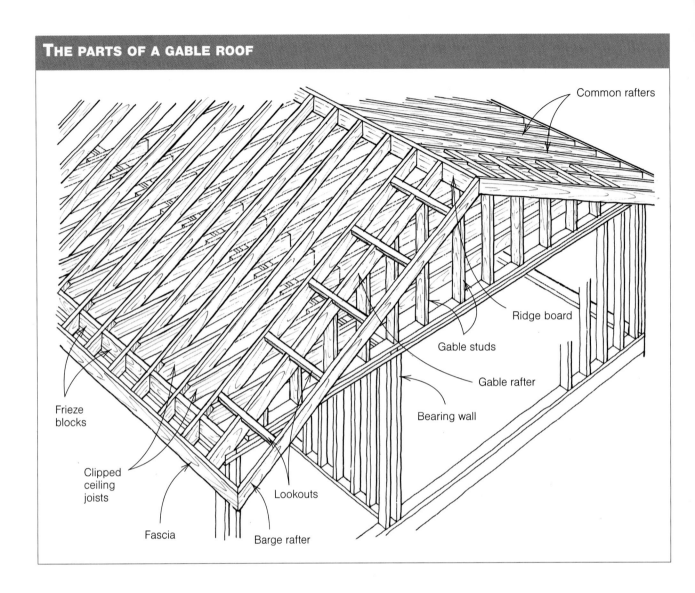

Common rafters

Ridge board

Gable studs

Gable rafter

Bearing wall

Frieze
blocks

Clipped
ceiling
joists

Lookouts

Fascia

Barge rafter

the span. When you know the pitch of a roof plus the true span (measure the span from outside wall to outside wall with a long tape) or the run, you can determine the length of the common rafters. To do this, try using a book of rafter tables (see Sources on p. 198) or a pocket calculator.

A 24-ft.-wide building has a span of 24 ft. To find the rafter length of a 4-in-12 pitch roof for this building, open your rafter-table book to the 4-in-12 page and look under the common-rafter table at 24 ft. to see that the rafter length is 12 ft. 7¾ in. If the span is 24 ft. 8 in., look under 8 in the inches column and add on an extra 4¼ in. That is the total length of the common rafter. It's really that simple, so don't make it difficult for yourself. After a few minutes with a rafter book, you can figure the length of almost any rafter for any pitch and any span. Subtract from this figure half the thickness of the ridge board (¾ in. for a 2x ridge) and leave enough extra wood to cover the length of the tails in the overhang.

GABLE-ROOF THEORY

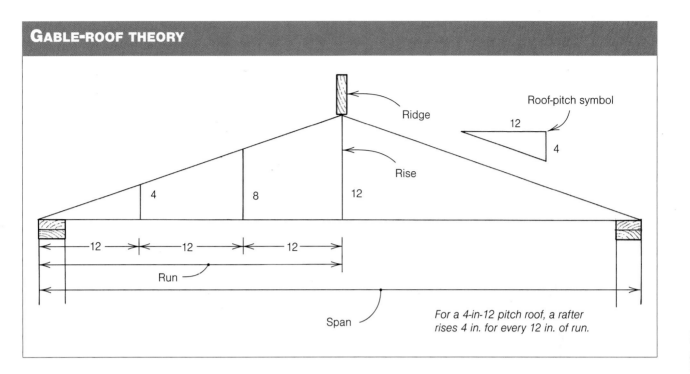

Roof-pitch symbol

Ridge

Rise

Run

Span

For a 4-in-12 pitch roof, a rafter rises 4 in. for every 12 in. of run.

It's also easy to determine rafter length with a calculator that has a square-root function. Knowing that $a^2 + b^2 = c^2$ is the key (this is the Pythagorean theorem, the formula for finding the lengths of the sides of a right triangle). If the roof pitch is 4 (a) in 12 (b), then a^2 (16) + b^2 (144) = 160; the square root of 160 is 12.65. The length of the rafter (hypotenuse) for a 4-in-12 pitch roof with 1 ft. of run is 12.65 in. (see the drawing on p. 144). If the rafter runs 7 ft., for example, multiply 12.65 by 7 to get 88.55 in., or 7.379 ft. Converting the decimal to fractions gives you a rafter length of 7 ft. 4½ in.

Laying out and cutting rafters

To determine the number, length (including enough for the rafter tail), and size of the rafters, you'll need to check the plans. If the rafters are spaced 16 in. o.c., divide the length of the building by four, multiply this figure by three, and add one more. Double the result to cover both sides of the roof.

If the rafters are spaced 24 in. o.c., the process is even easier. Just take the length of the building and add two.

These days, rafters tend to be made from 2x8s or larger so that they can be filled with adequate insulation to meet energy codes and to support heavy roof tiles or snow loads. Many of the roofs I cut and stacked years ago were made from 2x4s and 2x6s. Recently, I got a call from a family who lived in such a house. One night they heard a horrible sound above, like something breaking, and asked if I would please have a look-see. I crawled up in the attic, and they were right: Two rafters were split, and others were sagging. They had changed the roof covering from composition shingles to concrete tiles without adding extra supports to the rafters. Wet snow loads can cause the same damage.

Many buildings also have barge rafters (two on each end), that form the overhang on the gable ends. These rafters

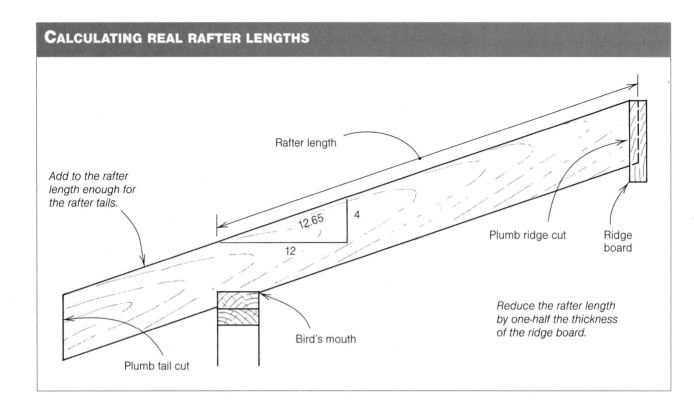

Add to the rafter length enough for the rafter tails.

Rafter length

12.65
4
12

Plumb ridge cut

Ridge board

Reduce the rafter length by one-half the thickness of the ridge board.

Bird's mouth

Plumb tail cut

are trim pieces that hang away from the building and are clearly visible to anyone who looks up. As you go through the rafter stock, lay aside four clean, straight pieces so that your trim will look good. But check the plans. Barge rafters may be smaller than the regular rafters or made from cedar, redwood, spruce, or pine.

One of the fascinating aspects of building a roof is that all the rafters can be laid out and cut on the ground. Then, as perfect as a picture puzzle, the parts fit together on the house frame to form the roof. It seems rather magical, but it's not difficult to do. Start at the beginning, by laying out a pair of common rafters on your sawhorses. First, though, make a rafter template out of scrap 1x or plywood that is the same width as your rafter stock (see the sidebar on the facing page), so that you won't continually have to use your small rafter square to lay out the rafters. I use this template

to scribe the ridge cut (a plumb cut on the rafter stock that fits against the ridge board) and the bird's mouth (the notch in the rafter that rests on the top wall plate).

To use the template, place it on rafter stock near one end and mark the plumb cut. Make sure the crown side is up. From the long point of this mark, measure along the top of the stock and mark the length of the rafter. Then align the template's registration mark with the rafter-length mark and scribe the bird's mouth. That's all there is to it. Be sure you have enough stock left over for the tail forming the overhang.

With the first rafter marked to length, make the ridge cut with your circular saw. Move to the other end of the stock and make the cuts for the bird's mouth, overcutting just enough to remove the wedge. Use this rafter as a pattern to lay out and cut the second rafter.

Use a small rafter square to scribe the ridge plumb cut at one end of the 1x6 template, as shown in the drawing at right. Move down the template about 1 ft. and scribe the heel cut (a plumb cut) of the bird's mouth. Extend this line across the top edge of the template. This will serve as your registration or guide mark when laying out the bird's mouth on the rafter stock. Then mark the level seat cut on the bottom edge of the template, which will be 3 1/2 in. long for 2x4 walls and 5 1/2 in. long for 2x6 walls. Add a 1x2 fence, and the template is ready for use (see the drawing below).

There is no need to lay out and cut rafter tails at this point. Instead, let the tails run long. Once the roof is built, a chalkline will be snapped across the rafters hanging outside the walls. The tails can then be cut in place, ready for fascia to be nailed to them.

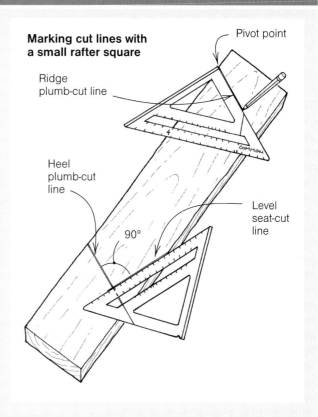

Marking cut lines with a small rafter square

Pivot point

Ridge plumb-cut line

Heel plumb-cut line

90°

Level seat-cut line

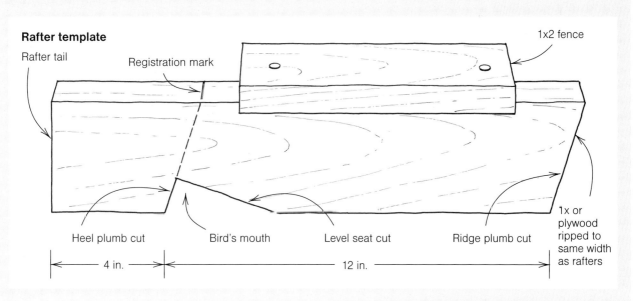

Rafter template

Rafter tail

Registration mark

1x2 fence

Heel plumb cut

Bird's mouth

Level seat cut

Ridge plumb cut

1x or plywood ripped to same width as rafters

4 in.

12 in.

Before cutting up all the expensive rafter stock, it's a simple matter to check to see that these first two rafters are cut properly. With a partner, pull up the two rafters, one on each side of the building. Hold them in place with the seat cuts snug at the plate lines. Place a short 2x ridge between the rafters at the peak, then check to see if all the cuts—both at the bird's mouth and at the ridge board—fit perfectly. When you are satisfied, use the first rafter as a pattern to lay out and cut the remaining rafters. Once the rafters are cut, carry them to the house and lean them against a wall, ridge end up. Rafter tails will be cut to length once the roof is built.

Like truss roofs, stick-built roofs have frieze blocks nailed between each rafter at the plate line that help stabilize the rafters. Cut the blocks slightly less than 14½ in. long for rafters at 16 in. o.c. and slightly less than 22½ in. long for those nailed 24 in. o.c. If blocks are set on the wall, they may have to be cut 1½ in. shorter (13 in.) because of the ceiling joist nailed to the plate.

Laying out and installing the ridge board

Before tackling the ridge board and installing the rafters, take the time to build yourself a safe place to work. Nail plywood strips left over from the floor sheathing on top of the ceiling joists under the ridge line to make a catwalk that's at least 2 ft. wide and that runs the full length of the building. There are times, especially when you have a high ridge or are working on a house without ceiling joists, that you will have to set up a scaffold. It's best to use a solidly built metal scaffold (you can rent these) to guarantee your safety. Anytime you work high up, be safe. Risks are for trained Hollywood stunt men.

A secure catwalk gives you a place to lay out the ridge boards, which need to be as straight as possible. The ridge board must be wider than the rafter stock so that the angled plumb cut of the rafter bears fully across the face of the ridge board. So if the rafters are 2x6, use a 2x8 for the ridge board. Begin the ridge-board layout at one end, marking it

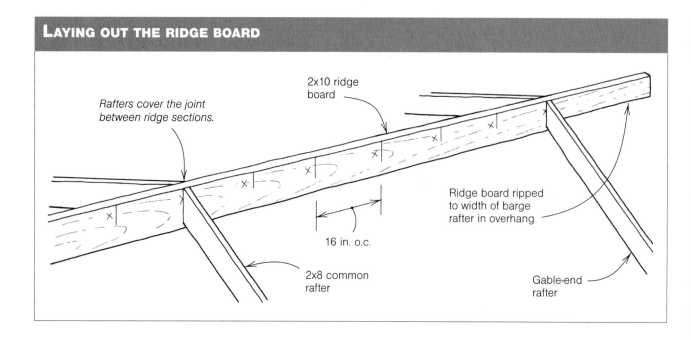

LAYING OUT THE RIDGE BOARD

Rafters cover the joint between ridge sections.

2x10 ridge board

16 in. o.c.

2x8 common rafter

Ridge board ripped to width of barge rafter in overhang

Gable-end rafter

every 16 o.c. or 24 in. o.c. If more than one board will be used to make up the ridge, cut the boards so that each joint falls in the center of a pair of rafters. Be sure to align the layout of the ridge board to that of the joists so that the rafters and joists tie together at the plate line. If both are spaced 16 in. o.c., every rafter will tie into a joist (see the drawing on p. 142). If the joists are 16 in. o.c. and the rafters are 24 in. o.c., a rafter will tie into every fourth joist.

Some builders like to let the ridge board extend out into the overhang and catch the ends of the barge rafters (see the drawing on the facing page). If you do this, rip the overhang part of the ridge board down to the actual size of the rafters because this section of the roof is exposed. Determine this length by measuring the face of the ridge plumb cut. For example, a 2x6 cut on an angle will be more than 5½ in. along the length of the cut.

Now comes the fun part. Nailing the rafters in place to the ridge board and to the wall plates and joists quickly gives the building frame a finished look. On most buildings, there is no need to pre-set the ridge at a predetermined height. Ridges are sort of like shoes. They go where they go. Setting rafters in place easily determines ridge height.

Begin by pulling up a straight, gable-end rafter. While one person holds the rafter at the ridge board, the other toenails the bottom end to the wall plate with 16d nails—one on each side of the rafter. Repeat this process with the opposing rafter. To hold them steady, tack a 1x brace from the rafters back to a joist.

Now move to the opposite end of the first ridge section and toenail another rafter pair in the same way. Next, pull the ridge board up between the two pairs of rafters (see the photo above).

Toenail a pair of rafters to the top plates, then raise the ridge board between the rafters. Nail the rafters to the ridge board with 16d nails. (Photo by Robert Wedemeyer.)

Drive two 16d nails straight through the ridge into the end of the first rafter, then angle two more through the ridge into the opposing rafter. I try not to nail in the top of any rafter, which helps me avoid dulling my sawblade later when I cut sheathing on the roof.

At this point, nail a 2x4 leg under the ridge board to a wall plate at both ends. These legs need to be the same length. If they aren't, it may mean that the walls are slightly out of parallel. Pull the nails out of the rafter pair at the top plate on the high end of the ridge and slide the rafters out a bit until the ridge rests on the 2x leg.

Be sure to nail the gable-end studs in plumb, trusting your eye or using a level. (Photo by Robert Wedemeyer.)

Plumbing the ridge

Just as you did on the truss roof, nail a long 2x4 on edge to the side of the building. Push the end rafters against the upright and install a 2x4 sway brace extending from the top plate to the ridge board at a 45° angle. Nail it between the layout lines at the ridge board so that it won't be in the way of a rafter.

After the initial ridge section is in place, raise the remaining sections in the same way, installing the minimum number of rafter pairs and support legs to hold them in place. At the opposite end, raise another 2x against the building and mark the ridge for length, plumb with the end of the building. Unless the ridge board runs out into the overhang, make the cut and nail in the second pair of straight, gable-end rafters.

With the entire ridge board in place, nail in the rest of the rafters and complete the roof frame. Nail each rafter into the ridge board with two 16d nails, then nail rafters to the ceiling joists with three 16d nails. The rafter should be toenailed to the wall with two 16d nails. Nail in several rafters on one side and then switch and do the same on the other side. Switch back and forth, or you may get too much weight on one side and cause the ridge board to bow.

Installing gable-end studs

Gable-end studs come built into gable trusses, but they have to be cut and fitted on the job site when building a conventional roof so that exterior wall coverings can be nailed on. Often, a 14-in.-wide vent is placed in the gable ends. To accommodate this vent (or other opening), measure over half the distance of the rough opening from the center of the ridge board and mark this distance on a gable-end rafter. Measuring down from this point to the plate gives you the length of the longest gable-end stud.

INSTALLING BARGE RAFTERS

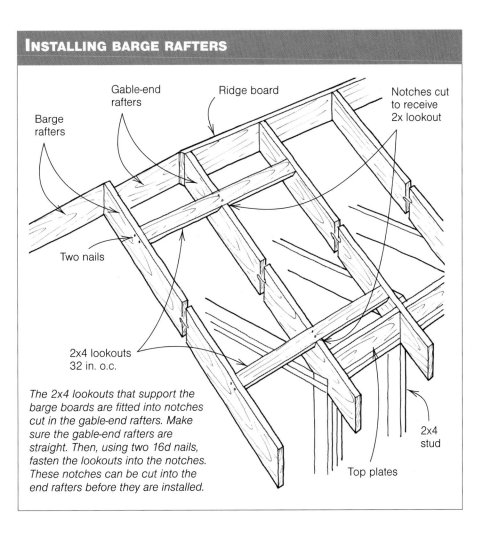

Barge rafters

Gable-end rafters

Ridge board

Notches cut to receive 2x lookout

Two nails

2x4 lookouts 32 in. o.c.

2x4 stud

Top plates

The 2x4 lookouts that support the barge boards are fitted into notches cut in the gable-end rafters. Make sure the gable-end rafters are straight. Then, using two 16d nails, fasten the lookouts into the notches. These notches can be cut into the end rafters before they are installed.

Rather than measuring the length of each individual gable-end stud, I use a little math to calculate the common difference in length of each successive stud. Divide the rise (4 in this case) by 3 and add the result and the rise together (4 ÷ 3 = 1.33 + 4 = 5.33, or 5⅜ in.). So, for example, if the first gable-end stud is 47 in. long, the next one will be 41⅝ in. (47 − 5⅜ = 41⅝). The next will be 36¼ in. long and so on. The tops of these gable-end studs are cut at an 18° angle, the pitch of the roof (consult rafter tables for this angle).

Nail the gable-end studs in plumb, trusting your eye or using a level (see the photo on the facing page). Be careful to

nail down through the rafter into the gable-end studs to keep from pushing the end rafter up. Don't inadvertently put a crown in this straight rafter.

Finishing the overhang

There are many ways to finish an overhang, from simple to ornate. Houses in the Southwest may have a stucco soffit. A Victorian beauty may be trimmed out with fancy gingerbread. But the trend in most areas of our country today is toward simplicity and economy.

The next step in finishing the overhang part of this big puzzle is to install the barge rafters. Lay the 2x4 lookouts into the notches cut in the gable-end rafters.

Nail them with two 16d nails into the first inboard rafter (see the drawing on p. 149). Sight down the end rafter to make sure it is straight, then nail the lookouts into the notches with two more 16d nails.

The gable-end rafter forms the upper part of the exterior wall and needs to be plumb and straight. I once got a callback on a house that had a badly bowed gable-end rafter that no one noticed until the shingles were on. While we were able to cut the nails that held the rafter to the roof sheathing with a reciprocating saw and correct the mistake, it took time and money. Like most building mistakes, it was correctable, but it would have been far cheaper to make sure the rafter was straight in the first place.

Next, check the plans to determine the length of the overhang. If it's 20 in. at the gable end, for example, subtract 1½ in. for the barge rafter and snap a chalkline at 18½ in. across the lookouts and across the ridge board if it extends into the overhang. This will ensure a straight barge rafter. Cut the lookouts and ridge board with a circular saw. Nail through the barge rafters into the ends of the lookouts with galvanized 16d nails. Because this framing will be exposed, make sure that the plumb cut at the ridge board fits tight and looks good.

Trimming rafter tails

Before the fascia can be nailed in place, the rafter tails must be marked and cut to length. The overhang can be easily measured out from the wall. If, for example, the overhang is 12 in. and the fascia stock is a 2x (1½ in. thick), measure straight out from the building line

Measure straight out from the building on the gable-end rafters 10½ in. and make a mark. This will be the cut line. (Photo by Roe A. Osborn.)

10½ in. and mark this point on the bottom edge of the rafters at both ends of the building (see the photo on the facing page). Snap a chalkline across the rafters, including the barges, to connect the marks. Use the rafter-cutting template you made earlier to mark the plumb cut on the rafter tails (see the photo below).

A professional carpenter can walk the plate and cut off the rafter tails. If this is too scary for you, then cut the tails from below while standing on a stable surface, such as a ladder or scaffold. Barge rafters are often mitered at a 45° angle along their plumb cut to receive the fascia. The mark on the barge rafters is the short point of this cut. This guarantees that the barge will be long enough to receive the fascia, which is nailed horizontally to the rafter tails.

Try to cut all trim material from the back side. Saw teeth tend to pick up wood grain and leave the upside of a board a bit shattered. This is finish work, so make every cut as clean as possible. Also, try to use long, straight stock for the fascia, just as you did with the barge rafters. Start by making a square cut with a 45° miter to fit into the barge rafter. The other end of this first board is cut at 45° also, with the cut falling over a rafter tail so that the next piece can be securely nailed to it with an overlap.

Now, working with a partner, nail the fascia into the barge rafter with 16d galvanized nails (see the left photo on p. 152). Because this is exposed, use a finish hammer, try not to miss the nail, and leave a nice, tight miter joint. Hold the fascia down a bit as you nail it to the rafter tails so that the roof sheathing can extend out over it and be nailed flush with the outside of the fascia. To find

Place the fence of the rafter-cutting template on each rafter and scribe a plumb-cut line at the mark. (Photo by Roe A. Osborn.)

Drive two 16d hot-dipped galvanized nails through the barge rafter and into the fascia. Make sure the miter joint is tight because it will be seen. (Photo by Roe A. Osborn.)

Place a piece of scrap wood on the top edge of a rafter extending beyond the rafter tail. Put the fascia snug against this scrap and drive one 16d galvanized nail high and another low. (Photo by Roe A. Osborn.)

exactly how high to place the fascia on the rafter, first place a scrap of wood on the rafter's top edge and extending beyond the end of the tail. Place the fascia snug against this scrap and nail it to the first rafter, driving the first nail high and the second nail as low as possible (see the right photo above). Then continue nailing the fascia to the remaining rafters, being sure to join fascia boards together over rafter tails with a 45° lap joint.

Preparation for building a soffit

Building other types of simple soffits is covered in Chapter 8, but sometimes preparation for building soffits can be done as the fascia is installed. The first type of soffit needs a subfascia (see the top drawing on the facing page). Cut the rafter tails back an extra 1½ in. Before nailing on the finish fascia, nail the subfascia to the rafter tails using the same stock as the rafters.

For the second type of soffit, cut a ¾-in.-wide by ½-in.-deep groove into the back side of the fascia (before it is installed) just below the rafter tails (see the bottom drawing at right). You can cut this groove with a table-saw-mounted dado blade or with a router.

Sheathing the roof

Years ago, when wood shingles were the norm, we used to sheathe roofs with 1x6 boards. Often, a roof was strip-sheathed (sometimes called skip-sheathed), where the builders left 4-in. or 5-in. gaps between each board to allow the wood shingles to breathe. If you live in an older house, look in the attic and you can often see this type of sheathing. But today, because composition shingles are more common than wood shingles and need a solid base, most roofs are sheathed with plywood or oriented strand board (OSB).

Sheathing a roof is much like sheathing a floor. Begin by measuring up 48¼ in. from the fascia on each end and snap a control chalkline across the rafters. You can work off the straight fascia edge, but I find it easier to use a chalked control line that's right in front of me.

On steep roofs, you can usually sheathe the first row or two while standing on the joists. If using OSB sheathing, take care to put the slick side down. I have stepped out on a frosty roof in the early morning and started skiing (for other safety tips, see the sidebar on p. 154). That's the way it is with the slick side of OSB.

The first sheet is always a bit difficult to get squared away on the roof and nailed directly on the control line, mainly because you don't have a good place to stand. As with floor and wall sheathing, make sure the edge of each sheet falls in the middle of a rafter. The ends can extend out over the barge rafter and be cut later.

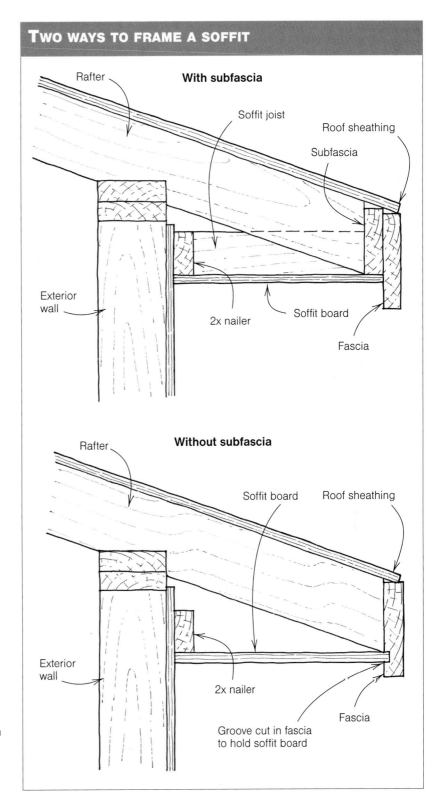

TWO WAYS TO FRAME A SOFFIT

With subfascia

Rafter

Soffit joist

Roof sheathing

Subfascia

Exterior wall

2x nailer

Soffit board

Fascia

Without subfascia

Rafter

Soffit board

Roof sheathing

Exterior wall

2x nailer

Fascia

Groove cut in fascia to hold soffit board

SAFETY RULES FOR SHEATHING A ROOF

• Roofs with pitches over 6-in-12 are too steep to stand on.

• When necessary, use approved safety lines to hold you when sheathing a roof.

• Don't wear slick-soled shoes.

• Be extra careful when working near the edge of the building.

• Sweep sawdust off sheathing panels because the dust will make the panels slippery.

• Stay off plywood that has ice on it, and be especially watchful early in the morning before the sun warms things up.

• When using sheathing that has one slick side, put the slick side down.

• Don't carry sheets in a strong wind because they'll act as a sail.

• On windy days, nail each sheet with enough nails to hold it securely until final nailing.

• Secure your tools so they won't slide off the roof.

• Never throw scrap wood off the roof without checking to see that no one is below.

Because composition shingles need a solid base, most roofs today are sheathed with plywood or OSB. (Photo by Roe A. Osborn.)

To cut the sheathing at the ridge on the roof, snap a chalkline along the ridge, set the saw to cut ¾ in. deep, and make the cut. The sheathing doesn't have to fit perfectly here because it will be covered by paper and shingles. (Photo by Roe A. Osborn.)

A last step in the roof-sheathing process is to trim the sheathing flush with the barge rafters at the gable ends. (Photo by Roe A. Osborn.)

A common nailing schedule for a roof is 6-6-12 (6 in. o.c. at the edges and joints and 12 in. o.c. in the field). When you nail sheathing on the gable end and overhang, take special care not to miss the rafters. Missed nails can be seen from below, and they don't draw the sheathing tight against the rafters.

Once you have the first row of sheathing down, start sheathing the second row. If you are using ½-in. plywood or OSB and the rafters are 24 in. o.c., you have to place metal clips on the edge of the panel between each rafter. The clips link the two sheets together so that any load between the two rafters is carried by the two sheets. Just like on a subfloor, remember to stagger the vertical joints. And remember to work safely, especially on steep roofs, nailing up 2x cleats as you go up and/or using safety lines as necessary to keep from sliding off.

Once the last row of sheathing is in place, snap a chalkline along the ridge and cut, with your sawblade set about ¾ in. deep (see the left photo above). Sheathing doesn't have to fit perfectly at the ridge because it will be covered with roofing paper and shingles. In some regions, the sheathing is held back from the ridge from 1½ in. to 3 in. so that a ridge vent can be run the length of the building to ventilate the attic.

Once you have one side sheathed, move to the other side and work the same way. When the entire roof has been sheathed, trim the plywood flush along the gable ends (see the right photo above) and finish nailing. Not long after the roof has been sheathed, builders in wet areas like to cover it with felt roofing paper to protect the entire structure from the elements until the finished roof can be installed.

7

STAIRS

Even complicated stairs become easy when broken down into simple tasks. (Photo by Roger Turk.)

Stairs, like roofs, come in many different styles and shapes. There are straight stairs, L-shaped or U-shaped stairs, winders (stairs that change direction over the course of several steps), and even circular stairs. They can be as basic as treads attached to a couple of stringers or as ornate as a double-helix beauty that spirals upward toward the sky. From the simple to the complex, every stair has the same basic purpose: to get us safely from one level to another.

What's more, every stair uses the same basic layout principles. So building stairways, like framing roofs, is actually quite easy to understand if you break the job down into simple tasks. In fact, you don't need many special skills or tools to build most stairs. What you will need to know are the names of stair parts, the codes regulating stairs so that they're safe for people to use, and a bit of math to calculate the number and size of steps. This knowledge, coupled with the ability to use a framing square to lay out the stair stringers, will allow you to cut and assemble the stair parts into a strong and durable stairway that is safe and comfortable to use. (To learn basic stair vocabulary and codes, see the sidebar on the facing page.)

Stairwell The hole in a floor through which a stair passes on its way from one level to the next.

Headroom The vertical distance from stair treads to ceiling joists. Must be at least 6 ft. 8 in.

Stringers The wooden members that run diagonally and support the treads and risers (also called carriages and horses). Three are required for most 3-ft.-wide stairs.

Riser The vertical part of a step. For safety, keep this figure near 7 in.

Tread The horizontal portion of a step (where you set your foot). Each tread needs to be at least 10 in. wide.

Landing A level place at the top and bottom of stairs (can also be a platform separating stairs).

Total rise The distance a set of stairs travels vertically from one finish floor level to the next.

Total run The total horizontal distance of a set of stairs from first tread to last.

Kicker A 2x4 secured to the floor that helps hold the bottom of the stair stringer in place.

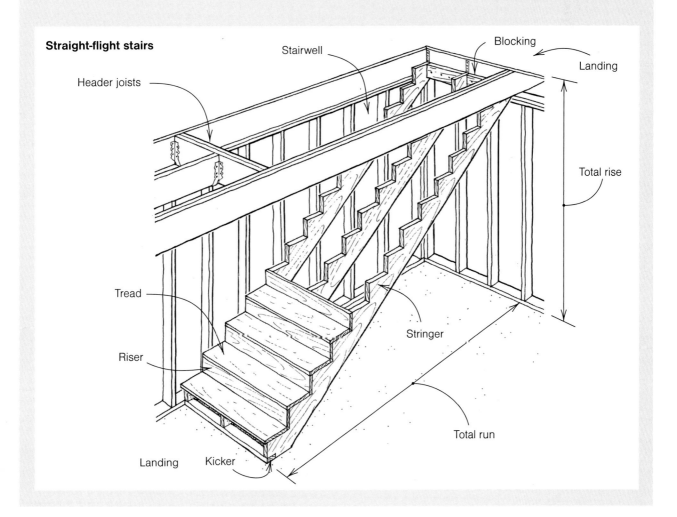

Straight-flight stairs

Stairwell · Blocking · Landing · Header joists · Total rise · Tread · Riser · Stringer · Landing · Kicker · Total run

STRAIGHT-FLIGHT STAIRS

Stairs and the stringers that support them come in different shapes and styles. Some stringers have a simple plumb cut at the top and a level cut at the bottom, with fixed cleats in between to hold the treads. Most stringers have notches cut in them where treads and risers are attached. Stringers that sit between walls and are hidden from view are called closed stringers. When they are exposed—and usually finished—they are called open stringers.

Like the gable roof discussed in Chapter 6, the straight-flight stairs covered in this chapter are basic and simple. At the same time, the skills necessary to build them are common to all stairs, no matter how complex they may seem. Once you know how to build a set of straight-flight stairs, you have the basic rise-run information you need to build other types.

Framing the stairwell

The first concern of stairbuilding is the stairwell (see the drawing on p. 157). Because they have to be wide enough for the stair structure and long enough for adequate headroom, stairwells take up a considerable amount of square footage. Most of us know what it's like to go up a narrow set of stairs, especially one with inadequate lighting. It's worse yet when you have to duck your head to

This seemingly complex stair of glass and maple is actually made up of simple elements. (Photo by Scott McBride.)

miss hitting the front edge of a stairwell. So for comfort and safety, codes require most stairs to be at least 3 ft. wide and have at least 6 ft. 8 in. of headroom along the total length of the stair.

When I can, I like to make stairs even wider than 3 ft., because more than people (like pianos and furniture) will be moved up and down. The average straight-flight stair will fit easily into a stairwell that is a minimum of 37½ in. wide and about 130 in. long. (To frame this opening, see Chapter 5.)

Seemingly minor details can have an impact on stairs. I've built stairs that fit between walls that were sheathed with ½-in. plywood, covered by ½-in. drywall, and had a ¾-in. skirtboard (stair trim) along each stringer. This meant that the rough opening had to be 39½ in. wide instead of 37½ in. Also, I like to leave an extra ½ in. so that all the stair parts fit easily in place. If you don't notice these details until the framing is complete and it's time to build stairs, you'll have to redo a lot of work to make it right.

Carpenters laying out the house frame also need to leave adequate room for landings. Because it's dangerous to open a door and immediately face a step down, building codes require a landing at the top and bottom. Many stairs have landings midflight, where you can stop to rest or make a turn and proceed in another direction. Landings have to be at least the same width and depth as the stairs, which means 36-in.-wide stairs require a landing that is at least 36 in. by 36 in. square. When snapping lines on the floors, building walls and laying out stairwells, remember that these clearances are finish requirements, so account for finish wall thicknesses (typically ½-in. drywall) on each side. This way you don't wind up with a landing that is 35 in. by 35 in. and not up to code.

Landings in the middle of stairs play no part in determining the total rise. They're figured as if they were large treads. They do make the total run longer, so if a landing falls midflight, seven risers up, for example, its height above the floor will be seven times the height of a riser. If the riser height is 7-in., the landing should be built at 49 in.

Determining total rise and run

One of the most important parts of stairbuilding is to determine the total rise, or vertical distance between finish floors that are connected by a stairway (see the drawing on p. 160). While figuring the distance between the two floors is simple, a problem can arise because stairs are usually built before the finish floors are in place. So the measurements are actually taken from rough floor to rough floor but must account for the finish floor material at both the top and bottom.

I once built several stairs in an apartment house, not realizing that the plans called for 1½-in. lightweight fire-resistant concrete on the upstairs landings. I was called back to explain why every riser was 7 in. except the last, which became 8½ in. once the concrete was poured. The next day I tore out the stairs and started over.

There are other problems when figuring total rise, especially for exterior decks and remodeling. Usually when I measure total rise, I hook my tape on the upper floor, pull it straight down to the lower floor, and read the measurement. But remember that the first tread lands a set number of horizontal feet away from the last tread. What's more, the floor or the ground between these two points may be sloping considerably. So for accuracy, carefully level straight out from

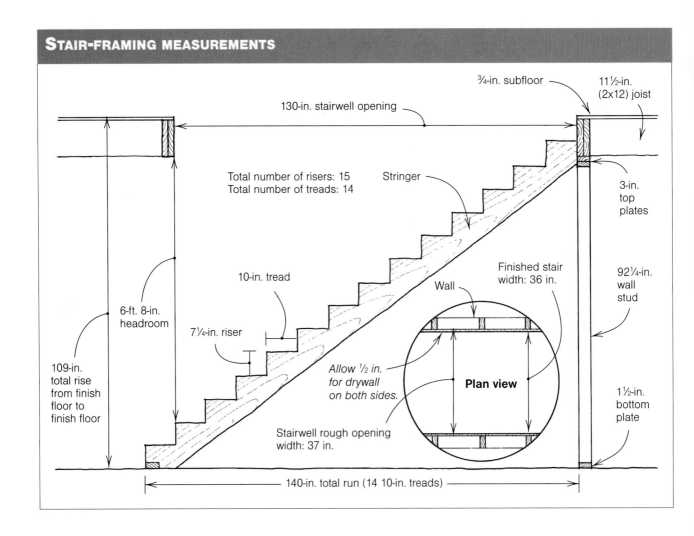

¾-in. subfloor

11½-in. (2x12) joist

130-in. stairwell opening

Total number of risers: 15
Total number of treads: 14

Stringer

3-in. top plates

Finished stair width: 36 in.

Wall

92¼-in. wall stud

10-in. tread

6-ft. 8-in. headroom

Plan view

7¼-in. riser

Allow ½ in. for drywall on both sides.

1½-in. bottom plate

109-in. total rise from finish floor to finish floor

Stairwell rough opening width: 37 in.

140-in. total run (14 10-in. treads)

the upper floor landing to a point directly over the lower landing before making the total rise measurement.

Unlike the total rise, which is a fixed number, the total run, or horizontal distance, can vary for a given set of stairs (see the drawing). This is important because treads can be made narrower or wider to allow the stairway to fit into the allotted space. While most straight-flight stairs run about 12 ft. on the level, the number of treads and their width determine the exact total run. If each tread is 10 in., for example, and the stair has 14 treads, then 10 in. x 14 = 140 in. for a total run of 11 ft. 8 in.

Calculating individual risers and treads

Once you've determined the total rise of a set of stairs, you can calculate exactly how many steps are needed to get to the second floor and how high each step will be. The total rise for a typical two-story house with 8-ft. walls (accounting for plates, studs, and joists) is often around 109 in., so I use this number in my calculations. Just remember that the first point in building any set of stairs is to measure the actual total rise accurately.

Some codes allow an individual riser to be up to 8 in. high. This is too steep for most of us and makes going up the stairway like climbing a mountain. But people tend to take shallow steps two at a time, which can be just as uncomfortable and dangerous. The angle of a set of stairs needs to be close to 35°, so wherever possible, I like to build stairs with a 7-in. rise and an 11-in. tread, which experience (and building codes) tells me is a safe and comfortable set of stairs for most people.

Divide 109 in. by 7 in. (the height of a normal step) and the result is 15.57 in. Because there can't be a partial step, round the result to a whole number to get the number of risers needed. If you divide the rise (109) by 15, you get 7.26, or 7¼ in., which is an acceptable rise. If you divide 109 by 16, you get a rise of 6.81 in., which is probably a little too shallow.

An 11-in.-wide tread makes for safer stairs. But if you increase each tread by 1 in., you increase the total run by 14 in. or 15 in., depending on the number of treads. That's okay if you have enough room to build a longer set of stairs. But like most things in carpentry, there is always more than one way to go. As you'll see, a 10-in. tread can be extended to 11 in. with no increase in the total run. So let's lay out and cut this 14-tread stair with 10-in.-wide treads and 15 risers that are 7¼ in. high. Because stairs have one less tread (14) than risers (15), the total run of these stairs will be 140 in. The upper landing takes the place of the last tread.

Laying out stringers

Treads and risers are supported by diagonal wooden members called stringers, carriages, or horses. As noted, finish interior stairs are normally at least 36 in. wide, a width that requires three stringers. You aren't penalized for exceeding code, however, and I like to use four stringers when the material is available. This ensures that the stairs won't feel bouncy.

A simple set of stair gauges (small screw clamps that fix to the square) attached to the framing square makes it easier to lay out stair stringers accurately. (Photo by Roe A. Osborn.)

The majority of rough stair stringers for a full-flight set of stairs are cut from 16-ft. or 18-ft. 2x12s. Pick out three or four good stringers that are straight and free of large knots and place them on sawhorses. I prefer a wood like Douglas fir for interior stair stringers because of its strength. I use pressure-treated wood for exterior stringers because they resist insect and moisture damage.

I use a framing square for stringer layout, and a simple set of stair gauges (small screw clamps that attach to the square) makes it easier (see the photo above). Screw one gauge at 7¼ in. (the unit rise) on the tongue, or narrow part, of the square, and the other gauge at 10 in. (the unit run) on the blade, or wider part. Begin the layout at the bottom end of the stringer with the blade downward. Mark across the top of the square with a sharp pencil and label this riser #1. Slide the square up and mark the next riser #2, and so on. Take your time and work accurately, making sure

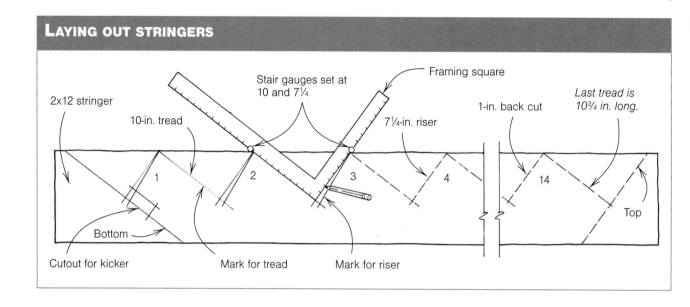

2x12 stringer

10-in. tread

Stair gauges set at 10 and 7¼

Framing square

7¼-in. riser

1-in. back cut

Last tread is 10¾ in. long.

1 2 3 4 14 Top

Bottom

Cutout for kicker

Mark for tread

Mark for riser

that each time you slide the square, you have the tread mark directly on the last riser mark so that each tread and riser are the same (see the drawing above).

I once built a set of stairs without using stair gauges. In the middle of the stringer, I made a mistake and laid out a riser at 8 in. instead of 7 in. Easy enough to do. I set the stringers and sheathed the treads and risers. When I walked up the completed stairs, I tripped on the 8-in. riser. I had the pleasure of building this set of stairs twice. Codes do allow for a bit of variation though. Even stairs don't have to be built to perfection. Riser height can vary up to ³⁄₁₆ in. from step to step, for example.

Often the stringer is attached to the upper floor system, one step below the level of the upper landing (see the drawing on p. 160). This means that the step to the landing makes the 15th riser, so lay out 14 risers on the stringer. Once the risers and treads have been marked on a stringer, finish with a level mark at the bottom of the first riser and a plumb mark at the end of the last tread (see the drawing above).

Now give the stringer a 1-in. back cut to make the treads 11 in. rather than 10 in. wide. This back cut doesn't change the total run, but it does change the look of the stairs by tipping the riser back and providing a wider (and safer) tread. Back cut the risers by slipping the riser gauge down the blade until the tongue of the square rests 1 in. in from where the riser mark meets the tread mark. Remark all the risers, making them slant back. The uppermost tread needs to be extended ¾ in. to allow for a riser board to be nailed against the landing header (see the drawing on the facing page).

Dropping the stringer

A simple adjustment often needs to be made at the bottom of the stringer to keep the first riser the same height as the rest, because if you nail a ¾-in. board to the first tread, for example, the step increases to 8 in. from 7¼ in. (see the drawing on the facing page). This is important for safety, because all risers need to be the same height. So subtract the thickness of the finish tread from the bottom of the stringer.

There are many different variations on this detail. If the subfloor is to be carpeted and treads sheathed with ¾-in.

DROPPING THE STRINGER

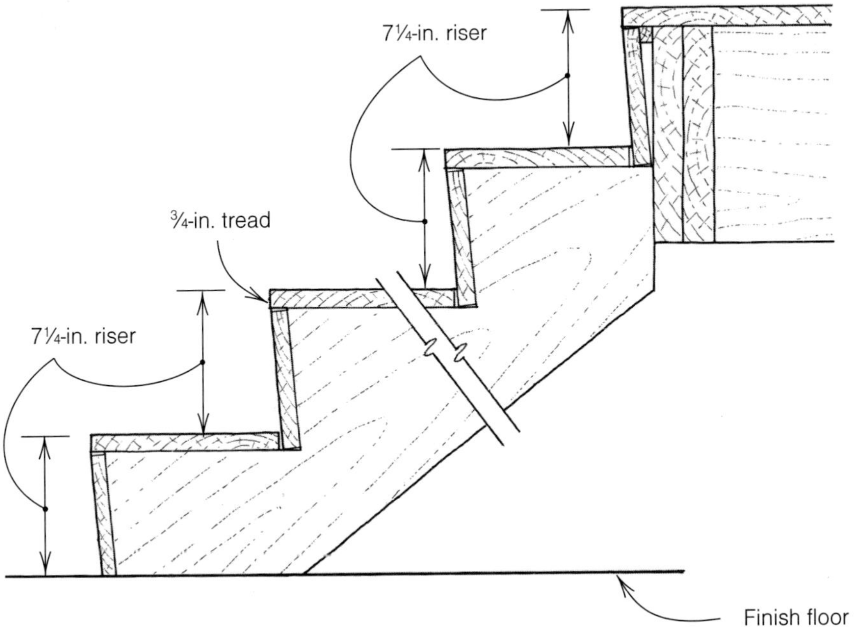

7¼-in. riser

¾-in. tread

7¼-in. riser

Finish floor

Once you've laid out the stringer, subtract from the bottom the thickness of the finish tread to bring each tread to the correct height.

plywood and finished with ¾-in. hardwood, the stringer has to be dropped by 1½ in. for every riser to be the same. If the stair is nailed to the subfloor and both treads and subfloor will be covered with ¾-in. hardwood, nothing has to be done. If the subfloor is sheathed with ¾-in. hardwood and treads with ¾-in. plywood and ⅜-in. hardwood, drop the stringers by ⅜ in. Again, you need to know the exact thickness of the finish floor and tread material before you can frame the stairs.

To help secure the bottom of the stair, lay out a notch for a 2x4 on the bottom front of the first riser. Just take a scrap of 2x4, hold it flush with the outside corner of the first riser, and scribe around it. This notch will rest on a 2x kicker that is secured to the floor (see the drawing on p. 157).

Cutting stringers

Take a moment to check that your layout is correct before cutting out all the notches on the stringers. I make two cuts—the horizontal (or level) cut that rests on the floor and the vertical (or plumb) cut that nails to the top header joist. The stringer should fit snugly at both top and bottom, and all the tread lines should be level. Sometimes, especially on concrete, the floor may not be dead level, which can cause the heel (back side) of a stringer to hit the concrete first and open up a gap at the toe (front). This results in an increase in the amount of rise on the first step up. If the floor is uneven, you'll either have to scribe a line across the bottom of the tread and make the cut so that the stringer fits snugly to the floor or shim the heel when the front hits first.

This basic unnotched stringer is frequently used for exterior stairs. I attach metal or wood cleats to the tread lines of the two side stringers and set them in place. Then heavy treads cut from 2x or even 3x material can be fixed to the cleats. Exterior stairs shrink and swell a lot, and it seems that every time a person

uses them, a nail tends to work loose. That's why I prefer using treated wood with bolts and deck screws rather than nails to hold exterior stairs together.

When cutting out the tread and riser lines on a stringer, start at the bottom and cut all the treads. Then turn around and cut all the risers. I to do it this way because it sets up a rhythm and is less tiring than switching back and forth. Stringers that will not be exposed and that will be supported by a wall can be overcut with a circular saw. Or you can finish the cut with a jigsaw or handsaw (see the photo below). If you overcut, be

The notch in the rough stringers can be overcut with a circular saw. If the stringers are exposed, finish the cut with a handsaw or jigsaw. (Photo by Scott Phillips.)

careful not to cut any more than is needed to remove the tread-riser notch, or you can seriously weaken a stringer.

Once the first stringer has been cut and checked for fit, it becomes your pattern. If the uncut stringer stock has any crown to it, turn it up. Then lay the pattern exactly on top of the other stringers and mark accurately along all the treads and risers with a sharp carpenter's pencil. Carefully make the remaining cuts, and you're ready to build the stairs.

Attaching stringers

Because a stairway is often asked to bear considerable weight, stringers need to be securely attached at top and bottom. There are several ways to attach a stringer to an upper landing, deck, or floor system (see the drawing at right). Whichever method you choose, the first step is to measure down on the face of the landing header one riser height (7¼ in. in this example) and carefully mark a level line across the header where the stringers will land. Think again about finish floors at this point. Remember what will cover the stair treads and the landing, and make adjustments to ensure that every step will be the same once all finish treads and floor coverings are installed.

I often support stringers by nailing a 1½-in.-wide, 18-in.-long metal strap (see Sources on p. 198) along the back edge of the stringer on the top end. I bend this strap around the stringer so the upper end can be nailed to the header joist of the landing, supporting it. On interior stairs, this strap will be hidden by a riser board. Blocks nailed between the stringers help stabilize them. Nail the first block through the side of the first stringer, flush with the top. Pull it up to the line on the header joist and nail it to the header. Then nail the strap to the header joist. Finish by

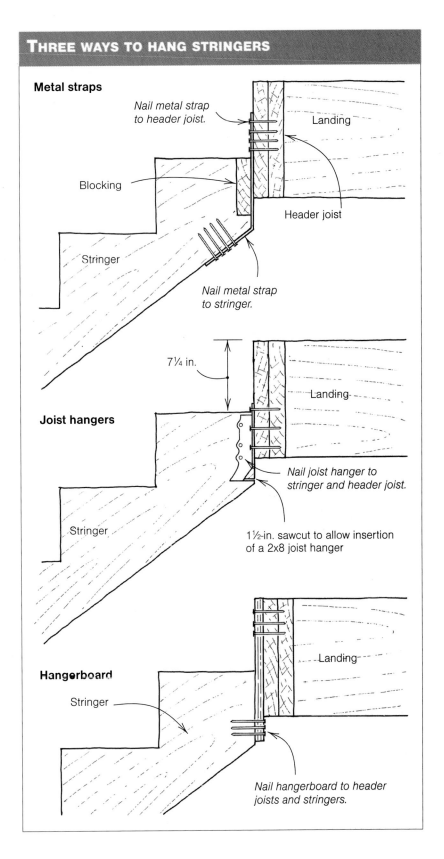

THREE WAYS TO HANG STRINGERS

Metal straps

Nail metal strap to header joist.

Landing

Blocking

Header joist

Stringer

Nail metal strap to stringer.

Joist hangers

7¼ in.

Landing

Stringer

Nail joist hanger to stringer and header joist.

1½-in. sawcut to allow insertion of a 2x8 joist hanger

Hangerboard

Stringer

Landing

Nail hangerboard to header joists and stringers.

A skirtboard, or finished stringer, which is cut to the shape of the stairs, is often installed between the stairs and the drywall to give a more finished look.

nailing in the second and third stringer in the same way. This set of stairs should be strong enough to hold people moving a refrigerator.

Another easy method for securing stringers at the top is with 2x6 or 2x8 metal joist hangers. Just make a horizontal cut about 1½ in. deep on the back of the stringer to house the bottom of the hanger. Nail the hanger to the stringer, place the stringer on the line below the landing and nail the hanger into the header.

A third method, using a hangerboard, also works well on exterior stairs because it can be left exposed. Take a piece of ⅝-in. or ¾-in. plywood (use exterior-grade, pressure-treated plywood for exterior stairs) and cut it about 15 in. wide and as long as the width of the stairs (36 in. normally). Nail the hangerboard to the face of the header joists, flush with the top of the landing. It should hang down no lower than the bottom of the stringer. Then strike a line on the board, down one riser height (7¼ in. for this stair). Hold the stringer to the line and secure it with nails or screws driven in through the back of the hangerboard.

With the stringers secure at the top, cut a 2x4 kicker as wide as the total width of the rough stairway (36 in. in this case) for the bottom of the stairs. Slip it into the notches on the front end of the stringers and fasten it to the floor. Then toenail the stringers to the kicker.

When setting stringers, remember to leave a bit more than ½ in. between the stringer and the wall framing so that drywall can easily slip between the stringers and the wall. Otherwise, somebody has to cut the shape of the stairs in the drywall to fit the stringer.

Skirtboards

Before nailing in the stair parts, a 1x skirtboard is often installed between walls and stringers (see the photo on the facing page). This piece of trim (often a 1x12) protects drywall from being dented by shoe kicks or vacuum cleaners. To cut the skirtboard, first snap a chalkline above the nose of the treads 3 in. or 4 in. and measure its length. Mark a plumb cut on the top of the skirtboard and a level cut at the bottom by using the 7¼-in. and 10-in. layout on the framing square (just as the top and bottom cuts on the stringers were laid out). Of course, be sure to leave enough room between the rough stringers and wall framing to accommodate the thickness of both the drywall and the skirtboard.

Cutting and installing risers and treads

If the stairs are going to be covered with carpet, the treads and risers can be cut from scrap material left over from sheathing. I use at least ⅝-in. plywood or oriented strand board (OSB) for the risers and ¾-in. plywood for treads. Scrap material can be ripped to width on a table saw or with a circular saw (carefully following a chalkline or using a ripping guide).

These rough treads and risers can also be covered with a fine, finished hardwood to give the stairs a custom look. Often, this is done later, when the house is nearly finished. To help you get a perfect fit, use a stair-tread gauge, a tool that fits from wall to wall, adjusts to fit out-of-square skirtboards, and gives you the exact length and shape of the tread or riser. Finish treads often have a nosing (1¼-in. maximum overhang by code) that projects out over the edge of each tread. I think that 1¼ in. is excessive because it is too easy to catch your toe on it as you go up the stairs, so I prefer no more than a ⅞-in. overhang.

Rough risers and treads don't have to be the exact width when they're being covered by carpet. In fact, it's better to cut them a bit narrow to eliminate the possibility that they will touch at the back side and create a squeak, which can happen when wood rubs against wood. And who needs squeaky stairs, especially if you're trying to sneak in late at night? So for stairs with 7¼-in. risers and 10-in. treads, rip the risers to 7⅛ in. and the treads to 9⅞ in. Cut them to the width of the rough stairway, or 36 in. long in this case.

Risers are nailed on first (see the photo on p. 168). The first riser usually has to be ripped an extra ¾ in. narrower than

Before nailing on the treads, first nail on the risers, driving two 8d nails through the stringer into each riser board. (Photo by Scott Phillips.)

the rest to compensate for the dropped stringer. Starting at the bottom, drive two 8d nails through the riser board into each stringer. Put the next riser in the same way, halfway up, to help straighten the stringers. Then go back to the bottom and nail on the rest of the risers.

When fastening the treads, use lots of construction adhesive between the treads and the stringers to help prevent squeaks that can develop as the wood dries out and nails loosen up. For extra insurance, secure the treads with deck screws, which are less likely to pull out than nails. Start at the bottom, run a generous bead of adhesive on the stringers and on the riser edge and secure each board as you go with three 8d nails or screws per stringer. When all the treads are on, try out the stairs. Finally, take a moment to admire the safe, easy access you have built to the next floor.

HANDRAILS

Handrails and guardrails come in many shapes, sizes, and materials. Like a seat-belt on a car, they are necessities for safety, but they can also be the highlight of a set of stairs (see the photo on the facing page). So not only do they need to look good, but they also need to be designed safely and built solidly, whatever their style or material.

Stairs are the most dangerous part of a house, and most building codes address stair and handrail design to some extent (see the sidebar on p. 170). A safe handrail is a key part of a safe stairway, whether it is a simple rail mounted on the wall with brackets or an elaborate balustrade (a horizontal rail with evenly spaced uprights that extend down to the stair treads).

Building a simple handrail

Elaborate balustrades can be expensive to build, and their installation is outside the scope of this book. But a safe and

Handrails are required by code, so they need to be safe and solid, but as this stair shows, they also can look good. (Photo by Kevin Ireton.)

sturdy handrail like the one that follows isn't difficult to build and can do the job just as well. Depending on the particular style of stairs I'm building, I sometimes use this sturdy, easy-to-use and inexpensive design.

To begin, run a row of scrap 2x10 blocks up the stair slope when framing the stairs. Nail them in the walls between the studs so that their center is about 34 in. above the stair nosing. After the drywall has been hung, come back and snap a chalkline above the stairs exactly where the handrail will be placed, typically between 30 in. and 38 in. above the nosing of the stair. Then drill a ⅝-in.-or ¾-in.-diameter hole near the top and bottom of the stairs and about every

3 ft. between, going through drywall and into the blocking directly along the line. Cut off 6-in. pieces of ⅝-in. or ¾-in. hardwood dowel (depending on the size of the holes) and glue them firmly in the holes.

After the walls have been finished, cut the dowels to length at about 2½ in. Next, get a long piece of 2x2 handrail (straight-grained Douglas fir or clear pine works well) and round the corners, sanding it smooth. Then hold the rail in position next to the dowels and mark it for drilling (a helper is handy for this step). Drill 1-in.-deep holes into the rail, apply glue, and tap the rail onto the dowels, being sure to leave it 1½ in. away from the wall.

• Every stair over three risers needs at least one handrail.

• Stairs 44 in. wide need a handrail on each side.

• Locate the handrail 30 in. to 38 in. vertically off the nose of the stair tread.

• Diameter of the railing must be 1½ in. to 2 in. for easy grasp.

• Leave a 1½-in. gap between the rail and wall on enclosed stairs.

• Extend the rail the full length of the stairs.

• Minimum guardrail height on landings or decks must be from 36 in. to 42 in.

• Balusters (uprights between handrail and treads or landings) must run vertically so that children can't climb on them.

• Spacing between balusters should not be more than 4 in. so that children can't squeeze through.

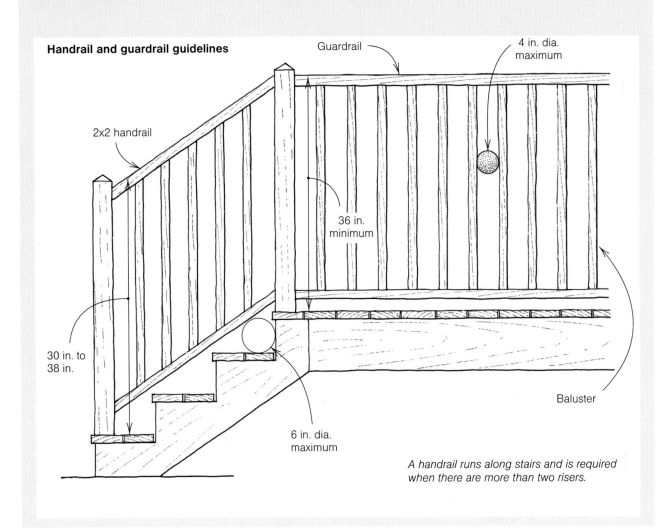

Handrail and guardrail guidelines

Guardrail

4 in. dia. maximum

2x2 handrail

36 in. minimum

30 in. to 38 in.

6 in. dia. maximum

Baluster

A handrail runs along stairs and is required when there are more than two risers.

A simple outdoor handrail or guardrail for stairs and decks can be made of naturally rot-resistant wood, such as cedar or redwood, or pressure-treated wood. (Photo by Dean Della Ventura.)

Building an exterior guardrail

Often, a handrail becomes a guardrail, enclosing an upper area like a landing or a deck. Like stairs and handrails, guardrails can be built using numerous designs and materials, but because they protect people from falling, they need to be safe and solidly built.

A guardrail design that I've often used for decks and balconies has a simple but classic look and can easily be modified—with fancy balusters, for example—for different situations (see the photo above). Although I prefer to work with cedar or redwood for these structures, here on the wet Oregon coast, we frequently use pressure-treated wood.

First, set 4x4 vertical posts every 8 ft. or so in the floor structure to hold the guardrail, notching and bolting these posts securely. Cut the posts 39 in. long, then cut and attach 2x4s laid flat about 3 in. above the floor deck between these posts. After nailing another 2x4 flat on top of the posts, cut 2x2 balusters at 40½ in., predrill them, and screw them vertically to the 2x4s with 3-in. deck screws. Plan your spacing so that there is no more than a 4-in. gap between each baluster.

Once the balusters are in place, cut and attach a 2x6 flat on top of the upper 2x4, which makes the total railing height 42 in. If you attach the upper 2x6 rail to the 2x4 from the underside, there won't be any penetrations to allow moisture into the rail, and it will look better.

8

FINISH DETAILS

Finish applied with care at the right places goes a long way toward making a house look pleasing to the eye. This includes installing doors and windows that are square, plumb, and level. (Photo by Rich Ziegner.)

Once there is a completed house shell, it's time to turn attention to the finishing details. Of course, much of this work—installing plumbing, heating, and electrical systems, roofing, and drywall, for example—is outside the scope of this book. But there is still plenty of carpentry work to do. In frame carpentry, it often doesn't matter if there are small gaps left here and there as the house is built. These gaps will all be covered "in the finish," as we say. What matters is that the house frame is square, level, straight, and plumb.

But more is needed when you start doing the finish work. I think it helps to approach finish carpentry with a different mindset than with frame carpentry. The work you do as a finish carpenter will be seen daily for the life of a building. Setting windows and hanging doors, adding exterior trim and siding, and trimming the interior all need to be done with care and precision.

WINDOWS AND DOORS

A finish carpenter's job is to make his work look pleasing to the eye. With practice, you can learn to split a pencil line with a sawcut—back cutting when necessary—so that exposed joints fit tightly. Doors and windows need to be set square, plumb, and level in their rough openings so that they work properly and don't allow moisture or air to penetrate the building envelope. Let's start with windows.

Setting windows

The majority of windows used today are aluminum or vinyl clad, and most have flanges that nail to the exterior wall and hold the frame in the opening. Wood windows with prefit casings are almost as easy to install.

Before fitting windows in place, do everything you can to prevent leakage and water damage. On the West Coast, we staple 6-in.-wide strips of felt or building paper over the housewrap around the window. These act as one line of defense against moisture. In wetter parts of the country, these strips are added over the flange, after the window is installed (see the drawing on p. 176). Cut strips of 15-lb. felt paper about 1 ft. longer than the height and width of the window. Staple one strip at the bottom of the rough opening and one strip along each side, lapping them over the bottom piece. Staple the top piece on after the window is set.

Next, lay down a good bead of caulk on the felt paper (see the photo at right), under where the window flange will be nailed. Squeeze out an extra-heavy bead at the top of the window to bed that flange in waterproof caulking. Even though this can be messy and take time, it's worth the extra effort because water leaking around the windows of a completed house can cause serious damage over time.

Temporarily lay a piece of ¼-in. plywood on the sill to bring the top of the window up to the correct height, then set the window in the rough opening with the aid of a helper (see the photo on p. 174). While one person holds the frame in place, the partner goes inside to check that the frame is centered in

Before nailing the window in place, lay down a good bead of silicone caulk around the entire opening under the window flange. This helps keep water from entering around the window frame. (Photo by Roe A. Osborn.)

the opening, the sill is level, and the jambs are plumb. There should be about ¼-in. clearance between the window and the rough framing all around. This gap will be covered later by window jambs or drywall. When windows are being set close together, make sure that they are level in their opening and with each other. Often, top and bottom trim runs straight across from window to

1. Check the rough opening for square, plumb, and level.

2. Apply felt paper and caulk to seal the window opening against air and leaks.

3. Use a story pole to mark and maintain uniform height of every window frame in the house.

4. Set the window frame in the opening and check the head for height and level and the side for plumb.

5. Check the window-frame diagonals for square before final attachment.

6. Nail or screw the window securely in place.

7. Open and close the window to see that it works with ease.

If the framing is correct, a window should fit easily in its rough opening. (Photo by Roe A. Osborn.)

After nailing the window in place, run another bead of caulk at the top of the flange, then staple the last strip of felt paper. (Photo by Roe A. Osborn.)

window, so any misalignments show up like weeds among the flowers in a garden.

In Chapter 5, I mentioned how I nail wall sheathing into the king studs with no nails in the trimmers so that when the windows are being set, it's easy to adjust the trimmers to fit the frame if necessary. When setting wooden windows, pull the trimmers tight against the window frame on both sides. Frames nailed directly to the jambs make for good, solid construction and eliminate the need for shims

Most windows that have nailing flanges can be held in place at each corner with 1-in. roofing nails, 8d nails, or drywall screws. But larger windows need more support. Drive another couple of nails into the flange between each corner. When setting wood windows, drive 6d nails through the jamb into the trimmer,

or drive 8d to 16d galvanized finish nails through the casings into the exterior wall frame. These nails are usually set below the surface with a nailset, and the holes are filled before painting. More and more carpenters are now securing windows with screws using a cordless screwdriver.

On the inside, wood windows need to be held straight and tight against the jamb with finish nails. Long wood windows will need to have the head jamb nailed to the header and the sill blocked level at the bottom.

With the window in place, run another bead of caulk along the flange at the top before stapling on the last strip of felt paper (see the photo above). If there is housewrap, make a slit in the housewrap, across the top and above the window, then tuck this last piece of felt into the slit. To further air-seal the win-

When doing finish work (particularly when remodeling an older structure), carpenters often run up against crooked floors, walls, and ceilings. I've found that when things are out of plumb or level, it's best to build parallel to that. The eye can see two lines that go away from each other much easier than it can see plumb or level. So, for example, if a window opening is out of plumb and can't be fixed, and if surrounding trim is parallel to the out-of-plumb opening, go ahead and set the window slightly out of plumb too. This way the side of the window will at least run parallel with the opening and be pleasing to the eye. This is particularly true when placing a new window next to an existing window or door that isn't exactly plumb. If the new window is perfectly plumb and level and the old one isn't, then both of them will read as crooked.

WINDOW FLASHING DETAILS

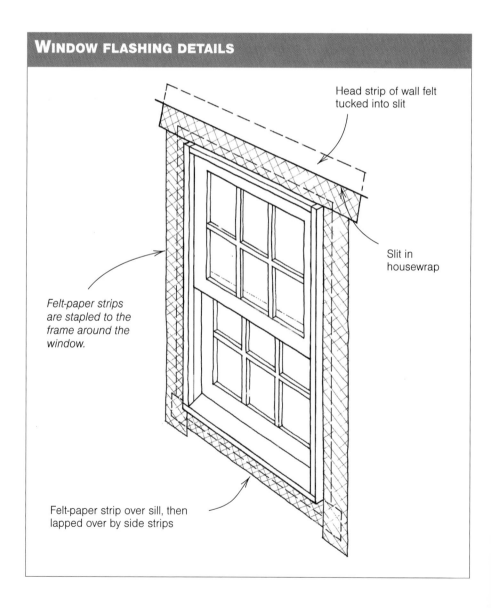

Head strip of wall felt tucked into slit

Slit in housewrap

Felt-paper strips are stapled to the frame around the window.

Felt-paper strip over sill, then lapped over by side strips

dow, move inside and seal the gap between the window frame and the wood framing with nonexpanding foam. Don't use expanding foam, which can bow trimmers and frames out of shape. Then open and close the window a few times to make sure it works with ease.

Setting exterior and interior doors

We've all lived in houses that have doors that stick, locks that are misaligned, and hinges that creak. After years of use, doors and windows that open and close with ease indicate that the folks who built the house knew and cared about what they were doing.

The majority of doors used these days are prehung and are installed much the same way as windows (see the sidebar on p. 178). Both doors and windows can be ordered with jambs wide enough for 2x4 or 2x6 walls (see the photo at right) and are usually available with factory-applied trim. Begin installing one of these units by stapling strips of felt paper around the opening. Then apply a good-sized bead of silicone caulk under the door sill and around the opening under the factory-applied trim.

An easy place for rot to develop is under the door sill, so take extra precautions to seal this area. I get several calls a year from people who want their rotted sill or floor replaced. Lay down a couple of layers of felt paper, lapping them up the trimmers and down over the outside edge. Do the same with some 10-in. metal flashing, cutting it into place with tin snips.

With the door placed in its opening, check to see if the sill is resting flat on the floor. If the floor isn't level, the low jamb side will have to be shimmed so that the door won't hit the head jamb when closed. I like to cut a long, thin shim under the sill so it will have good bearing.

Part of the job of installing a prehung door is to lay a good-sized bead of silicone caulk under the door sill and around the opening under the factory-applied trim. (Photo by Charles Miller.)

Take time to ensure that the door will open and close with ease. On prehung doors, there should be about a ⅛-in. gap between the door and the jamb head and sides. On exterior doors, the weatherstrip should seal at the bottom without binding.

1. Check to see that the floor is level and the trimmers are plumb.

2. Apply felt paper and caulk to exterior doors to prevent leaks.

3. Set the door frame in the opening. If the floor isn't level, pick up a jamb leg so that the door won't stick on the jamb head when closed.

4. Check to see that door jamb edges are flush with the face of the drywall.

5. Check that there is about a 1/8-in. gap between the jambs and the door and that the door opens and closes freely.

6. Nail the hinge side first, directly to the plumb trimmer.

7. Nail the lock side to the trimmer; shim where necessary.

8. Nail through the door casings into the exterior wall.

9. Cross-sight so that jamb sides are parallel.

If you have a pneumatic nailer, fasten the jamb to the trimmer stud with 8d nails. Sinking the fasteners behind the weatherstrip helps to hide the nail holes.

SHIMMING

Shims are time-consuming to use and tend to fall out as wood shrinks. You can eliminate shims if you use the clipping technique to hold trimmers securely in place (see p. 130). Clipping will also allow you to nail the jamb directly to the trimmer.

For many years, trim carpenters have been using drywall screws in place of shims. Screws work as adjustable shims. They can be driven into the bottom plate, for example, to hold baseboard plumb and square. You can also use screws to help level, plumb, and square cabinets as you install them. On the rare occasion when I need a shim (as when I want to pry two boards apart), I can quickly make one by ripping a slice off the edge of a 2x.

If you set the trimmers plumb so that the rough opening is $\frac{1}{4}$ in. larger than the door-frame assembly, you should have enough room to move and adjust the frame slightly. If the trimmers weren't set plumb, you have to plumb and shim every jamb, making sure they are straight and true.

The door has to be open when nails are driven through the jambs. Usually I nail or screw the hinge side of the jamb to the trimmer stud first with an 8d nail or screw gun, sinking the fasteners behind the weatherstrip near the hinges (see the photo on the facing page). Later, these holes can be filled and painted. Nailing through the exterior casing (just like with wood windows) further stabilizes the door frame.

There will be about a $\frac{1}{4}$-in. gap on the lock side of the door between the framing and the jamb, so this side needs to be shimmed to keep it straight and in place for the life of the house. I carry 3-in. by 3-in. blocks of $\frac{1}{8}$-in., $\frac{3}{16}$-in., or $\frac{1}{4}$-in. plywood to use for shims. If you use shingles for shims, be sure to push them in from both sides so you have a level bed to nail the jamb against (for more on shimming, see the sidebar above). The thin plywood blocks seem more solid to me, and I place them about 6 in. from the top and bottom, as well as one above and one below the door latch. These too can be secured with nails or screws hidden behind the weatherstripping.

Keep closing the door to make sure the $\frac{1}{8}$-in. gap is maintained between the jamb and the door. Once the frame is nailed securely in place, check once again to make sure that the door opens and closes with ease.

While much the same process is used to set interior prehung doors, they don't have a sill, which makes them floppy and harder to handle. Again, I like to set the hinge side first, hard against the trimmer. Jambs should be flush with the drywall on each side of the opening, because any irregularity here makes it harder to install door casing.

Nail these jambs off by driving five sets of 6d finish nails toward the edges of the jambs, one close to the top, one close to the bottom, and three sets spaced evenly between. I also replace one screw from each hinge going into the jamb with a longer 2-in. screw so that the trimmer supports the door and not just the jamb. End by cross-sighting the jambs to ensure that they are parallel (for more on cross-sighting, see the sidebar on p. 180).

Cross-sighting ensures that a door fits accurately in its frame because the jambs are parallel to each other. You can cross-sight with strings, pulling two from corner to corner diagonally across the frame. If the strings just touch in the middle, the jamb sides are parallel. A faster way to do this is by eyeballing. Stand beside the wall about 3 ft. from the frame and sight along the side jambs to see if they line up with each other from top to bottom (see the drawing below).

When a house frame has been well plumbed and lined, jambs cross-sight easily. If the jambs aren't parallel, place a 2x block against the bottom plate near the frame and hammer it until the wall moves enough so that both jamb sides line up. Then drive a 16d toenail into the bottom plate to hold it in place. If the jambs are terribly out of parallel, check to see what the problem is—the wall might be badly out of plumb and need correction.

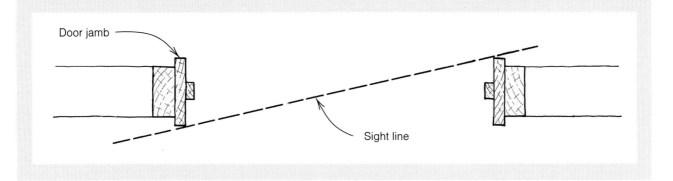

Door jamb

Sight line

Installing door hardware

Most prehung doors and their jambs are predrilled and premortised to accept the door lockset and dead bolt. Even then, you might need to whittle and adjust to install the lockset accurately. Although every lockset comes with installation instructions, here are the basic steps that I follow.

If the door is predrilled, insert the spring-bolt latch into its hole and mark around the outside of the face plate. I do this with a utility knife or sharp pencil to get a close fit. Remove the latch and carefully mortise with a sharp chisel to a depth equal to the thickness of the faceplate (about 1/8 in.). Then reinsert the latch into the hole, fit the faceplate into the mortise, and screw it flush with the door edge. If the door edge is pre-

mortised, chisel out the corners so they are square before installing the latch. The knob assembly slips through the spring-bolt latch, and two longer bolts hold the knobs together (see the photo on the facing page).

Next install the strike plate. If it's premortised, fit it in place just like the latch. It's best to predrill the screw holes here so you don't split the jamb. If the jamb isn't premortised, place the strike plate over the hole and trace around it as you did for the latch bolt, then carefully mortise within the traced lines to a depth of about 1/16 in.—the thickness of the strike plate.

After the knob assembly is slipped into the door, screw two long bolts in to hold the knobs together.

It's often hard to get the strike plate to set correctly. When things are right, the door shuts and locks and is held firmly against the door stop or weatherstripping. Many strike plates have a lip that protrudes down into the jamb hole. So if the door rattles back and forth, you can bend this lip outward a bit until the latch fits firmly against it. If the latch won't quite drop into the strike hole, try using a flat file to remove a bit of the metal along the front edge of the metal plate.

If this doesn't work, the strike plate itself may have to be moved. Measure in on the door edge (door-stop side) to the flat side of the latch. On the jamb, place the tape measure against the stop and transfer the measurement taken above to locate the front inside of the strike plate. If the strike plate is remounted, the extra holes will have to be filled so that they can be sanded and painted.

Victorian houses are well known for their intricate and elaborate exterior trim, which is beautiful to see but difficult to maintain. (Photo by Charles Miller.)

EXTERIOR TRIM

I live near several Victorian houses, which are notable for their intricate and extensive exterior trim. While I admire the craftsmanship on these houses, I'm always thankful that I'm not the one responsible for their upkeep.

In this section, I'll talk about cutting and installing basic exterior trim. While it may not be as ornate as the trim on a Victorian beauty, it's far less time-consuming to install and maintain, which is an important consideration in our fast-paced world. There are many ways to trim a house, and a house that looks quite ordinary can suddenly take on a whole new character just by using another style of trim.

Building soffits

Soffits are used to cover exposed rafter tails and roof overhangs. West of the Mississippi, the tendency is to leave the eaves open with rafters exposed. In the East, houses often have a soffit that fills the gap between the fascia and the wall. Many of these soffits are quite elaborate and ornate, but the trend in house building is toward simplicity. Elaborate soffits require a lot of material, special moldings, and considerable labor and cost to build.

EAVE WITH SOFFIT

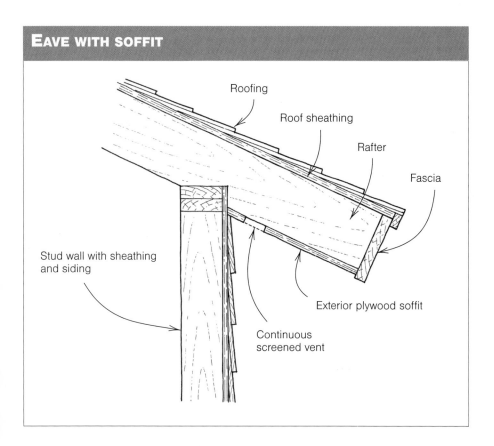

Roofing

Roof sheathing

Rafter

Fascia

Stud wall with sheathing
and siding

Exterior plywood soffit

Continuous
screened vent

The drawing above shows an easy soffit to build. It has rafter tails cut square, and once the fascia is nailed to the tails, the rafters can be sheathed with exterior plywood, 1x cedar or pine, or even covered with stucco. A common way to cover this soffit is to take a long board, butt it against the fascia, and nail it to the rafter tails with 8d galvanized nails or drywall screws. Break all joints over a rafter tail so the ends can be nailed into it. Then install a strip of continuous screened vent (the vent has a lip that fits under wood and is easy to install). Next, nail in a second board to fill the gap between the vent and the wall.

If you cut the rafter tails plumb, you can build a level soffit (see the drawing on p. 184). To prepare for this soffit, install a subfascia or cut a ¾-in. groove in the fascia during framing. Next, level over from the bottom of the subfascia or top

of the groove to the wall and make a mark on each end of the building. Connect these two marks with a chalk-line and nail 2x stock flat against the wall along the line with a 16d nail into each stud. If you plan on installing a continuous vent—or if the distance between the wall 2x and the subfascia or groove is more than 16 in.—nail short joists between these two points every 16 in. or 24 in. Now you can cover the soffit as described previously.

There are many ways to close in the ends of a soffit. One way is to let the wall covering extend over it. The overhang at the gable end of the building, running from the eave to the ridge, can be covered much the same way, especially if the barge rafter is supported by 2x lookouts. Nail in a few more flat 2xs, one at the fascia and another at the ridge. Now you can cut soffit stock,

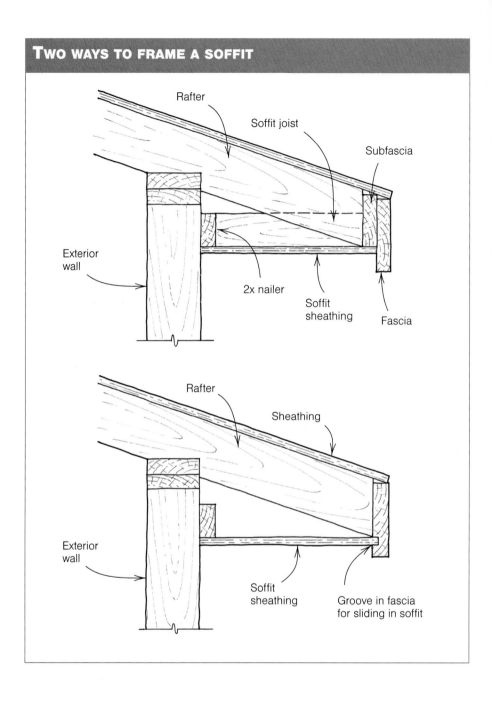

TWO WAYS TO FRAME A SOFFIT

Rafter

Soffit joist

Subfascia

Exterior wall

2x nailer

Soffit sheathing

Fascia

Rafter

Sheathing

Exterior wall

Soffit sheathing

Groove in fascia for sliding in soffit

plywood, or siding boards to the width of the overhang and nail it to the look-outs running up the gable end. Fit the stock tight to the barge rafter, but don't worry if it fits loosely against the wall, because this joint can be covered by siding and trim. Use 6d galvanized nails or screws, because they won't go through the sleepers and into the roof covering.

Installing exterior trim

Trim makes a house look neat and inviting. It helps give a house its distinctive look. Use good, straight, kiln-dried stock and install it with care so that it will last a long time with little maintenance.

This book deals with just a few of the basic trim options. To begin, I often use 1x cedar or pine for corner boards,

At the corners, I often nail a 1x3 on one side and install a 1x4 on the opposite side so that it laps the 1x3. Once lapped, both trim pieces look like a 1x4. (Photo by Roe A. Osborn.)

around windows, and where the siding meets the frieze blocks. But thicker stock is available for trim. It's common to see four-quarter (true 1 in.) material, five-quarter (1¼ in.), or even 2x (1½ in.) trim. Most types of siding —particularly lap siding (clapboards)—fit better against thicker trim stock. The thicker stock stands out farther from the building and hides the ends of the siding.

Houses seem to look better with corner boards, which define the house's outlines and are easy to install. Starting at a gable-end corner, use a small rafter square to scribe the roof pitch (4-in-12, for example) on one end of a corner board and make the cut. Place this piece against the building, flush with the wall edge and butted up to the roof sheathing or soffit (see the photo above).

Corner boards extend down onto the foundation, ½ in. or so below the rim joist or sill plate. So mark at this point and cut the corner board to length. Nail it flush with the corner of the building—or even ¹⁄₁₆ in. proud—with 8d hot-dipped galvanized nails. Other options for fastening exterior trim include noncorrosive aluminum nails, stainless-steel nails, or galvanized drywall screws. Try nailing a few scrap 1x cleats up the opposing wall to butt the corner board to, because the actual corner, once it is wrapped with building paper, is often hard to locate precisely.

Pull the cleats off and you're ready to start on the other side of the corner. This piece runs from beneath the end rafter, soffit, or frieze block to the same distance below the sill, and laps over the

first corner board. To make the corner symmetrical, be sure to rip the thickness of the trim stock off the first board before nailing it into place. If you're using 3½-in.-wide by ¾-in.-thick stock, for example, rip ¾ in. off the first piece of trim (or 1¼ in. off 4-in. by 1¼-in. stock). When the second piece of trim is nailed over it at the corner, both pieces will be the same width. After marking it and cutting it to length, nail it to the wall and to the other corner board. Some carpenters connect this joint with waterproof glue. Take care driving nails into the edge of the first board so that it doesn't split out; angling the nails in toward the corner can help. Trim out the remaining outside corners the same way.

Inside corners trim out a bit differently. I often use a piece of 2x2 (1½ in. by 1½ in.) and nail it directly into the corner from the rafter down, overlapping the foundation by ½ in. The siding can butt directly to this board from either direction, leaving a bit of corner trim showing.

If the windows and doors aren't already cased, now is the time. Clad windows often are trimmed picture-frame style (with mitered corners) using a type of trim known as brickmold. The trim boards are nailed snugly against the window frame to cover the flange. Framing a window is pretty straightforward: Cut one 45° miter on a piece of trim, place it in position, mark it for length, and then cut a 45° miter at the other end. I find it easier to hold a board up to the window and measure it in place rather than using a tape measure (see the photo at left). Repeat this process all the way around, nailing the trim in place with 8d galvanized finish nails staggered and spaced 16 in. o.c. Finish the process by nailing through the miters to close them up and hold them in place.

After fitting the miter joint at the top, scribe the miter on the bottom. Mark the miter cut at the window corner and make the cut. (Photo by Roe A. Osborn.)

If the trim is to be painted, prime or paint the end grain of these miter joints to keep water from soaking into the trim. You can also put a bit of caulk or waterproof glue, such as Gorilla Glue (see Sources on p. 198) at this point before nailing the joint together.

Nailing trim over flanges can be a problem. The thickness of the flange can cause the trim to tip and open up the miter joint. Try slipping thin strips of wood behind the trim to bring the nailing surface up level with the flange. All of these tasks take time, but this is trim that will be seen by everyone. Taking the time to do it right shows you care about your work.

It's a good idea to install either wood drip edge or aluminum flashing at the top of horizontal trim (for example, at the top of a window). Both are quick and easy to install and help divert water away from the wood underneath. A kerf, or groove, cut in the underside of wood sills and drip edge helps prevent water from creeping back into the wall.

If using a wider casing, try butting the joints instead of mitering. Wood has a tendency to move as it dries out and the house settles, which makes miter joints open up. Let the top and bottom pieces run past the opening and the side pieces butt up to them. I sometimes run a 1½-in.-thick piece at the top and bottom and 5/4 (1¼ in. thick) stock between. This creates a reveal, which, unlike a flush surface, can dry out and move and still look good.

EXTERIOR BEVEL SIDING

Unlike framing, where you can leave a small gap now and then, siding needs to fit properly everywhere. If the horizontal boards are running out of level or don't fit well at the corners, doors, and windows, it's noticeable from the next county. Not only do gaps in siding look bad, but they also might allow water and cold air to enter the building.

While there are many different types of siding styles and materials available, in this section I'll talk about how to apply bevel (or clapboard) siding. Years ago, clear redwood, cedar, and spruce siding were widely available. These were easy to work, free of knots, looked good, and stayed flat. Unfortunately, such quality siding isn't readily available these days. Most of what we have to work with comes from second-, third-, or fourth-growth trees, often curls in the sun, and is *spendy* (as we say in Oregon). Because of this, many builders use a wood or cement-base composite siding made of OSB. This manufactured siding is preprimed and 7/16 in. thick with no taper. It ranges from 6 in. to 12 in. wide and is available in lengths of 16 ft. and longer. If using composite siding, read and follow the manufacturer's recommendations for specific application instructions.

Siding should be nailed into studs whenever possible, rather than relying on ½-in. plywood or OSB sheathing to hold the nail. So the first thing to do is mark stud locations on the housewrap. The best way to do this is to mark the stud layout at the top and bottom of the wall, then snap vertical chalklines at these marks.

1½ in., leaving a 6½-in. exposure. This ensures that moisture won't wick up behind the siding. So on the story pole, measure up 6½ in. and mark across the 1x2. Then make a mark at every 6½-in. point from there at 13 in., 19½ in., 26 in., and so on. These marks indicate the bottom of every course.

There is another consideration when laying out siding. Frequently you can adjust the courses a bit so that the bottom of one course of siding fits directly on top of the window. Another course can be adjusted so that it lines up with the bottom of the window. This looks better to the eye and reduces the amount of cutting you have to do. So instead of a 1½-in. lap, you may need to lap a few of the bottom courses 1¾ in. Then you may need to change the lap to 1⅜ in. to come even with the top of the window. The story pole is a handy place to mark these adjustments. Make course changes gradually. The eyes rarely notice a ¼-in. change in exposure from one course to the next.

With the layout on the story pole complete, transfer the marks on it to each piece of vertical house trim. Take it to the corner, hold it flush with the bottom of the trim, and transfer the marks (see the photo at left). Do the same at the side trim around doors and windows.

Transfer the marks on the story pole to each piece of vertical house trim. The marks will ensure that the siding will be the same height on all sides of the house. (Photo by Roe A. Osborn.)

Laying out siding

To ensure that each course (or row) of siding is the same height, make a story pole from a straight length of 1x2. Cut it to the same length as the corner trim that runs from the frieze blocks to ½ in. down onto the foundation. If you're using 8-in.-wide lap siding, for example, each successive course of siding will overlap the previous course by at least

Installing siding

Composite siding has a single row of nails driven about 1 in. from the top, hidden by the second row. Other types of lap siding nail near the bottom of the course, about 1 in. from the butt. You have to be careful when using a pneumatic nailer for this job. If the pressure is too high, the nail could be driven too deep, breaking the surface of the siding, compromising the nail's holding power and leaving a place where water can enter. When installing siding with a hammer, use hot-dipped galvanized nails or stainless-steel, ring-

8d galvanized nails 1 in. from the top of each course and spaced 16 in. o.c.

8-in. siding board

Nailed into studs

1½-in. overlap

6½-in. exposure

1-in.-wide starter piece

Siding extends below starter 1 in.

To begin the installation of horizontal lap siding, nail on a ⁷⁄₁₆-in.-thick by 1-in.-wide strip at the very bottom of the wall, flush with the bottom of the sill plate. Just remember to prime all raw edges for moisture protection. (Photo by Roe A. Osborn.)

nail flush with the bottom sill plate and tip the first course of siding out so that it will match successive rows (see the drawing at left). Rip these strips from siding boards. They don't have to be ripped perfectly because they will be hidden by the first course of siding. It's a good idea to keep a paint bucket handy and cover all raw edges to protect them from moisture.

Actually cutting and nailing up the siding is a process I always find exciting. The house is finally being closed in against the weather and begins to take on a finished look (see the left photo on p. 190). Composite-siding manufacturers recommend that both ends of the siding be held back ³⁄₁₆ in. from the trim to allow for expansion and waterproof-

shanked nails. Other, thinner types of beveled wood siding can be nailed on with 4d or 5d nails.

Regardless of whether you use an air nailer or a hammer, the first step is the same. Install ⁷⁄₁₆-in.-thick by 1-in.-wide strips along the bottom of the walls (see the photo above). These starter pieces

Once the siding begins going up, the house acquires a more finished look. However, it's important that siding be primed on all sides, including the back and especially the cut ends to prevent moisture problems. (Photo by Roe A. Osborn.)

Where a great deal of rain is likely, it's a good idea to tack 4-in. by 12-in. felt strips behind all butt joints on horizontal siding. These strips provide extra protection against moisture intrusion. (Photo by Andrew Engel.)

ing. This is a big gap for finish work, but it leaves enough room for a good bead of caulk to help keep water out. A smooth bead of paintable, latex-silicone caulk will be hard to notice once it is painted.

In my experience, the expansion and contraction of composite siding in most parts of the country is minimal. You may be able to put a bead of caulk underneath the siding and fit it tight to the

trim, which is what I sometimes do when installing wood bevel siding. In cases like this, take time to talk to builders and carpenters in your area and see what they recommend for the particular type of siding that you are using.

Start on a side of the building where you can begin with full-length pieces. As a general rule (and this applies to studs, rafters, headers, siding, or any work that a carpenter does), always start with the

To match the angle of the roof on the gable ends so that the siding fits perfectly against the roof sheathing, make a template that matches the roof pitch. Use the template to carefully scribe the cutlines on each piece of siding. (Photo by Roe A. Osborn.)

longest pieces first, because the cutoff ends can normally be used elsewhere. If you cut the short pieces first, you may not have enough long stock left to complete the job. Remember to cut the siding so that the ends fall over studs for secure nailing.

Because these cuts need to be made accurately and cleanly, this is a good place to use a sliding compound miter saw. If you use a circular saw, cut from the back side to prevent tearout on the front side. Use a small rafter square as a guide for your circular saw to help make a square and accurate cut.

On sections longer than 16 ft., snap horizontal chalklines to keep the courses straight. While composite siding is quite uniform, wood siding can have crowns and twists that can be straightened by nailing them to a chalkline. In areas that get a lot of wind and rain, many builders

cut 4-in. by 12-in. strips of felt paper and slip one behind every joint where two pieces of siding abut (see the right photo on the facing page).

Cutting siding to fit the gable ends is a bit more difficult than sidewalls, because the cuts are no longer square. To mark these cuts, which are the same pitch as the roof, make a simple pattern from a piece of siding that's cut to the roof pitch (see the photo above). Use a small trim saw for making these cuts and clean them up with a block plane.

Working up the gable end, measure down 1½ in. (the amount composite siding laps) from the top of the last installed board at each end. A measurement with the tape held along these marks will give you the long point of the next board. An easier way to do this is to mark the lap on each board before it is nailed in place. Lay the next board on

Above openings, install a filler strip to prevent the next course of siding from tipping inward when nailed. It's also a good idea to caulk the tops and sides of window and door openings before nailing on the siding. (Photo by Andrew Engel.)

these lines and mark it to length, which eliminates the need to drag out your measuring tape. Now you can place the template on these points, scribe cut marks on the siding, make the cuts, and nail the piece in place. If you can't get a perfect fit between siding and roof or eave soffit, you can cover this gap later with trim, which can be as simple as a 1x2 or 1x3 nailed on top of the siding.

Cutting around doors, windows, and gable-end vents needs to be done neatly and carefully. At the top of openings, install a filler strip to tip the lap siding out (see the photo above). And remember to caulk joints around window and door openings. Caulk, unlike diamonds, is not forever, but it does help repel water. Caulk carefully at the tops and sides of windows and doors before nailing on siding.

INTERIOR TRIM

Once the drywall is up and the painters have sealed and finished the walls, the task of installing interior trim, window surrounds, casing, baseboard, and aprons can be started. Years ago we used to trim with wide baseboards, fancy casings, and elaborate crown moldings. While big-budget houses still often have these material- and labor-intensive trim details, the trend for more modest houses has been toward simpler and less expensive trim styles.

Trimming windows

Unlike wood-framed windows, most vinyl-clad and aluminum-framed units don't come with wood stools (often called sills) or wood jambs. Some people put in a wood stool and let drywall cover the wood trimmers and header. I like to make wood surrounds, or jambs, and

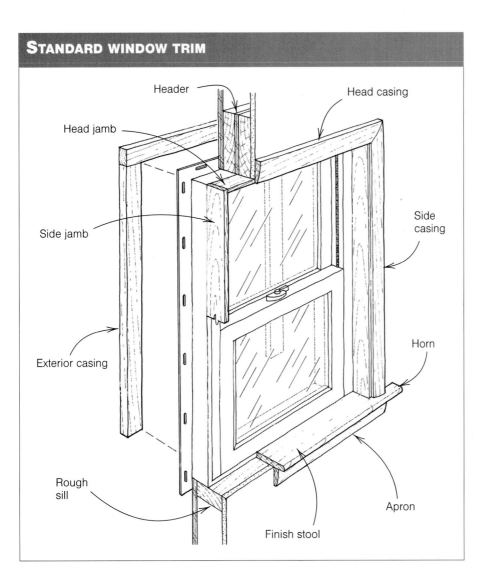

Header

Head casing

Head jamb

Side casing

Side jamb

Exterior casing

Horn

Rough sill

Apron

Finish stool

case them with trim. I think the wood gives a home a bit more warmth and style, and it's not hard to do.

I usually install the stool first. I like to use thicker material for this piece of trim (like 4/4 or 5/4 stock). Oak, pine, or spruce make beautiful stools that can be stained or finished clear, or you can use paint-grade pine or even medium-density fiberboard (MDF). The overall length of the stool is equal to the width of the window opening plus the length of the horns (ears that extend out beyond the casing). The length of these

horns depends on the width of the side casings, plus the amount the horns extend beyond the casings, usually about ¾ in. (see the drawing above).

As a general rule, stools are wide enough to protrude about 1½ in. beyond the wall plane. But this can vary, and the window stool I have by my writing desk sticks out beyond the wall 3½ in. and is wide enough to hold an open book. Many folks like an even wider stool in the kitchen to set flower pots in the sun.

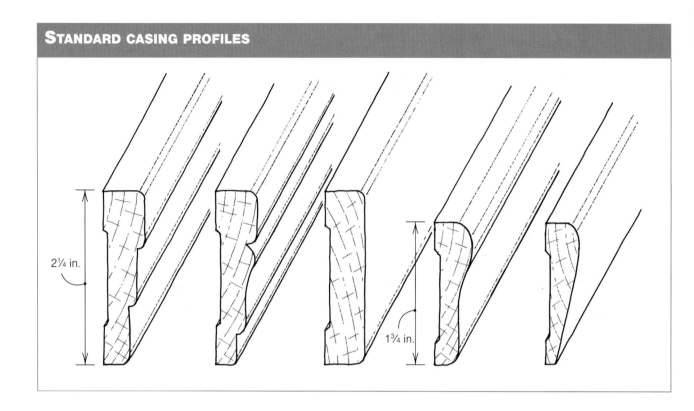

After cutting the stool to length and laying out and cutting the horns, test fit it against the window. You want to make sure that the edge fits tightly against the window and that the horns fit tightly against the drywall; sometimes it takes some work with a block plane to get everything right. Although this is simple trim, every piece of trim in a house needs to fit just right to account for irregularities in the walls, floors, and ceilings.

Windows can often be ordered with jambs for specific wall thicknesses (for example, 2x4 or 2x6 construction), but sometimes you'll need to cut and add jambs on the job. First, measure in from the face of the wall surface to the window frame in several places around the window. If these measurements are close, you can rip stock to this uniform width. I generally use a table saw and clean up the cut with a block plane. If the measurements vary widely, cut to

length a head piece that is wider than the wall thickness, then hold it in place at the top of the window and scribe a cutline by running a pencil along the drywall. Repeat the procedure with the side jambs. Jambs can stick out past the drywall about 1/16 in. to make a tight joint with the casing. Once properly fitted, nail the jamb head and sides to the rough header and trimmers with 6d finish nails.

Installing casing

Casing hides the joint between the drywall and door jamb or window surround. It comes in many styles, from 1x square-edged stock in varying widths to milled casings (see the drawing above). When casing doors, I buy 14-ft. lengths to cut down on waste. Sometimes door casing is available in 7-ft. pieces that have a 45° miter already cut on one end. Like exterior casings, doors and windows can be either picture-framed (with 45° miters at the corners) or wider trim can

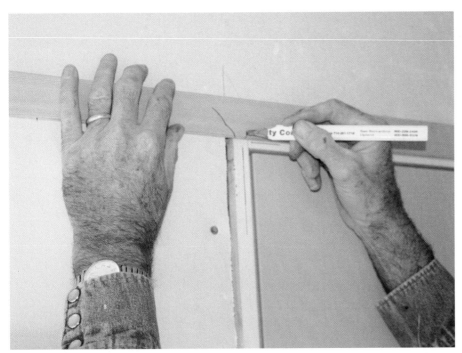

Instead of using a tape measure, get more accurate measurements by holding the casing stock in place and marking it.

be butt jointed. I generally nail casing back from the edge of the jamb about 3/16 in. to leave a reveal.

Reveals make life easier for a carpenter. When wood pieces are nailed flush, they absorb moisture or dry out, moving back and forth in the process, so that flush pieces seldom stay flush. Carpenters learned long ago to step casings back from the door edge 3/16 in. or so. This creates an attractive shadow line and makes it hard to see variations.

Install the side casings first. The short point of the miter should stop 3/16 in. past the top of the inside edge of the head door jamb or window surround. Rather than use a tape measure, hold and mark the casing stock in place (see the photo above). Mark the 3/16-in. reveal from the inside edge of the jamb in several places and nail the casing into the wall and the jamb with a pair of 6d

finish nails about every 16 in. Don't drive these nails home like a 16d framing nail, but let them stick up (proud) slightly above the face of the wood, setting them later with a nailset so they can be hidden with putty in preparation for painting. Or you can use an air nailer that drives and sets finish nails. If you are using hardwood casing, you may have to predrill to avoid splits.

Once the side pieces are in place, it's easy to find the length of the top piece. Cut a miter on one end of the top piece and match it to the miters on the side pieces to see if the cut is accurate. Then hold it in place to mark the location of the second miter. Before nailing it in place, a dab of glue in the joints will make for a long-lasting miter joint.

A window apron, usually made from casing material, is nailed under the stool to hide the joint between drywall and sill. Measure across the window casing

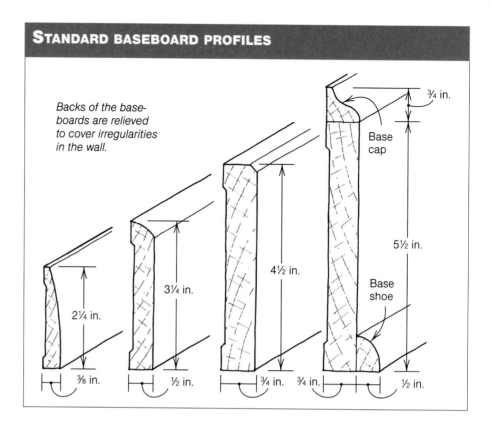

STANDARD BASEBOARD PROFILES

*Backs of the base-
boards are relieved
to cover irregularities
in the wall.*

¾ in.

Base
cap

5½ in.

Base
shoe

2¼ in.

3¼ in.

4½ in.

⅜ in.

½ in.

¾ in.

¾ in.

½ in.

from outside to outside to get the length of the apron. There are several ways to finish off the end of aprons. You can cut them square or give them a 15° back cut and nail them directly below the windowsill.

Installing baseboard

Baseboard hides the joint between the drywall and the floor, so most finish floors are installed before the baseboard. On carpeted floors, baseboard can be installed ahead of time, but hold it up about ½ in. so the carpet can tuck underneath.

Baseboard comes in many different styles, ranging from simple flat stock of various widths to milled trim to built-up baseboards composed of two or more pieces (see the drawing above). It's best to buy long lengths so there will be fewer joints. Start installation on long

walls first, opposite the door, cutting a piece square on each end to fit from wall to wall. Work from this piece toward the door, making the final cut a square one against the casing. Thin, modern trim can be nailed with 6d finish nails directly into the bottom plate about every 16 in. Wider, thicker trim needs further nailing into studs to draw it tightly against the wall. Mark the location of these studs before nailing.

Unfortunately, walls and floors are seldom totally straight and level. While simple baseboards are thin and bend easily to conform to irregularities, heavier moldings will need to be scribed and planed to fit the wall and floor contours. The use of base caps and base shoes is another solution to this problem. They can be flexed to fit tightly against the wall and floor surface without scribing. When the baseboard will be

Nowadays, baseboards are usually fitted together at outside corners by using regular 45° miter cuts on each piece. And many carpenters do inside corners the same way. But traditionally, inside corners have been joined, particularly with detailed baseboards, with what is called a coped joint (see the photo below). While these joints may look tricky, they aren't hard to do. In fact, I find cutting these joints to be kind of fun.

First, cut a 45° miter on the end of a piece of trim that will fit in the corner against the baseboard that is already nailed in place. Then, with a coping saw, cut along the outline of the exposed end grain, tipping the saw back a few degrees to give the wood a slight back cut (see the drawing below). This allows the leading edge of the coped cut to fit crisply and cleanly against the installed baseboard, making a tight-fitting joint that won't open up.

This joint is also useful for other situations where different types of trim, such as a chair rail, meet at a corner.

Coping trim at inside corners creates a tight-fitting joint.

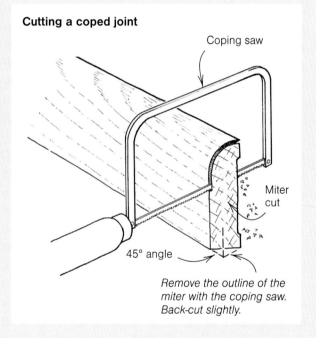

Cutting a coped joint

Coping saw

Miter cut

45° angle

Remove the outline of the miter with the coping saw. Back-cut slightly.

painted, builders often fill the gap between the baseboard and the wall with paintable latex caulk.

I have a lightweight chopsaw that I use to cut baseboard. I carry it from room to room, set it on the floor, and cut baseboards to length on the spot.

Some painting needs to be done, cabinets set, closets finished, and electrical, plumbing, and heating work completed, but the end is in sight. You can start thinking about moving in, baking bread in your oven, and planting some roses outside.

SOURCES

HAND TOOLS
Empire Level Corp.
Box 868
Waukesha, WI 53186
(800) 648-7654

Stanley Tools
14117 Industrial Park Blvd.
Covington, GA 30209
(800) 648-7654

Zircon Corp.
1580 Dell Ave.
Campbell, CA 95008
(800) 245-9265

POWER TOOLS
Black and Decker
701 E. Joppa Rd.
Towson, MD 21286
(410) 685-3390

Bosch-Skil Corp.
4300 W. Peterson Rd.
Chicago, IL 60646
(312) 286-7330

DeWalt Tool Co.
Box 158
Hampstead, MD 21074
(410) 685-3390

Makita Tools
14930 Northern St.
La Mirada, CA 90638
(800) 462-5482

Milwaukee Tool Corp.
13135 W. Lisbon Rd.
Brookfield, WI 53005
(414) 781-3600

Porter Cable
Box 2468
Jackson, TN 38305
(800) 321-9443

RotoZip Corp.
1861 Ludden Dr.
Cross Plains, WI 53528
(800) 411-5571

HAMMERS
Dalluge Tools
2217 S. Laura Linda
Santa Ana, CA 92704
(714) 546-5298

Hart Tool Co.
13120 Arctic Circle
Santa Fe Springs, CA 90670
(800) 331-4495

Ted Hammers
6152 Mission Gorge Rd.
San Diego, CA 92120
(800) 645-2434

PNEUMATIC NAILERS
Danair, Inc.
Box 3898
Visalia, CA 93278
(800) 232-6247

Hitachi Koki Tools
3950 Steve Reynolds Blvd.
Norcross, GA 30093
(770) 925-1774

Pacific Construction Sales, Inc.
857 Thorton St.
San Leandro, CA 94577
(510) 614-0765

Senco
8485 Broadwell Rd.
Cincinnati, OH 45244
(800) 543-4596

TOOL HOLDERS
Diamond Back USA
Box 347179
San Francisco, CA 94134
(800) 899-2358

Occidental Leather
60 W. 6th St.
Santa Rosa, CA 95401
(707) 522-2500

JAPANESE TOOLS
Hida Tool & Hardware
1333 San Pablo Ave.
Berkeley, CA 94702
(510) 524-3700

Japan Woodworker
1731 Clement Ave.
Alameda, CA 94501
(510) 521-1886

Takagi Tools, Inc.
337-A Figueroa St.
Wilmington, CA 90744
(714) 557-3663

MISCELLANEOUS TOOLS AND SUPPLIERS
Big Foot Saw Adapters, Inc.
Box 92244
Hendersen, NV 89015
(702) 565-9954
Allows you to safely use a 10-in. blade on a 7¼-in. worm-drive saw.

Calculated Industries
4840 Hy Tech
Carson City, NV 89706
(800) 854-8075
Handheld calculators and estimating tools.

Faspac, Inc.
13909 N.W. Third Ct.
Vancouver, WA 98685
(800) 847-4714
A wide variety of self-tapping screws.

Gorilla Glue
Box 42532
Santa Barbara, CA 93140
(805) 963-2234
All-purpose, easy-to-use polyurethane glue.

Griset Industries, Inc.
Box 10114
Santa Ana, CA 92711
(800) 662-2892
Saw guide with clamps for cutting material up to 8 ft. long.

Insty-Bit
2310 Chestnut Ave.
Minneapolis, MN 55405
(612) 381-1060
Easy-to-use bits for drilling pilot and countersink holes with a quick-change adapter.

Judson Enterprises
1642 Baltimore Pl.
Escondido, CA 92025
(619) 741-9895
Compact, T-handle screwdriver.

Linear Link
2347 Whithall Rd.
Muskegon, MI 49445
(800) 635-5465
Chainsaw adapter for a circular saw.

McFeely's Tools
Box 11169
Lynchburg, VA 24506
(800) 443-7937
Square-drive screws, nail and tool holders, sandpaper, sawblades, as well as construction books.

National Nail Corp.
2964 Clydon SW
Grand Rapids, MI 49509
(800) 746-5659
Specialized nails and hammer to attach exterior insulating sheets and housewrap.

New England Products
348 Dover Pt. Rd.
Dover, NH 03820
(603) 749-1230
Plastic clips to store cords, hoses, and tools.

Olive Knot Products
Box 188
Corning, CA 96021
(916) 824-5280
Saw guide for cutting material up to 8 ft. long.

Oxi-Solve, Inc.
12055 Universal Dr.
Taylor, MI 48180
(800) 594-9028
Biodegradable tool cleaner.

Pairis Enterprises
2151 Maple Privado
Ontario, CA 91761
(909) 923-7742
Specialized tools like the layout stick for framers.

Portable Products
5200 Quincy St.
St. Paul, MN 55112
(800) 688-2677
Nail aprons, cloth, and plastic tool organizers.

Prazi Beam Cutter
118 Long Pond Rd.
Plymouth, MA 02360
(800) 262-0211
Chainsaw adapter kit for circular saws.

Proctor Products Co., Inc.
210 8th St. S.
Kirkland, WA 98033
(425) 822-9296
Wall jacks for raising heavy framed walls.

Qual-Craft Industries
Box 559
Stoughton, MA 02072
(800) 231-5647
Wall jacks for raising heavy framed walls.

R&A Tool Co.
935 American St.
San Carlos, CA 94070
(415) 593-0946
An attachment for a circular saw that blows sawdust from the cut line.

Simpson Strong-Tie Co.
Box 1586
San Leandro, CA 94577
(800) 999-5099
Wide variety of metal building hardware.

Trus-Joist Corp.
Box 60
Boise, ID 83707
(208) 364-1200
Manufactured floor and roof joists.

Utility Composites, Inc.
3925 W. Braker Ln.
Austin, TX 78759
(512) 305-0270
Plastic nails for pneumatic nailers.

BOOKS

Brand, Stewart. *How Buildings Learn.* New York, NY: Penguin Books, 1995. *What happens to buildings after they are built.*

Haun, Larry. *The Very Efficient Carpenter.* Newtown, CT: The Taunton Press, Inc., 1992. *A step-by-step manual on advanced framing.*

Harwood, Barbara Bannon. *The Healing House.* Hay House, Inc., Box 5100, Carlsbad, CA 92018. *Thoughts about building houses for people instead of just for profit.*

Manning, Richard. *A Good House.* New York, NY: Grove Press, 1993. *The daily joys and troubles of building your own home.*

Mussell, Barry. *Roof Framers Bible.* Box 2065, Stockbridge, GA 30281: M.E.I. Publishing, 1994. *Gives rafter lengths for both equal and unequal pitched roofs.*

Sloane, Eric. *Sketches of America Past.* New York, NY: Promontory Press, 1986. *Offers a reverence for the wood and tools we work with.*

Stiles, David and Jeanie. *Treehouses.* Boston, MA: Houghton Mifflin, 1994. *A book for those who still dream.*

Walker, Lester. *The Tiny Book of Tiny Houses.* Woodstock, NY: The Overlook Press, 1993. *Some ideas on what can be done with small houses.*

INDEX

Publisher: **Jim Childs**

Acquisitions Editor: **Steve Culpepper**

Editorial Assistant: **Carol Kasper**

Technical Editor: **Andrew Wormer**

Editor: **Thomas McKenna**

Indexer: **Harriet Hodges**

Layout Artist: **Suzie Yannes**

Photographer, except where noted: **Tony Mason**

Illustrator: **Vincent Babak**

WESTERN DISTRICT LIBRARY
ORION, ILLINOIS 61273